The Dream is Real

My life on the airwaves

Bob Davis
My stories as told to Jeff Bollig

outskirts
press

About the Authors

Credit: Kansas Athletics

Bob Davis:

Bob Davis is a storyteller - and an outstanding one at that.

For 48 years, Davis told his stories on a broadcast platform touching nearly every level of competition from high school, to small college, to large university, to minor league, to major league sports. With his distinctive deep voice tinged with passion and emotion, he told a story that made us feel like we were right there. Primarily on the radio, hearing a game with Bob Davis on the call was certain to entertain.

Born May 27, 1944 in Iola, Kan., he moved to Independence when his dad took a sports editor position with the *Independence Reporter*. It would be the start of Davis's love affair with sports and sharing it with others. The family would move to Manhattan and then to Topeka where he graduated from Topeka West High School and Washburn University. After a year in law school, Davis pursued his dream of being a broadcaster. After getting 50 rejection letters, he landed a position at KAYS radio in Hays, Kan, in 1968. He would spend the next 16 years there doing high school and small-college sports play-by-play.

In the summer of 1984, Davis was selected to be the radio voice of the Kansas Jayhawks, a position he would hold for 32 years. During that time he had a 20- year run as the sports director at KMBZ radio in Kansas City (1985 - 2005). He also spent 16 years calling Kansas City Royals baseball on radio and television (1997-2012). He retired from the Royals after the 2012 season and the Jayhawks after the 2015-16 academic year. In addition, Davis broadcast games for the Wichita Aeros Triple A baseball club, the NCAA Women's Final Four, the Big Eight Holiday Basketball Tournament, Missouri Tiger basketball and was a highly-sought after speaker.

Davis's honors include:

- 14-time winner, Kansas Sportscaster of the Year Award
- Winner Hod Humiston Award for Outstanding Contributions to Broadcasting (1991)
- Member, Kansas Association of Broadcasters Hall of Fame (inducted 2006)
- Member, Fort Hays State University Hall of Fame (inducted 1990)
- Two-time winner, Oscar Stauffer Award for Excellence in high school sports
- 2001 named to Dick Vitale's "Sweet Sixteen" list of best college basketball broadcasters.
- Honored by the Kansas Legislature as April 28, 2016 was designated as "Bob Davis Day" in the state of Kansas.
- Topeka West High School Hall of Fame

Davis and his wife Linda, who served as his radio spotter early in his career, reside in Lawrence. Their son Steven has pursued a career in sports broadcasting, calling high school, college and minor league sports on radio and television. He and his wife Katie (Towner) live in Kansas City and have four children Landon, Will, Millie, and Hattie.

Dedicated To:
My wife Linda, our son Steven and daughter-in-law Katie, and our grandchildren Landon, Will, Millie and Hattie; My late father Les, mother Vera, and brother Jim; The fans of the Indians, Monarchs, Tigers, Jayhawks and Royals; My wonderful broadcasting friends across Kansas and the nation; and those who made the effort to listen to me do what I loved.

Jeff Bollig:

Credit: Jeff Bollig

Jeff Bollig is a life-long Kansan. His love of sports was fueled at an early age by participating in youth athletics, going to sporting events with his father, Marion, and listening to Bob Davis on the radio. Many a night was spent lying on the living room next to the wooden console stereo or in bed with a tiny transistor radio perched on the nearby nightstand.

A 1980 graduate of Hays High, Bollig attended Fort Hays State as a freshman, then completed his education at the University of Kansas. He received a master's degree in sports administration from Wichita State. He would later work in the KU athletics department and the Big Eight Conference. He has worked on the KU scorer's table for men's basketball games since 1996 and held the same position at the Big Eight/Big 12 Tournament for the same time period. He has served in a working capacity at every Big Eight/Big 12 Tournament since 1986.

Bollig has co-authored two books with his good friend and former boss Doug Vance. The first, "Beware of the Phog: 50 Years of Allen Fieldhouse" was written in 2005 to commemorate the 50th anniversary of the grand facility. In 2008, the duo published "What it Means to Be a Jayhawk" a compilation of short stories about legendary Jayhawk athletes.

He resides in Olathe with his wife Laurie. Their daughter Courtney is working in higher education in Washington, D.C., and son Kyle is completing his master's degree at Ohio University in Athens, Ohio.

Dedicated To:
My wife Laurie, daughter Courtney and son Kyle;
My late father Marion, mother Shirley, brothers Joe and John,
and sisters Coleen and Camille:
The community of Hays, Kansas and its people (a wonderful place to grow up); and
Jayhawk fans everywhere.

Table of Contents

NOTE: *The Friends of Bob are individuals who have been a part of Bob's life. Some for a lifetime, others for a moment in time. Together they contribute to the story of his life, sharing insights, adding humor and providing details. Their contributions are direct quotes with only minor editing for clarity and brevity.*

Acknowledgements i

Foreword: Kevin Harlan, CBS Sports, TNT, Westwood Radio; University
of Kansas, 1982 iii

Preface: Jeff Bollig v

Introduction: Max Falkenstien, Jayhawk Broadcasting Legend ix

Chapter 1: Finding Sports 1

Chapter 2: Running From the Law 5

Chapter 3: Right Place, Right Time 13
    Sidebar: The Brilliance of Bob Schmidt 18
    Friends of Bob: Mitch Holthus, Dave Armstrong, Errol Wuertz, Gerard
    Wellbrock, Larry Friend, Mike Kennedy, Bill Hancock 19

Chapter 4: Go, Tigers, Go! 23
    Sidebar: A Rhyme for Every Season 33
    Friends of Bob: Bill Morse, John Mason, Joe Rosado, Gary Sechrist,
    Mark Watts, Billy Hall, Chuck Brehm, Mike Kennedy, Bonnie Lowe 35

Chapter 5: Growing Up in Hays, America 40
    Sidebar 1: The Best of the Best 49
    Sidebar 2: Nick Pino's Shoe and Satchel Paige's Gun 52
    Friends of Bob: Larry Weigel, Alan Billinger, Don Slone, Steve Bates,
    Clair Augustine, Mike Leikam, Randy Johnson, Garret Schmidt,
    Father Earl Befort, Father Mike Scully. 54

Chapter 6: Setting Up on the Kaw...59

    Sidebar 1: The Birth of the KU Network 69

    Friends of Bob: Monte Johnson, Larry Brown, Gary Bedore,
    Gary Bender, Bernie Kish, John Baker, Mark Turgeon 71

Chapter 7: New Faces take the Jayhawks New Places 74

    Sidebar 1: Tuxedo Tony Sands...89

    Sidebar 2: We'll Play Anyone, Anytime, Anywhere 91

    Friends of Bob: Danny Manning, Dean Buchan, Glen Mason,
    Richard Konzem, Roy Williams, Tony Sands, Doug Vance,
    Alonzo Jamison, Bob Newton, Chris Piper.......................91

Chapter 8: Eight is Not Enough 98

    Sidebar: Larger than Life 107

    Friends of Bob: Bill Self, Mark Mangino, David Lawrence, Mike Leas,
    Doug Vance, Chris Theisen 109

Chapter 9: Changing of the Guard 113

    Sidebar: My Offices: Stadiums, Arenas, Ballparks and More 129

    Friends of Bob: Tom Dore, Dick Vitale, Jeff Hawkins, Eric Heft,
    Blair Kerkhoff, Tim Allen, Jim Marchiony 133

Chapter 10: Waving the Wheat and Waving Goodbye 137

    Sidebar: Within Earshot 151

    Friends of Bob: Bill Self, John Morris, Chris Piper.....................155

Chapter 11: Back to the Station 157

    Friends of Bob: Noel Heckerson, Nate Bukaty 159

Chapter 12: Always Royal..161

    Friends of Bob: Lynn Splittorff, Denny Matthews, Pat Shea,
    Ryan Lefebvre, Tony Muser, Kevin Kietzman, Kevin Shank,
    Max Utsler, Mike Sweeney, Don Free, Pat Scott, Mike Swanson..............171

Chapter 13: My Partners 177

    Sidebar 1: And Thanks to Our Spotter, Linda Davis 184

    Sidebar 2: Max and Me 185

    Friends of Bob: David Lawrence, Greg Gurley, Chris Piper,
    Kevin Shank, Nate Bukaty, John Rooney, Jim Nantz, Holly Rowe,
    Al Wallace, Andy Landers...189

Chapter 14: Believe in Yourself 194

    Friends of Bob: Steven Davis...196

Afterword: Wyatt Thompson 198

Acknowledgements

THE NAMES ON the cover are but a tip of the iceberg when it comes to recognizing the people who were vital in delivering the final product. It would not have been possible to get to the finish line without the assistance of countless individuals who were so giving of their time. While our goal is to identify all those contributors, we know we will unwittingly miss a few. Please know that we are grateful to everyone who provided a story, fact-checked a note, provided a photo, reviewed the contents and/or provided encouragement.

We offer a tip of the cap to Kevin Harlan and Wyatt Thompson for their respective writing of the foreword and afterword. Two outstanding broadcasters, they are even better friends. Some 50-plus people took our phone calls to share stories of their relationship with Bob Davis and/or the events that occurred during their interaction. Writing a book takes time and effort, but it sure was fun talking baseball with former Royals manager Tony Muser; promising former Plainville High School football coach Larry Friend - now 84 years old - that you'll need a few minutes of his time, only to end up sharing stories for more than an hour; or recounting with broadcasting peers, coaches and athletes the seemingly endless litany of stories and jokes. Those conversations only reinforce the fact that it's the relationships you develop during your life that are more valuable than any trophy, ring or award.

There are certain individuals who were always there to return a call, text or email: Richard Konzem, Doug Vance, David Lawrence, Bob Newton, Kevin Shank, Chris Theisen, Linda Davis, Steven Davis, Randy Johnson, Kent Goodwin, Kyle Goodwin, Gerard Wellbrock, Brian Schumacher, Dustin Armbruster, Alan Billinger, Mary Lang of the TMP-Marian Alumni Association, Mark Watts, Steve Gerstner and Al Wallace. The quality of the book would be lacking without the contribution of several outstanding photographers. Those are noted in the individual photo credits. Special thanks to the award-winning artist John Martin and graphics specialist Bonnie Henson for providing the cover design. The most thankless role in production of a book is editing, but in Laurie Bollig we had one of the best editors around.

Lastly, we appreciate the support of two outstanding Kansas-based companies who provided resources to help get the book across the finish line: Dillons (Dillons.com) and Rally House (RallyHouse.com). It shows the respect and admiration they have for Bob Davis and the impact he had on people throughout the Sunflower State.

Foreword

Credit: *John Filo/CBS*

By Kevin Harlan CBS Sports, TNT, Westwood Radio

University of Kansas 1982

VOICES CAN NAVIGATE us to an earlier time and memory that triggers your thoughts and imagination. I've always thought that your imagination, your "theater of the mind," is perhaps the most powerful tool we possess. Words ignite it. Voices deliver it. Pictures in our minds painted by the words and inflection with voices guiding our journey. Indelible images in our mind's eye. Radio has that effect. It is still incredibly impactful. Listening to the words of someone telling a story, or a broadcaster describing an event or a game, capturing the moment and action with their inflection, emotion, adjectives and reporting skills is an art.

And for KU fans, remembering the history of the Jayhawks basketball and football seasons, with the accompanying soundtrack of the voice of Bob Davis was unforgettable. His unparalleled emotion in every big call in every big KU game is our soundtrack. Different players, different seasons, same voice. His voice and those plays are married forever. In fact, the voice and those memories are so intertwined that sometimes you're not sure which was better, the call by Bob or the play itself. Either way, Bob Davis's voice is the soundtrack. Vivid description. Edge-of-your-seat drama.

Bob has the most unique crescendo of a big call that I have ever heard. But because he is a Kansan, a product of the midwest, his delivery is warm and folksy, friendly, the kind of voice you'd like company with during a drive down I-70, through the middle of the state, like so many of us have had with Bob. And that style played perfectly in his 16 years on the Royals Major League Baseball radio and TV broadcasts, as well broadcasting the Jayhawks. His style, while dynamic on the big plays, was the perfect fit. And his voice is as identifiable as the Jayhawks mascot itself. Final Fours. Bowl games. He's done it all. I think of Bob's versatility to jump from sport to sport, and marvel at how tremendously skilled he was, regardless of the microphone he held.

No higher praise can be made of a broadcaster than to have that kind of resume, broadcasting major college sports, major league baseball and all the things in-between like hosting and reporting, which Bob did in a career that spanned over five decades. Decorated as a 14-time Kansas Sportscaster of the Year, and inducted into the Kansas Broadcasters Hall of Fame, there is no greater honor than to be recognized and voted on by your peers, those who do what you do and know the challenges of the profession. Years ago, Bob, me and others shared a lunch on a fairly regular basis in Kansas City, and during those meals we would laugh and tell stories, reminisce and playfully complain about the business, and life. It was time well spent with a friend.

I'd like to think that's what he meant to listeners through the years as well. A friend who was there during the various parts of our life, describing wins and losses, heroism and failure. About five years ago, Gary Bender and I drove into Lawrence and met Bob and Tom Hedrick for lunch. All, at one time, the Voice of the Jayhawks. I respect these men immensely. They are my heroes. Thinking of the history at that table, the accomplishments of these men, the lives they touched through their broadcasts, is overwhelming. So rare to get this opportunity, we took a picture of the four of us and I treasure it as much as any I have from my profession.

I miss seeing and listening to my friend Bob. I think about him and hear him in my mind from years gone by, and sometimes hear his highlights on the radio when the show drifts back to the past. I guess when there is a book written about your life, it means that your career has probably concluded. Perhaps it has ended, but for the thousands and thousands of fans across Kansas and the Midwest who listened to the Jayhawks and Royals, and Fort Hays State before that, a Bob Davis broadcast meant a familiar voice, an emotional delivery, and a love of sports that embraced the listener. You could just tell in his voice how much he enjoyed having you along for the ride. He was a welcome companion when driving, walking, working in the yard or doing whatever because that's what a friend does.

He was familiar and comfortable. When I think of Bob, I feel blessed to have had his wonderful voice, and friendship, in my life. And I don't get sad because I don't hear it as much anymore, but rather smile because I listened and admired and respected the professional, and friend. In my mind's eye, I can hear Bob broadcasting. I hear his voice and his words and listen to his description filter through my mind, the pictures that those words paint, and the passion they produce, and I imagine the generations of fans touched by the voice of Bob Davis the same way.

Preface

By Jeff Bollig

STEVE JOBS, THE late co-founder of Apple, once said good storytellers are among the most powerful people in the world.

Their words inspire and motivate. They inform and educate. They make us laugh and cry. They capture and keep our attention. They take us to places we've never been.

Who hasn't picked up a book and hours later found themselves still turning the pages? Who hasn't binge-watched episode after episode of a television series on Netflix? Who hasn't listened to their Spotify playlist over and over again? We all have. Why? Because we like the story being told to us.

Being a good storyteller is a wonderful gift. People hang on your every word. They set their schedules so that they hear your next message. They even share what you have to say over and over again.

Bob Davis was a sports broadcaster for 48 years. He got into the business because he liked sports and he wanted to tell people about what was happening on the baseball field, the basketball court and football gridiron. As a youth, he was mesmerized by the passion and excitement the announcers possessed in delivering their call of the game. He listened to sports whenever he could, setting a goal that someday, he would have the same impact doing the same thing Al Helfer, Harry Carey, Jack Buck, Merle Harmon and Dev Nelson did.

He wanted to be a storyteller of sports.

After sending out tapes and resumes to some 50 stations all over Missouri and Kansas, Davis finally got his chance as an afternoon disc jockey, playing middle-of-the road music in the middle of America. Hays, Kan., is probably best known as the half-way point between Denver and Kansas City -- a good place to stretch your legs and get a soda. It was the place Davis came to get some experience and then hit the road to a bigger market as fast as he could.

This is where our worlds intersected for the first time. As a young child growing up in Hays, sports was a big part of my life. To have Bob telling me stories on almost a daily basis was inspiring and entertaining.

The authors review statistics on the plane ride home during the 1987-88 season. Credit: Jeff Bollig

Davis found his grass was plenty green in Hays. He quickly became popular with the listeners and successful as a professional, earning state broadcasting awards on a regular basis. If there were anyone who had rock-star status in the community of 20,000, Bob had it. He rocked and rolled Hays, America for 16 years.

Davis was selected the Voice of the Kansas Jayhawks in the summer of 1984, a position he would hold for 32 years. To this day, former Kansas Athletics Director Monte Johnson says Davis is the best hire he made in his tenure on Mt. Oread. In 1997, Davis added the duties of television and radio play-by-play for the Kansas City Royals. Captivated by the sport since he first saw a teenage Mickey Mantle in the old Kansas-Oklahoma-Missouri league, Davis spent 16 years calling Royals baseball (11 on radio and five on television).

I consider myself fortunate to have listened to Bob Davis broadcast sports for all of his 48 years in the business (those memories from the first few are a little fuzzy). Like so many others, I was drawn to his deep booming voice, uber descriptive delivery, quick wit and sense of humor. He had you feeling like you were right there in the front row even though you were nowhere near the venue.

And while Bob has few peers when it comes to telling a good story, getting him to write a book that tells a story was not an easy task. It took several years of cajoling by many people. "It's not about me, it's about the players and coaches," he often said.

So, we made a deal. Bob would share stories, but only if he could do so with the help of his friends. The following pages feature Bob Davis telling his story of a life in broadcasting, with dozens of others adding their own anecdotes - some humorous, some intriguing, some not known to the masses until now. The contributors run the gamut from a fifth-grade Sunday School student, fellow broadcasters, former student-athletes, coaches and close personal friends.

I hope you enjoy reading it as much as I did in working with Bob to produce it.

Introduction

By Max Falkenstien

Bob Davis: A Terrific Announcer but An Even Better Friend

NOTE: *The following text comes from the book "A Good Place to Stop, 60 Seasons with Max and the Jayhawks" written by the late Max Falkenstien and Matt Fulks. Published in 2007. Portions of this chapter are used elsewhere in the book. Reprinted with permission from Ascend Books/Powerhouse Publishing, Matt Fulks and the Falkenstien family.*

DURING MY 60 years with KU, I had a chance to work with some great radio partners, such as Gerry Barker, Bob Fromme, Al Correll, Jerry Waugh and Jim Fender. But in 1984, I moved from the play-by-play chair over to color analyst when Bob Davis came to Lawrence from Fort Hays State University, where he'd been an announcer for many years.

When I was invited to serve as a color commentator to Bob's play-by-play description, I had many reservations. It wasn't going to be easy going from telling what was going on, as I had done for about 38 years, to why it was happening.

But Bob made it so easy for me that we soon settled into a pattern that fans really seemed to enjoy. First of all, Bob had listened to me for years and I think he respected what I had done. Secondly, he was not burdened with the big ego that is so common in our business. He and I just settled into a conversational pattern. He would say what was happening, and I would remember things from the past and relate the close relationships and confidences I had with the players and coaches.

Most importantly in the long run, we laughed a lot and had fun. Bob has a **GREAT** sense of humor and is quick-witted. Thousands of people told us that whenever a game was on television, they would mute the sound and listen to "Bob and Max" on the radio. They liked hearing the same guys on every game, not different announcers who didn't know the people nearly as well as we did.

The 1984-85 broadcast team Max Falkenstien, Bob Davis and Bob Newton (engineer),
Credit: Kansas Athletics

One of my phrases was "Don't Make Me Laugh," because Bob would start telling a story, and we would laugh so hard that I would become hoarse, which made doing the game that night more difficult than it might have been. After many years, one or the other of us would start a story, and everyone in the group would remember it, and jump to the punch line, and then we all would laugh. We saved a lot of time that way!

Our partnership of 22 years is probably one of the longest pairings in college sportscasting history. Of course, just up the road, Denny Matthews and Fred White called Kansas City Royals games together for 25 years. Partnerships at the college level, however, tend not to last as long. Dick Vitale named us as a pair to his Sweet Sixteen of basketball broadcasters in the nation, the only twosome from one school in the whole country.

There are so many great stories from our time together, it's impossible to remember all of them. And, frankly, some probably are best forgotten. But there are a few memorable moments that pop into my head immediately.

Bob and I always had fun on trips. We liked the same kind of food. Home-cooked style, mostly. Greasy was okay. We always joked that if our wives wouldn't go into a place, it probably would be perfect for us. Once, when we stayed at a beautiful resort, The Inn At South Mountain, in Phoenix, Bob and I would walk out to our rental car and drive a couple of miles to eat at the Waffle House.

Those are the kinds of things we remember more than the games. One of Bob's great lines is, "This would be a great trip if we didn't have to do the games."

One of the funny incidents of many happened during the 2002 NCAA Tournament. The Hawks were in Madison, Wisc., for the Midwest Regional, where they played Illinois and Oregon. Bob, his wife Linda and I went out to dinner one night at a nice restaurant that someone recommended. Verne Lundquist, who is one of the nicest guys in the whole business, was there with his CBS-TV partner Bill Raftery and a couple other guys. As we were being seated, we saw the group and waved to each other.

The waiter came by and said, "The silver-haired gentleman over there would like to buy you folks a drink."

Bob said, "Well, thank you. Please thank Mr. Raftery, but tell him we are a couple of tee-totaling Kansans over here. But we appreciate the offer."

A few minutes later, the waiter came back and said, "Mr. Raftery wants to know if you'd rather have the money instead." (Of course we said yes!)

Over the years, Bob and I have walked to breakfast through the icy cold of Anchorage, Alaska. We've eaten dinner in Maui, Hawaii, as the sun has seemingly set into the Pacific. And we have lined up at Joe's Stone Crab Restaurant in Miami. While there, Kansas State Senator David Wysong saw us at the end of a long line of those waiting to get in. He left for a few minutes to talk to the maitre'd. In a few moments he came back and said, "Follow me," and the maitre'd announced, "Governor Wysong's party" next. We always figured he slipped the maitre'd $50 or so. But from that moment on, Dave has always been "Governor Wysong" to us.

Bob and I like to go to zoos. We have visited many to kill time on game day. We have visited the Richard Nixon Presidential Library in Yorba Linda, Calif., and the George Bush Presidential Library in College Station, Texas. Bob is well-versed in history and has a great memory. He seems to know the words to every country-western song ever written, yet he almost always listens to sports-talk radio while in the car. Not me. I get tired of hearing the same jerks express the same opinions over and over.

You can probably tell that Bob and I laughed more often than we can count. Although I had some apprehension about going from play-by-play to color — only because I didn't really know if I could do it — when he came to KU in the fall of 1984, working with Bob for the final 22 years of my broadcasting career couldn't have been more enjoyable.

As more and more honors fell my way, it seemed that Bob was always the guy to emcee the event or to introduce me for the award. He always did a terrific job. Surely he must have gotten tired of that, but I never sensed it, and he was always gracious and complimentary to me. There are not a lot of guys around like that, so I will always be indebted to him. I was pleased that he was inducted into the Kansas Broadcasters Hall of Fame in 2006, and I am sure many more awards will come to him in the future.

CHAPTER 1

Finding Sports

AS A CHILD, I was largely in my own little cocoon, mostly unaware of the world around me. I had my family, friends, school, sports and filled the remaining time just messing around.

Sports was something I enjoyed and followed closely. I played baseball, collected baseball cards, listened to games on the radio and read newspapers. I loved everything about sports. At the time, however, it did not register to me that they were a big part of our society. Once I got into high school and college, I began to understand just how important sports were in our lives.

I believe it's the live nature of sports that creates widespread interest among people. Nothing is predetermined or rehearsed. There's real drama in athletic competition and it is that element that drew me to broadcasting. To be able to tell the story as it unfolds is exciting. As Jim McKay would say in the opening of ABC's Wide World of Sports, you have the thrill of victory or the agony of defeat every time the game is played.

Being in broadcasting, I quickly learned that people hung on every word uttered about their team. Whether it was the local high school, the college or university, or the pros, people take great pride in associating with "their" team. Being a fan allows them to experience a wide range of emotions. Whether it is a crisp Friday night under the lights for a high school football game, a Saturday afternoon basketball game in a warm basketball arena or the glamour of big-time professional events -- we come together as one to support our coaches and players. I am not sure there is anything else that builds community quite like sports.

I was fortunate to have an up-close and personal seat to sports as a child. I was born to Les and Vera Davis in Iola, Kan. (May 27, 1944). My dad was actually overseas on duty in World War II when I was born and when he returned, he sold shoes. We moved to Independence in the late 1940s when my father got the job as the sports editor at the *Independence Reporter*. It was a great opportunity for him and me because we had the high school, junior college and then in the summer, minor league baseball.

The Independence Yankees were the Class D affiliate of the New York Yankees and played in the old KOM (Kansas-Oklahoma-Missouri) League. In the league's last year in 1952, the local Yankees became the Independence Browns, an affiliate of the St. Louis Browns. The league had teams from southeast Kansas - Chanute, Pittsburg, Iola, Independence; northeast Oklahoma - Ponca City, Miami, Bartlesville, Blackwell; and southwest Missouri - Carthage. It was like that all over America and perhaps why baseball became known as America's pastime. Small communities with fans jamming small ball parks to watch future major league legends.

I would sit in the stands with my mom but sometimes got to go up in the small press box with my dad. He would keep score and do the public address announcing, and then the next morning would write the game story for the afternoon paper. Some great players passed through that league. A few went on to the major leagues. The most famous, of course, being a teenager by the name of Mickey Mantle who played shortstop for the Independence Yankees in 1949. Independence won the title that year. Mantle had a strong arm and was unbelievably fast. He was truly a once-in-a-generation player and of course a Hall of Famer. But my favorite player was Bill Virdon. He was a terrific defensive player in centerfield. My dad said Bill Virdon was the first player he saw who took his first step at the crack of the bat, turned and ran to a spot and would be waiting for the ball to come down into his glove.

Virdon would go on to have a long playing and managerial career in the majors. He retired in Springfield, Mo., and I would run into him later in life when there were reunions in Independence. There is a little museum featuring artifacts and information from the KOM League in Independence. If you are ever in the area and are a baseball fan, I encourage you to drop by for a visit.

Because I hung around my mom and dad at the games for the most part, I did not get to meet any of the players or coaches. I was still pretty young -- not yet hitting double digits in years of age. But I did love the actual baseball with the horsehide and stitching. My dad would regularly bring me a ball, and sometimes it would have an autograph. I may have one of the bigger baseball collections from the KOM League. One is even autographed by Mick Mantle.

Being the son of a sports editor, I read *The Sporting News* religiously, scouring the box scores and stats. Even though my dad was a sports editor, he wanted me to be a little more diverse in my interests. One day after spending quite a while with my nose stuck in the paper, he said, "son, you'll never get anywhere reading the blankety-blank *Sporting News*!"

Every afternoon in the summer I would tune to the local radio station, KIND, and listen to Mutual Broadcasting's Game of the Day for Major League Baseball. We had one of those big ol' wooden console sets that was about four feet tall with the radio and record player. I would lie on the floor and listen to the deep baritone voice of Al Helfer. That is when I fell in love with broadcasting for the first time. Mel Allen, who later had the television show This Week in Baseball preceded Helfer. Then Buddy Blattner, who would go on to do the Royals (1969-75), was joined by Dizzy Dean to do national games, first on radio, then on TV. They were fun to listen to. Buddy was actually a former major league player, so he knew the game. He rubbed off on me and heightened my love for baseball.

My dad got out of the sportswriting business and he entered the insurance industry. We moved to Manhattan, living there in 1954-56 and then moved to Topeka in 1957. That opened up my world to the Big Seven Conference. You had great coaches like Phog Allen at KU, Tex Winter at K-State, Bud Wilkinson at Oklahoma, Henry Iba at Oklahoma State and so many others. Then you had great basketball players at both KU and K-State like (Wilt) Chamberlain, (Bob) Boozer, and of course Oklahoma was a dominant football program. The 1950s were such a great time for the Kansas and Kansas State basketball programs as they both went to the NCAA Final Four and were highly ranked.

I did not know much about college sports and the great teams and athletes until that point. In Manhattan I listened to Dev Nelson do Kansas State sports. He was fun to listen to and was an outstanding broadcaster. It was a real treat for me to get to know him once I got in the business. He was from the small town of Marquette, Kan., and was an absolute peach of a person. There was no finer guy than Dev. He could have gone on to do bigger markets. He almost had the A's job, but he was content doing Kansas State and he did it well. My neighbor and I would walk down the street to Ahearn Fieldhouse and get in a basketball game for fifty cents. Of course, that was the 1950s, but still, only fifty cents!

We'd go to the old stadium at Kansas State to watch football. The first college game I ever saw there featured future Wildcat All-Big Eight running back Gene Keady. He was a remarkable four-sport standout at Larned High School and was drafted by the Pittsburgh Steelers. He played football, baseball, basketball and ran track in high school and at Garden City Community College. When he went to Kansas State, he dropped basketball because legendary coach Winter told him he was not good enough to play there. Interestingly, Keady became a basketball coach, starting at Beloit High School, then onto Hutchinson Junior College, then as an assistant to Eddie Sutton at Arkansas and eventually the successful head coach at Purdue.

We'd also drive over to Lawrence on occasion for games. We had some relatives with tickets to KU basketball and we'd get to see some of the great KU stars. I was amazed at how big the fieldhouse looked from the outside. When it was constructed, it was on the edge of town in a field and stood there like some fortress. Little did I know it would later become the place where I worked. It also had special meaning to me as my grandfather Edwin Davis was among the general carpenters who helped build the fieldhouse.

I also listened to the KU Network throughout high school and into my college days at Washburn University in Topeka. You had some great announcers in that position through the years: Merle Harmon, Monte Moore, Bill Grigsby, Gary Bender, Tom Hedrick and Kevin Harlan. And of course, you had Max Falkenstien, who was not part of the network, but did both KU and K-State games for WREN in Topeka. Those guys were really respected and they didn't last long at KU because the professional teams came and grabbed them. I thought the guys at Wichita State Gus Grebe and Rick Weaver were good as well.

One thing I don't think people of the state of Kansas realize is just how good the broadcasters were and continue to be in this part of the nation. They do not take a backseat to anyone. I'd like to think that not only made people's lives more enjoyable, but fueled their passion for sports. There's no doubt I learned a great deal listening to them. And, to later get in the profession and meet them was quite an experience -- or I should say, an honor.

Moving to northeast Kansas as a 10-year-old in 1954 opened my eyes to professional sports in Kansas City. I listened to Merle Harmon and Larry Raye, and later Ed Edwards and Bill Grigsby call the Kansas City A's baseball games. I learned just how big of a deal pro sports were in grade school, when my dad took me to my first game at old Municipal Stadium for my birthday when the A's played the Yankees. I remember taking binoculars so I could get an up close perspective. My dad said I never put them down the whole game. That game left quite an impression on me. This was "**The**" show. I could see why sports were such a big deal to people.

Looking back, I now realize that sports were everything to me as a young child and teenager. I was not a particularly good athlete. I tell people I got into broadcasting and not sportswriting like my dad because I was not a good speller and in those days you did not have spell check. But back then radio was the main broadcast delivery for sports and it seemed like I could never get enough of it. I couldn't begin to count all of the hours I spent listening to the radio.

As I would learn, I was not alone in my passion for sports. All you have to do is look at the television ratings, player salaries, sponsorship dollars, merchandise sales, stadium attendance and the abundance of sports talk radio to see the popularity. It's been said that sports are the toy department of life. That may be true, but society's past challenges proved just how fun -- and necessary -- those toys are for us.

CHAPTER 2

Running From the Law

I ATTENDED TOPEKA High for two years and finished school at the newly-opened Topeka West. My first job was delivering the *Topeka Capital Journal* during my high school days, so you could say I was in the media business at a young age. At Topeka West, I was the sports editor of the school paper and they even let me name it, *Campus View*, which I believe is still the name. As an aside, I was later selected to the Topeka West High School Hall of Fame, going in the same year as the band "Kansas." Talk about different ends of the spectrum.

I would go on to Washburn for college, but changed my source of income to selling men's clothing. I enjoyed history, so I chose that as my college major, knowing it would be helpful if I were to go on to law school. My father thought the law was an honorable profession. He was happy I decided to take that route.

And, that is how it went until I received a letter in the mail in 1967 informing me my military deferment was up. So, after my first year of law school, I headed to Fort Polk, La., for Basic Training and Advanced Individual Training. I was a refueling specialist for helicopters. But that was not the only change going on in my life at that time. I never gave up on my love for broadcasting. I told myself before I left for Louisiana that if I was going to pursue an announcing career, now was the time. I was determined to do it, I just did not know how to go about making it happen.

When I returned to Topeka four months later, I was faced with the difficult task of telling my dad that I was not going back to law school and was becoming a broadcaster. I think he was more disappointed than mad. He thought law was a noble means to support a family.

I had some inkling of what was involved in broadcasting. While I was in high school, I had a cousin who worked at KTOP radio in Topeka. I would go to the station with him on occasion and he would let me speak into the microphone. I told him I wanted to be a sports broadcaster some day. He said that would be like riding a dead horse. In other words, I would go nowhere doing that. But during the 60s there was an explosion of sports and jobs were being created. I had also taken some broadcasting classes at Washburn, so it wasn't as if I was starting from zero.

To become a broadcaster, I attended Career Academy, located in the old Skelly Building on The Plaza in Kansas City. It was a four-month program where I learned how to broadcast, do basic production and engineering, and honed my skills as a broadcaster. While I was in school, I sent out more than 50 applications for jobs in Kansas and Missouri. I couldn't get a sniff. The replies were all the same: "We don't hire anyone without experience." I was despondent. How do you get experience if no one provides the opportunity?

As a side note, Merle Harmon, who was the first broadcaster for the KU Network and went on to do the Kansas City A's, was part owner of that school. I would send him letters asking him about the profession and he would always write back. I later got to meet him and we became good friends. He was such a nice man and always had time for me. He gave me some great advice.

Disappointed, but not deterred, I learned of an opening for an afternoon disc jockey position at KAYS radio in Hays. My dad was friends with Merle Blair, who was from Independence and ran KTOP radio. He knew the people at KAYS, and even though he had not heard me broadcast one word, he put in a good word for me. I sent in my tapes with fingers crossed. I had passed through Hays going to and from Topeka and Denver, but never spent time there until I interviewed in the summer of 1968. I had lunch with television general manager Bernie Brown and radio general manager Bob Churchill at the Ramada Inn on Vine Street. It was the longest drive back to Topeka not knowing if they liked my tapes and how I did in the interview. I had it going for me, at least, that I did not spill anything on me during lunch.

A week or so later - although it seemed like an eternity -- I received a call from Bernie and was offered the job. I sensed they thought I could do a pretty good job and I would come fairly inexpensive. My first salary of $400 per month, with a $10 talent fee for each game I broadcast. I didn't care what I was making. I was ecstatic. It wasn't a job in sports, but my goal was to just get my foot in the door, get some experience and then look for a sports job somewhere else.

While I consider myself to have earned the job on my merits, there were some elements of luck involved. First, having the connection with KTOP radio was good fortune. But the biggest stroke of luck came in that KAYS owner and general manager Bob Schmidt was not in town for my interview. Several years later he told me if he would have been there that day, he never would have hired me. He never offered a job to anyone for a full-time position without experience.

I reported to work in August 1968 and was on the air from day one. I'd do a noon TV show with Errol Wuertz, reading the news and doing the weather. Then I had my DJ duties from 1 to 4 in the afternoon, I operated the camera for the 6 p.m. television newscast and read the sports for the 10 p.m. show. Our music was considered middle of the road so we could appeal to everyone. I always joked with Bob, though, that we could make more money if we played polka music in this community, which was settled by the Volga-Germans.

There were some sports broadcasting opportunities early in my career. After just a few days on the job, I broadcast a state American Legion baseball tournament because our sports director was attending a funeral. It was the first sporting event I ever called. In the fall, I would join news/sports director Keith Cummings on broadcasts of games featuring the two local high schools and Fort Hays State University.

Keith, who was from Sylvan Grove in Lincoln County, was an excellent broadcaster and much respected by his peers for his talent. I really learned a great deal from him. He knew of my career aspirations, so I always felt he was preparing me to be a lead play-by-play guy. I just hoped it would come sooner than later.

I have always said that to be successful in broadcasting, you have to hook up your eyes and your mouth together and eliminate your brain. Sounds easy enough, but it isn't always the case. Although for me, there wasn't much of a brain to eliminate. So I had no problems.

Even though it may come naturally, there are times when it is difficult to get the words out. Early in my career I had this recurring dream that there would be the opening kickoff and then I couldn't say anything. Nothing would come out. Thankfully, that never occurred, but every announcer gets tongue-tied once in a while. People asked me if I ever got nervous, and the answer would be -- yes. It wasn't a lot, but I know I was extremely nervous doing my first sports event ever, the American Legion tournament in Hays in August 1968.

Bob Schmidt made it clear that it was important for me to pronounce the names correctly. That was his nature. He was attentive to detail and he knew that where I came from there weren't a lot of Pfannenstiels, Leikers, Staabs or Weigels. So Bob sat down with me to go over the correct pronunciation of some of the more difficult player names. He reminded me: "I will be listening."

I would put the first football and basketball games at KU in that category. And, I remember being a little on edge for my first Royals game. For those "first" games, you had people hearing you for the first time, or had people who helped you along the way listening. I did not want to let them down.

My opinion about sportscasting is you can study it, you read a book about it, and you can have guys lecture to you about how to do it. But in the end you've just got to do it to get better. And, you must never get away from the foundation of a good broadcast. As the play-by-play guy, your job is to grind away at the basics, what is the score, where are we in the ballgame, who's ahead, where is the ball, and it is continuous bookkeeping. That is the challenge and the fun.

I just love radio. There are so many forms of communication now, but what could be better than a human voice? Radio is one-on-one communication. You're sitting with a guy in his car driving along, or the guy that has a radio in his shower — now how intimate is that?

Being a little nervous is generally a good thing. When you are on edge just a bit, it keeps you focused on the job at hand. If you get too comfortable, you begin to lose contact with the game. I wouldn't get nervous necessarily because I thought I would screw up, it was more that something would go wrong. It could be something to do with getting on air, missing a piece of equipment or having a travel mix-up. My mentor at KAYS, Keith Cummings would say you should leave the station early enough so you can stop for a quick bite to eat and change a flat tire, and still be there in time to get set up for the game.

When you are in the business as long as I have been, you are going to have some travel issues that make things interesting. Weather is understandable. Running into an airplane, being attacked by unruly fans and equipment malfunctions not so much. In 1987 on the road at Auburn, the Jayhawk football team went straight from the plane to the bus on the tarmac. The driver cut the corner a bit too tight and ran into the wing of the plane and cratered the top of the bus.

In 1990, the football team was flying back from Miami when that ominous announcement came over the intercom: "Ladies and gentlemen, the captain asks that everyone fasten their seatbelts and assume the crash position." Thankfully, it was a false alarm.

The Kansas basketball team was playing at California in 2006. Right next to the arena, the Kansas City Chiefs would play the Oakland Raiders at Oakland-Alameda County Stadium. As we drove through the parking lot, Raider fans began pelting our bus with garbage. Only later did we learn the sign in the front of the bus said "Kansas."

Sometimes your travel schedule just does not allow for any time cushion and you pray everything goes right. One September, I did a Royals game on Friday night in Detroit. I got up early to catch a flight to Kansas City and was met by Johnny Rowlands of "Newschopper Nine" fame. We took a helicopter ride to the helipad at Lawrence Memorial Hospital where my family rushed me to the stadium for an 11 a.m. kickoff. Years later we played a football game in Columbia and that night played a basketball game in Las Vegas versus top-ranked Florida. In the past, Max and I had split up and did one or the other. But Lew Perkins wanted me to do both games, so after the football game we hopped on a private jet and made it to Las Vegas in time. Now, that is what I call a true day/night doubleheader.

Of course, you had the "big game" such as a national championship, bowl game, or matchup against a ranked team that also brought a little extra fanfare. I wasn't necessarily nervous because I wasn't playing in the game, but I did feel some added excitement. I think almost every broadcaster would tell you there is some extra adrenaline when the ball is kicked off, at the opening tip, or with the first pitch. Naturally, when the game ends you are tired -- as much mentally as physically. Something that I had to get accustomed to was the pure frequency of Royals baseball games. When you are doing a game every day for a period of two weeks and going on all those road trips, it can tax you. You have to pace yourself. Every game cannot be Game Seven of the World Series.

Then, there is the prospect that you get sick and cannot do the game. Thankfully, I cannot ever remember missing a game due to illness. I did play hurt, but if the players can tape an ankle and get back out there, then I can suck it up for a few hours. The one thing broadcasters fear the most is a throat or voice ailment. A cold or sore throat that can wreck a broadcast. I remember we were in Alaska for the Shootout and I was doing my first Kansas basketball game and I had a cold. My throat was so sore. I thought there was no way I was going to make it. Thankfully, I got through it. The only other time I came close was the 2008 NCAA title game. I woke up with a sore throat and told my family I was not sure I was going to make it. I rested my voice all day then adrenaline carried me the rest of the way.

You have to periodically rest your voice and drink plenty of liquids. I drank a great deal of water and soda, but I heard guys swear by coffee or warm tea with some lemon or honey. Throat lozenges are always in the briefcase. I had not counted how many games I had done over my lifetime until I decided to do this book. But in general I did 16 years in Hays calling 20 football, 50 basketball and 25 baseball games each year (1,520 total). At KU, I did 374 football and 1,198 basketball games (1,572 contests). For the Royals, I did 1,848 games, meaning over my career I called just under 5,000 sporting events (4,940). Throw in weekly coaches shows, TV shows, pre- and postgame shows, commercials, highlight videos and banquets, and that adds up to a lot of stress on the vocal cords.

People ask about my style. Your style is developed by who you are and knowing your audience. I worked for a local radio station, and the Jayhawk and Royals networks. My audiences were predominantly fans of Hays High School, Thomas More Prep High School, also in Hays, KU or the Royals. It was okay for the broadcaster to want the Indians, Monarchs, Tigers, Jayhawks and the Royals to be successful. Certainly, you want those teams to win. But you have to be impartial in reporting the events of the game. In that regard, I saw myself as a reporter and an entertainer. I wanted to have fun doing the game and wanted the listener to enjoy following it. When I worked games such as the NCAA Women's Final Four, I still felt it was important to have passion and show excitement, but it was more a neutral approach based on your association with the teams.

You also have to develop a bit of a thick skin to be in this business. People are going to criticize you on what you say, how you say it, and when you say it. My advice to young broadcasters is to first consider the source of the feedback and then be honest with yourself on what you need to do to improve. There's a story about Phog Allen and his reaction to the criticism he would receive about his coaching. He said, "if the postman stopped at every barking dog, the mail would never get delivered." In other words, you cannot get so caught up in the naysayers that it keeps you from getting your job done. But in the Midwest, people are so nice. Even when there was criticism, it wasn't mean spirited. If people took the time to write or leave a message, I would call them back.

But as a whole, people have been so nice to me. I enjoyed when people stopped to talk to me and say hello. They would come up to me and say, 'You don't know me but I really feel like I know you.' That is about the best compliment you could possibly receive — to have someone feel like they know you because they listened to you on the radio.

Breaking into the industry was difficult when I started and continues to be so today for young broadcasters. I talk to so many young kids who remind me of what it was like in my early days of broadcasting -- they are just looking to get their foot in the door. Virtually every station wants you to have experience, but how can you get experience if no one is willing to provide it? That is why you often end up in a smaller market in jobs that might not match your interests or exact training. You might want to be a play-by-play announcer at first, but you just want to get your foot in the door. Heck, I got my start as a DJ and camera operator.

Another misnomer is that the best announcers are in the big markets. I have listened to plenty of radio people in small communities who were excellent professionals. Broadcasting is broadcasting. To be good, you have to have talent, but also work hard and get a few breaks along the way. I've referenced what a wonderful succession of broadcasters Hays has had over the years. It seems like each one was better than the person who came before. The current guy, Gerard Wellbrock, is the best of them all. My son Steven has done 12 years of minor league baseball and absolutely loves it. The difficult aspect for them is broadcasters are hanging on longer it seems, so the top jobs don't open as much.

Speaking of top jobs, the guys on the network level often have agencies behind them to schedule appearances, pursue endorsements or handle other arrangements. I was my own agent - which might explain a lot of things - but if I was a bit quicker you never know. The Royals were in Anaheim and I came around the corner and practically ran into super agent Scott Boras. I introduced myself and he replied, "oh, I know who you are, I watch you all the time." Somewhat stunned, I let him get away before I asked if he wanted to be my agent.

I've mentioned previously that my goal was to be in Hays only a short time and get to a place where there was major college or professional sports. I remember talking to former KU Network broadcaster Tom Hedrick, who was outstanding in his day. He said to me, "Robert, you can be a big leaguer in a small market." That kind of changed my perspective. I stayed in Hays so long because I enjoyed it and we were doing good work. I could have stayed in Hays my whole career and have been happy.

The technology involved in the broadcast changed immensely over my time in the business. In Hays, I was essentially a one-man band and not a technical marvel at that. For home games, we had what was called a Marti unit hooked to an FM antenna. The sound would be sent back to KAYS and the station would send the signal out over the airwaves. But that would only work for short distances, maybe 15 miles at the most. For road games, our engineer developed a unit where I plugged in a phone line and the sound went back to Hays and up in the air.

At KU, the network had just moved from the "flagship" concept to satellite distribution. KANU, the public radio station on campus was the flagship, which meant it distributed the signal on behalf of all of the stations on the network. When Learfield Communications took over, the signal was sent over phone lines to Jefferson City, Mo., and then distributed via satellite to the network stations, who would then put it on air. Over the years, I am sure listeners could tell the sound improved as the technology advanced. It went from sounding like listening to the game over a phone to a clear, clean signal. A key development later on was sending the signal to the network distribution via ethernet rather than phone line.

There is no doubt television cut into our radio audience, but we weren't overly bothered because we knew we had a large audience First, there weren't very many games broadcast on television until the late 1980s. Second, we had many rural and small-town fans who did not have access to games on cable. And third, people weren't always able to be in front of their TVs during the game, so they listened to us: people in cars, farmers in the field, the kid mowing the lawn. It was always considered to be a plus for stations to carry Kansas athletics and the revenues continued to go up, so we knew there was a good listening audience.

I'd like to think there was a fourth reason people listened to us on the radio -- and that was because they liked our broadcasts. We heard this loud and clear once television started to delay signals and our calls did not sync up with the action on television. Our network administrators' phone lines and email inboxes were quite busy with fan complaints. The technology of sending the television signal up on satellite caused us to be slightly ahead of the TV announcers. But once the Super Bowl halftime wardrobe malfunction of Janet Jackson occurred, television decided to put on an even longer delay. So, engineer Bob Newton found a piece of equipment in England and had it shipped to us that addressed the issue. The only problem is the fans in Allen Fieldhouse and Memorial Stadium listening on their headphones started to complain that we were too far behind live action. We stuck with the delay until the television one got extended even more, then went back to the original timing.

The broadcasting fraternity is close. I believe that is so because we all face similar challenges and we know that our employment status can change with a switch of an AD, a coach or a network provider. I always enjoyed meeting up with my peers at home and on the road. A highlight of the season was at the Big 12 Tournament where on the night before the tournament we would go out to eat as a group. I believe we could sell tickets to that event! Even though I am retired, I am still invited to the dinner. At first, I thought the only reason was to pick up the tab.

Speaking of my friends around the league, I would be remiss if I did not say a word about those who are no longer with us. Bob Barry, Sr., was a legend in the state of Oklahoma and broadcast both the Cowboys and the Sooners. He had a great sense of humor and we probably shared more jokes than I did with others in the league. Everyone loved to have Bob tell a joke because he started laughing with the first word he uttered. He was a friend of all. His son, Bob, Jr. was a chip off the old block -- great sense of humor and personality. He was a sports anchor for KFOR-TV in Oklahoma City, but his life was taken much too early in a motor scooter accident in 2015.

Pete Taylor was a veteran play-by-play voice for Iowa State. He also had a wonderful sense of humor, but you wouldn't know it by meeting him the first time. His partner, Eric Heft, played basketball at Iowa State and graduated in 1974. Pete was going the games solo, so he grabbed Eric, who was also doing some Ames High School broadcasts in 1979. The 2020-21 season will be Eric's 42nd. A night that rocked the league and college sports was January 27, 2001 when the Oklahoma State basketball team had one of its three planes headed from Denver to Stillwater go down just southeast of Denver. Ten members associated with the program died that night, including play-by-play voice Bill Teegins. A professional in every sense of the word, Bill is missed.

Right Place, Right Time

I THOUGHT I had died and gone to heaven working at KAYS.

I knew little about the station before taking the job, but quickly learned there was a high level of talent and professionalism there. Bob Schmidt and local Hays businessman Ross Beach were co-owners. Bob was also the general manager and more hands-on with the operations. They always said they wanted KAYS to be recognized as the best station between Kansas City and Denver.

I would argue it was. In the day, we had people like Bob Schmidt, Bob Churchill, Bernie Brown, Ed Briley, Errol Wuertz, Mike Cooper, Bob Templeton and others. They were professionals in every sense of the word and extremely dedicated to their craft. A lot of them moved on to bigger markets.

I have been blessed many times over in my career, but I never expected perhaps my biggest break to happen so soon after I got to Hays. In the fall of 1968, Keith Cummings announced he was leaving to become a news director in Lansing, Mich. Bob Schmidt elevated me to the position as sports director after I was on the job only two months. He himself did play-by-play for a while, so my guess is he had an inkling I would eventually get the hang of it. But it was going to be a challenge for a 24-year old having to replace such a popular voice on the radio. It was my big break. I was a little nervous.

For a short while, I kept my original duties and added play-by-play for Fort Hays State and the two high schools, Hays High and Saint Joe's (St. Joseph Military Academy, which later became Thomas More Prep in 1971). I was thrust into reporting on the November elections that first year. Errol and I would provide local and county results, then threw it to Walter Cronkite for state and national reporting. That was a big election on all levels. Bob Dole, who was from nearby Russell, won his first U.S. Senate election, and Keith Sebelius, the father-in-law of former Kansas Governor Kathleen Sebelius won Dole's U.S. House seat. The presidential race was Nixon vs. Humphrey. To tell you how new television was, we were still in black and white, but the national network was in color.

I was in a bit of a unique setting. For a town that size (approximately 15,000 at the time), it was unusual to cover two high schools and a college, plus all the area schools. You also had summer baseball with the American Legion team and a semi-pro team, the Hays Larks. I was always running between games, but that was such a great experience. I was fortunate at that young age to be at such a well-run operation at KAYS. And because I was single for the first couple of years, I would spend a lot of time at the station.

A few years into my tenure, Bob (Schmidt) asked me to be station manager. I stopped being a DJ and cut back on television to take on the new duties. I also picked up some advertising sales responsibilities. I did the manager thing for a while, but I would find myself working 18-hour days and doing games on the weekend. It just got to be too much. I had added football and basketball coaches shows for both local high schools, and then for the five area high schools - WaKeeney, Ellis, Victoria, LaCrosse and Plainville; and the coaches shows for Fort Hays State, as well.

I would broadcast all of the Fort Hays games for football and basketball. During football season, I did whichever high school was out of town on Friday, then drove back to Hays if Fort Hays was home, or wherever they were on the road. Talk about some interesting road trips. Try doing a football game on Friday night in Liberal, Kan., and then a Saturday afternoon game in Wayne, Neb., (that would be 510 miles). We racked up a lot of miles. I would work in some games featuring the area schools when I could, and would regularly do the Mid-Continent League Tournament (teams like Ellis, WaKeeney, Plainville, Stockton, Phillipsburg, Victoria, Hill City) in the mid-season on the Fort Hays campus.

I met so many coaches at those smaller high schools who were just wonderful people. Guys like Larry Friend at Plainville, Earl Barber at Wakeeney, Tom Bowen at Ellis, Scott Stein at LaCrosse, John Vincent at Victoria. I know I am missing several others, but they were all great to work with. They were so accommodating and excited to tell you about their players and community. The weekly interviews were 5-10 minutes, but our chats carried on much longer. Even after I moved, I would keep in contact with many of the coaches I worked with in the area.

One of the great blessings of my broadcasting career was doing high school sports. You could not help but soak up the atmosphere in these small western Kansas towns. The pageantry of the bands and cheerleaders, the aroma of popcorn in the air, and the enthusiasm of the crowd was special. The town would be dark except for the glow of the lights from the football stadium. The basketball gyms were usually small, hot and loud. A lot of students get out of school today and want to go to the big-time right away. But I felt I would have missed out if I had not done high school games. I think if you ask Wyatt Thompson, who was at Abilene High School and followed me at KAYS and now is at Kansas State; Mitch Holthus who did Pratt High School,

Kansas State and now the Chiefs, and Mike Kennedy who did Chanute High School, Pittsburg State University and is now the voice of the (Wichita State) Shockers, and they would tell you the same thing. I have a special respect for those guys who took that route.

Most of the time while in Hays I would do the games solo. At times, there would be an occasional guest analyst or conversationalist. For a while, my wife Linda would be my spotter and statistician - until our son Steven was born in 1981. Gene Jacobs, who was the sports information director (or SID) at Fort Hays State joined me for a few Tiger games and would jump on some high school broadcasts from time to time. Jacobs was a popular German surname in Hays, but he would joke that he was the one who got away. He was from Ohio. Once in a while I even had a Catholic priest join me. Father Earl Befort was a big sports fan and would occasionally take a seat next to me for the Thomas More Prep games. I really had to be on my good behavior then.

For the most part, I drove to all the games either by myself or with Linda when she was my spotter for football. But there was one coach who wanted me to go on the bus with the team. Al Billinger, the long-time basketball coach for Thomas More Prep would invite me to travel with them. A great athlete in his own right at Fort Hays State, Al was definitely a character. Competitive and tough-minded, his teams always played hard and were quite successful. Our bus driver was Father Earl. I figured we were in good hands with the Padre at the wheel as there would be someone up above guiding us. That proved to be the case as on the return trip from Lyons a semi-truck was in our lane headed straight for us. Father Earl calmly pulled the bus off the side of the road and the truck went by. Father Earl earned player-of-the-game honors.

It wasn't the last time a little divine intervention saved me in my travel activities. In 2005, I wanted to be in attendance at our son Steven's first game he broadcast solo in Casper, Wyo. The Royals just happened to be in Denver and it was an off day, so my plan was to drive up to see him. Much to my dismay, there was not a single rental car available in the entire city as the U.S. Women's Open golf championship was in town. I reached out to a few people and had no luck. Then, remembering TMP instructor Father Mike Scully was on assignment in Denver, I reached out to him and explained my plight. Not only did Father Mike get me a car, but he joined me for the trip.

I may have been a Methodist, but the priests and staff at TMP were good care of me. One time on a road trip back to Hays we started to slip and slide because it was icing. Jack Schramm, who was a recruiter and fundraiser for the school, turned to me sitting a few rows back and said, "Bob, come up here and sit by me. If Jesus is a Methodist I want to get as close to him as possible!"

When I first got to Hays, Thomas More Prep was known as St. Joseph's Military

Academy and they went by the Cadets. It was an all-boys Catholic school with some out of town students and later became TMP, which was run by the Capuchin priests, in the early 1970s. The school became co-ed when it merged with the Catholic girls high school located not too far away, Marian High School, in the early 80s. Obviously, being a military prep school, discipline was an important element of the instruction. I wasn't sure if Al had me go with them to be a positive influence on the kids, or if it was the other way around.

Working so many games afforded me to meet many people around the state. And, my job took me on the road everywhere over the course of 16 years. Hays High and Thomas More Prep were rivals, but the Indians were one classification higher than the Monarchs in terms of regional assignments. That meant my travels took me on regular basis for high school games to Dodge City, Garden City, Great Bend, Liberal, Salina, Manhattan, Junction City, Lyons, Nickerson, Pratt, Larned, Abilene, Scott City, Colby, Goodland, Russell, Hoisington and all the Mid-Continent League stops. Fort Hays had great rivalries with Washburn, Emporia State, Pittsburg State, Kearney (Neb.) State, several Colorado teams in the days of the Rocky Mountain Athletic Conference, and then the Missouri schools when the move was made to the Central States Intercollegiate Conference and the Midwest Intercollegiate Athletic Association.

There were great rivalries, great arenas, great fan bases and great characters playing and coaching the game. It was just a different time than it is now. Doing high school and small college sports meant you were friends with every athletic director, football and basketball coach, broadcaster, sports editor and so on. You enjoyed all of the personalities. I loved every minute of it -- well, except the late night drives home.

It wasn't as if it were **ALL** fun and games. I broadcast some Fort Hays State baseball games over the years and early in the 1969 season I did a solo call of a 21-0 loss to Southern Colorado. Earl Hobbs, the coach called me and I did a big gulp. I was this young, 25-year-old new broadcaster and thought I had really screwed something up. He said, "Sorry you had to put up with that shit! See you tomorrow."

I was also fortunate that Bob Schmidt had ownership in other stations and that gave me the chance to do other sporting events. He owned KFEQ radio in St. Joseph, Mo. so, for a period of time I would do the old Big Eight Holiday Basketball Tournament for KFEQ and KAYS. He also owned a radio station in Alliance, Neb., and CBS affiliates in Ensign (KTVC), Goodland (KLOE) and Wichita (KWCH). Ensign was the smallest city in the nation to have a commercial radio station. They placed the tower there so it could serve Dodge City, Garden City and Liberal. The Montreal Expos had an affiliation with the Wichita Aeros, so I got to do Triple A games on KWCH in the early 1980s.

I also did a handful of KU games on radio as a fill-in for the KU Network when the school would televise a big matchup, featuring teams like Kentucky, Louisville and Kansas State. The network radio play-by-play guy would move over to TV.

As I had mentioned before, my original plan was to stay in Hays no more than a few years and then leave after I had the experience. But I was happy there and it was such a good station, I felt there was no need to be in such a hurry to leave. Plus, Bob (Schmidt) was always good about letting me do other events such as the Big Eight Holiday tourney, KU and the Aeros. In 1983, John Rooney, the voice of the St. Louis Cardinals, called me with another such opportunity.

I had met John when he was the play-by-play guy for Pittsburg State in succeeding Mike Kennedy. Rooney was now doing Missouri Tiger basketball games. That year, he had about 12 conflicts and wanted to know if I was interested. Bob was all for it, so I filled in for John and enjoyed the continuity of several games. The people at Missouri were great to me. And, because Fort Hays State's mascot was a tiger and its colors were black and gold, I did not have to change my apparel.

I mentioned Mitch Holthus as a broadcaster that I respect for the road he took. Not many know that path almost took him to Hays. Because Fort Hays State basketball moved to Friday-Saturday games, I was unable to do as many high school games as I had hoped. So the decision was made to hire someone who could help do other games. Mitch interviewed and was offered the position, but he had just heard about an opening at WIBW and accepted the offer in Topeka. You could say it worked out well for him.

I was now going on 15 years in Hays and in that time I had been approached about other opportunities throughout that time. In 1973, I came in second to Don Fischer for the Indiana play-by-play job. It would have been interesting to work with Bobby Knight, but Don was a local from Terre Haute, Ind., and he was a perfect selection. Then, in summer of 1984, I was contacted about my interest in the open play-by-play job at Kansas.

I had applied two other times for the position and obviously did not get the job each of those times. I went into both the Indiana and the Kansas situations knowing one thing for certain. I had a great job in Hays and if I never went anywhere else, I would be happy. Kansas was in the first year of its network being the sole originator of games and it was managed by Learfield Communications in Jefferson City, Mo. It just so happened that Learfield had the rights to Missouri games when I filled in for Rooney. My third attempt would either be a charm or I would strike out -- but do so swinging.

The Learfield connection turned out to be a plus for me. Kansas Athletics Director Monte Johnson would have the final say, but having Learfield in my corner was big. I did not know Monte, but I later found out that Kansas Sports Information Director Doug Vance had shared an article about me with Johnson early in the search process. I submitted tapes of my work and interviewed. I got the job and in 1984 began a 32-year run with the Jayhawks.

The Davis family was excited. But we knew leaving Hays would be difficult. We had made so many friends and KAYS was truly a great place to work.

Chapter 3 Sidebar: The Brilliance of Bob Schmidt

I don't know if I worked for a person who was more impressive than Bob Schmidt. He had such a large presence at the station -- as the co-owner and general manager -- and in the community. He was so well respected for his business sense and benevolence. People admired him.

He would tell us that we were here to serve the community, provide entertainment, offer an advertising vehicle to businesses and make money while doing it.

Bob grew up 25 miles south of Hays in LaCrosse and went to Fort Hays State, majoring in broadcasting. He had a golden voice and still kept a presence on the air, even though he was managing the station. But make no mistake, his goal was to run the business. He was a capitalist in the nicest sense of the word. He was not overbearing, but when he needed to be firm he was. He cared deeply about people. Because of that, you did your best to please him. And it made you happy to do so. Everybody did - they respected him that much.

Bernie Brown once said of Bob, "he's the only guy I know who could be comfortable eating at the swanky Tavern on the Green in New York or at Effie's Hamburgers in Rush Center (population 170)."

Former KAYS sports directors (L to R): Kay Melia (deceased), Bob Schmidt (deceased), Bob Davis, Wyatt Thompson, Steve Webster, Gerard Wellbrock (current). Credit: Bob Davis

Bob carried so much weight in the business that he was selected as the chair of the CBS Affiliates for a while. Here's a guy from little ol' Hays, Kan., rubbing elbows with the boys from New York, Los Angeles, Chicago and the other big markets. He was always getting under their skin by poking fun at their big city ways and use of $100 words. He good naturedly threatened them by saying he was planning to have the meeting in Hays and he was going to take them out to chase rabbits. He chided them because he had his number listed in the phone book and the others didn't. One time after he returned from a CBS affiliate meeting, he sent everyone on the board a Hays phone book with the inscription: "Not Much of a Plot, But a Helluva Cast of Characters."

He was on so many local, state and national boards and giving of his time. I think people quit counting all the organizations he belonged to and to which he contributed resources. He gave without wanting anything in return.

I always said he could have been President -- of CBS or the United States -- if he wanted such a position. He was that sharp and that good of a person. But he loved Hays and western Kansas. He did not want to go anywhere else.

From time-to-time, a group of us would prod him to run for governor of Kansas. We knew he would not do it because he had a business to run, but there was some seriousness in our effort. Terms were two years in those days. Bernie Brown said that he hoped Bob would run, "because he would be out of our hair for two years and he'd have the state making a profit in no time at all." He was joking about the former, but definitely not the latter.

He did not have a big ego either -- he was just a regular guy. He owned Sweetwater Ranch, north of Hays, but kept some horses in an open field next to the station. He would periodically go out and ride. We called him the Marlboro Man because he would light up his pipe while riding.

Towards the end of my time in Hays, Bob knew there were a few jobs that I had interest in. He was always supportive of me, but wanted to make sure that if I left, I was receiving a good deal. To be sure, there was no one I have ever met like Bob Schmidt. The further I get from my days at KAYS, the more I realize how fortunate I was to have him in my life. I would not be where I am today if it weren't for his guidance.

Chapter 3 Friends of Bob:

Mitch Holthus: Play-by-Play, Kansas State University, 1983-96; Kansas City Chiefs, 1996 - Present. Per capita, the state of Kansas definitely holds its own in terms of quality play-by-play broadcasters produced. I think that comes from a certain work ethic, knowing your audience, respecting the audience and respecting the game. Look at those people who started out doing high school games and have had the opportunity to do college or professional sports. The Ness City - LaCrosse game is as important to them as the Royals versus the White Sox. They respect their audience and the fact this game is important to their listeners. People hang on your words, so it is an awesome responsibility to tell that story and be professional in doing it.

The thing that made Bob so good was his ability to translate the excitement of the event for the listener, and activate all the senses. It's not about just being excited or being loud. It comes in the pace, the timing, the descriptions and the story he told. With Bob, you absolutely know what is happening and the environment in which the game is being played.

Dave Armstrong: ESPN, Jayhawk Television Network, 2002 - Present. I first met Bob Davis in 1979 as I worked on the television side at KAYS in Hays. I remember walking in the studio and heard him recording a spot. He was the only guy I have ever known who cupped his hand over his ear, almost as if it was a headset. There was this loud booming voice and an amazing description. I thought to myself, "my gosh, if I am ever going to be as good as him, I really need to step it up."

Bob was so generous. He always had time for me and other young announcers. I remember after I left Hays for Wichita and KKRD (later became KSNW) we'd talk weekly and he would help me to become a better play-by-play broadcaster. He was that way with everyone. He always had time for you. He was so good and so loved by the people of Hays. I think that is the reason he stayed there so long. And, he loved them back. What made Bob so good is he captured the moment better than anyone. He would get excited and was able to get you excited. But it wasn't about him. It was about the action on the court or on the field. It was not fake at all. And he did it without using the word "we." He wanted the team to win, but he wasn't a homer in doing the games.

Errol Wuertz: Production Director, KAYS radio and television station, 1967-78. I thought we all worked well together at KAYS to deliver the best radio and television we could. But we did have our fun, too. Our routine after doing the 10 p.m. newscast was to go out to the Wagon Wheel for a hamburger and beer. The owner, Andy Lang always knew what we wanted and it became our hangout. One time we brought news anchor Bob Chaffin with us and Andy asked who he was. We never let Chaffin forget just because he was a TV star, not everyone knew his name.

Back then, you had to be able to think on your feet because in TV and radio, not everything goes as planned. We were filming high school football previews and on this particular day we went to Stockton. Everything was going fine until the film jammed in the camera. We had two options. Either fix it right there in the broad daylight and lose everything by exposing the film. Or, find some place that was pitch dark and fix it. After some thought, I told Bob that if he helped me get in the trunk of our car and close it, I could then fix it. After I was done, Bob let me out and we went back to shooting.

Gerard Wellbrock: Voice of the Fort Hays State Tigers, 2008 - Present. I would not be where I am today without Bob Davis. I grew up in Hays listening to him do Fort Hays and high school sports; and followed him when he left to do KU and the Royals. I can't remember wanting to be anything other than a sports broadcaster. I sent a tape to him when I was in college for a critique and he got back to me right away with a thorough response. That tells you how good a person he is.

I don't think it is too strong to say he is a legend, not only in this area, but around the league, too. People ask about him all the time. He was popular -- I should say he is popular -- even though he has been gone for 35 years. He was inducted into the Fort Hays State Hall of Fame in 1990. That honor is usually reserved for coaches, athletes and administrators. It tells you how highly people thought of Bob.

KAYS radio has quite a legacy of broadcasters and I feel fortunate to be part of that group. About 10 years ago, we began holding a reunion of people who were sportscasters dating back to the 1950s each summer. We lost Kay Melia and Bob Schmidt recently, but you have Bob, Wyatt Thompson, Steve Webster and myself. I tell those guys they were so good, that I don't belong with that group. I am the only one of those who has not won a national basketball title at Fort Hays -- and they let me know about it!

Larry Friend: Head Football Coach, Plainville, Kan. High School, 1968-88. Bob is just a tremendous person and friend. He was busy at the radio station and doing Fort Hays and Hays and TMP sports, but still found time to do the weekly "Coach's Corner" interviews with several of the smaller schools around Hays. We'd talk each week for about 10 minutes, and then we'd hang on the line for what seemed to be another half hour to shoot the breeze. What I liked about Bob, is even though we were small high schools, he treated us no different than when he was doing work for the bigger schools or Fort Hays. He made us feel special. The radio show was important because they promoted football, our town and our kids. I really enjoyed listening to Bob do games because he had so much energy and excitement. He was always so descriptive and sharp in his broadcast. I always felt it was an honor to talk to him.

Mike Kennedy: Voice of the Wichita State Shockers, 1980 - Present; (Chanute High School [KKOY radio] 1971-73; Pittsburg State [KOAM radio] 1973-76). The play-by-play guys in the state of Kansas have always had a real camaraderie because we realize how difficult it is to break into the business and that many of us got our start doing high school sports. You look at people like Bob, Mitch Holthus and Wyatt Thompson, and they all were Kansas high school grads and started doing high school sports. That was my path as well. Kansas is not a state of major metropolitan markets, so the opportunity is not as great. I also think there has been a great respect for those who came before us because of the quality of their work and the ethical manner in which they went about it. The people at the major universities or bigger stations were never too busy to help. I remember when Wichita State and Kansas met in the 2015 NCAA Tournament in Omaha, Bob and I were afforded the opportunity to spend some extended time together. We did some radio shows together and had some great conversations. It was like old times. It was wonderful.

I can appreciate Bob's love for baseball and growing up in small-town America watching minor league baseball. When I was at Chanute and Pittsburg, there were many people who would speak fondly of the old KOM League. It was their chance to see the major leaguers of tomorrow, including a young Mickey Mantle who played shortstop for Independence. In fact, my first broadcast at Chanute was an American Legion baseball game at the community ballpark where the Chanute team in the KOM League used to play. In a relatively small geographic area you had several small towns with minor league teams. It was America's pastime.

Bill Hancock: Associate Commissioner, Big Eight Conference; Director, Division I NCAA Men's Basketball Championship; Executive Director, College Football Playoff. In 1978, a guy with a sly grin showed up to broadcast the Big Eight Holiday Tournament from Kemper Arena. He shuffled his feet, rubbed his hands together and said, "Hi, I'm Bob Davis from Hays, Kansas. I hope you will have us."

Of course, we were happy to have Bob and KAYS-AM. Bob paid the rights fee— it wasn't much more than the price of a hotdog—and KAYS was in business. As Humphrey Bogart said to Claude Rains at the end of *Casablanca*, that was the beginning of a beautiful friendship. The fact that I remember Bob's earnest, clever sincerity more than 40 years later says everything about him. He is truly an extraordinary, unforgettable Kansan with a warm smile and quick wit. At our house we still quote "Bob-isms." He is a wordsmith; the Shakespeare of the airwaves. Bob didn't change a bit when he moved up to a dream-come-to-true position as voice of the Jayhawks. He always opened the door and let us into his and Linda's lives. Their son Steven was like a son to all of us.

Go, Tigers, Go!

MY EXPERIENCE WITH the people of Fort Hays State was wonderful. The campus always had so much energy. It was a picturesque setting of limestone buildings with beautiful landscaping tucked in the southwest corner of the city. There was a traditional campus quad crisscrossed by sidewalks and protected by a canopy of large elm, ash and oak trees. It was surrounded by quaint neighborhoods and Big Creek, which wound itself from the northwest to the southeast corner of campus.

The institution also serves a vital service to western Kansas in particular, producing teachers, nurses, scientists, business leaders, artists and more. It is the only four-year college on I-70 located between Denver and Salina, Kan. - a stretch of 433 miles. Today, the campus and enrollment continues to grow because of a key decision made years ago. There was an emphasis placed on distance learning, opening up education to the world. Because of that, it has the third largest enrollment of all state universities with 5,000 on campus and 10,000 accessing it on the world wide web.

The sports teams, where I had most of my focus, were the Tigers and their colors were black and gold. Nothing unusual about that, until you consider the influence of the University of Missouri on those selections. Fort Hays was actually created as a branch of Emporia State in 1902. History has it that shortly after his arrival as school president in 1913, William Lewis sought to create an official mascot and colors. He thought it should have gold to represent its roots with Emporia State. But being a native Missourian and a fan of the University of Missouri, he selected black as a second color and the name of Tigers as the mascot.

Cade Suran was the athletic director when I arrived. He had been a successful basketball coach at Wellington High School before coming to Fort Hays. At Wellington, he coached some outstanding basketball players. On the same team he had Ernie Barrett, who went on to be an All-American and led Kansas State to a Final Four, Jerry Waugh who was All-Big Seven at Kansas and later would coach Wilt Chamberlain at Kansas as an assistant coach, and Harold Rogers, an All-Missouri Valley performer at

Oklahoma State. He also coached Bob Blazer and Rex Curtis, who came with him to play at Fort Hays. Blazer would be a long-time teacher and coach in the Hays Public School System, while Curtis would become a successful businessman.

Cade was short in stature but was a ball of energy. He was an uptempo basketball coach who did not care if your man scored 20 points as long as you scored 21. He was well-respected and well-liked on campus and in the community. He had a great sense of humor and had great fun with me in always critiquing my broadcasts the next day.

The residents of McMindes Hall on the Fort Hays State campus thought highly of Bob Davis. Credit: Bob Davis

Chuck Brehm replaced Suran as basketball coach, coming to Hays after coaching Dodge City to the 1964 national junior college title. One of his stars was Galen Frick who would go on to play at Kansas State. Years later he would coach Brent Frack at Fort Hays. I would tell people Brehm was the only person ever to coach both Frick **and** Frack. A good athlete in his own right, Brehm's Fort Hays teams were tough, physical and competitive. He also built his teams around Kansas high school kids, adding a few out of state players here and there.

One of the more memorable seasons came as the Tigers won the Rocky Mountain Athletic Conference in 1971. They capped it off with a 101-99 overtime win over Western New Mexico on its home court in Silver City, located in far southwest New Mexico. Gary Ritter, from Norcatur, Kan., hit the shot that sent the game into overtime and the bucket that won it -- both in the final seconds.

The win meant the Tigers would play KCAC champion Friends University of Wichita for the right to play in the NAIA national tournament the next week. But a huge snow storm wreaked havoc on the return trip to Hays. The team chartered two planes for the round trip. Assistant Coach Bud Moeckel and big men on one plane, and the guards, radio crew, athletic director and Brehm on the other. The plan was to leave after the game, but a fuel pump malfunction kept the team overnight. The next day we refueled in Amarillo, Texas, and the itinerary called for the team to go to Enid, Okla., and then into Hays. The weather continued to get worse and after getting airborne, the plane carrying big men was diverted through Denver, and the other continued to Hays.

With blizzard-like conditions in Hays, the pilot had quite a tussle on his hands landing the plane. As he announced our final descent and the pavement appeared, Suran broke the tension by saying, "I sure hope this isn't Main Street." The group in Denver got snowed in for four days. They finally arrived in Hays with only time to shower, pack and jump on the bus to Emporia. The team did not have one full practice in preparation for Friends, and fell, 92-85 to end the season.

The unique thing about that group is the starting five of Daryl Apel (Belpre), Leneal Locke (Natoma), Daryl Stockstill (Geneseo), Mike Gaskill (Muscotah) and Dave Okeson (Weskan) each came from small Kansas communities. The aggregate population of those five towns was less than 1,500. I was as close to that team as any. Today, I keep in touch with many of them, along with Chuck (Brehm).

Joe Rosado came from Clinton Area Community College in Iowa, replacing Brehm who had retired following the 1977-78 campaign. Joe grew up in New York and played baseball at Illinois. Whereas Chuck's teams were a bit more patterned and disciplined, Rosado's emphasis was to play uptempo and score as much as you could. He eclipsed the .500 winning percentage mark in his third year, going 17-16. One of the losses was on the road to Division I San Diego State, which featured a guard by the name of Tony Gwynn. He would go on to be one of baseball's all-time best hitters and a Hall of Famer. In Rosado's fourth year, the Tigers won the Central States Conference title, NAIA District 10 championship and advanced to the NAIA national tournament in Kansas City, finishing with a 30-4 record in 1980-81.

That team came from near and far. Max Hamblin (Page, Ariz.) and Mark Wilson

(Columbus, Ohio) were the first team all-league guards. The three other starters were honorable mention all-league picks, Bill Giles (Hays High School), son of former Fort Hays State football coach Bill Giles, Lionel "Zuke" Hamer (Lakeview, S.C.) and Cesar Fantauzzi (Arroyo, Puerto Rico). Hamer was a physical specimen, while Fantauzzi (Fan-too-zee) had great personality on the court -- and a name that play-by-play and public announcers loved to say. It would be Rosado's last campaign. The following season was a bit of a transition. But the spotlight would shine again the next year in 1982-83.

Fort Hays Athletic Director Bobby Thompson, who previously served as football coach, scored a major coup in landing Grand Canyon's Ben Lindsey to coach the Tigers. Lindsey had reached the NAIA national tournament seven of the last eight years with two national titles, but his tenure at FHSU was one of the more bizarre in college sports. He had hoped to get the Arizona job that was open along with the FHSU position, but the Wildcats had lured Kansas State head coach Jack Hartman away from Manhattan to be their next coach -- at least they thought so. A plane was sent from Tucson to Manhattan to bring him back for a press conference, but Hartman was not on it when it returned. Arizona was back to square one and turned to Lindsey who had been on the job at Fort Hays for all of one day in April 1982.

My only interview with Lindsey was by phone just before he left for the Hays Airport. As strange as it was, the move made sense. You don't turn down a Division I offer to coach. Unfortunately for Lindsey, he would be fired after a 4-24 campaign and was replaced by Hall of Famer Lute Olson after coaching the Wildcats only one year. I remember asking Bobby what he was going to do next and he said, "I am going to get the guy who is next on my list, Bill Morse."

Thompson acted so quickly that he had Morse on a plane to Hays in no time. In fact, Morse actually ended up bumping into Lindsey, who was flying back to Arizona, in the Hays airport. This wasn't LaGuardia or O'Hare. With only a baggage handler and gate attendant, it was hard for two of the best small college coaches in America to miss each other. Morse had not had any appreciable contact with Fort Hays State, so he picked Lindsey's brain in the airport terminal. Even though he had not coached one game, Lindsey told Morse it was a job he should strongly consider taking.

Morse came to Hays from Hillsdale (Mich.) College after having finished fourth at the NAIA national tournament in 1981. He instantly made the Tigers a national power casting a wide net for recruits. Among those was All-American Nate Rollins, a transfer from Marymount College in Salina. The story on Rollins is that he actually decided to transfer to Fort Hays before Morse was hired, but made it official after the announcement. He was the first coach I saw use different colored towels and signs to call plays. It was a technique he picked up from watching Michigan State during his days at Hillsdale. They worked most of the time, and quite well I might add.

Morse was a Jekyll and Hyde on game day. He was an extremely demonstrative coach on the sideline, which earned him more than a few technicals during his career. But on his postgame radio shows -- win or lose -- he was calm. I remember our postgame interviews at the NAIA tournament where the final two wins came in overtime. The broadcast crew was worn to a frazzle as the final buzzer sounded, but Morse was cool, calm and collected as he did his radio show.

Fort Hays finished third at the 1983 NAIA national tourney and followed it up with back-to-back championships in 1984 and 1985. The 1983 tournament was noteworthy in that the Tigers beat Chaminade, 85-76, in the third-place game. Earlier that year, Chaminade upset Virginia in Hawaii. Fort Hays fans were chanting "Bring on Virginia" during the game. In the 1984 semifinals, the Tigers took an 86-84 overtime win against Chicago State on a buzzer-beating baseline jumper by Joe Anderson. He was only in the game because three starters had fouled out. Anderson hailed from Toledo, Ohio, so naturally when he hit the winning bucket I called him Joe "Holy Toledo" Anderson.

The title game the next night was a 48-46 grind-it-out overtime nailbiter over Wisconsin-Stevens Point. The Tigers' largest lead of the night was two and the Pointers' was four. The game was tied in the first half at every two point interval until Stevens Point scored late to take a 20-18 intermission lead. Dick Bennett, who was the Pointers head coach, would later coach Wisconsin. His son, of course, is Virginia head coach Tony Bennett. Their star player that year was former Portland Trailblazer Terry Porter, the tourney MVP. Rollins, guard Raymond Lee and Edgar Eason, a transfer from Southern Mississippi, made the all-tourney team for the Tigers.

Morse was a master motivator and used a variety of psychological ploys to motivate his players to greater performances. He even went as far to send forward Dan Lier to a psychologist to improve his rebounding. The ironic thing about that as I found out listening to him on a podcast with current Tiger play-by-play voice Gerard Wellbrock is that today, Lier is a highly-successful motivational speaker. But the irony doesn't end there. One of his clients for a period of time was his NAIA title game opponent, Terry Porter while he was an NBA head coach.

That would be the last game I would call as the voice of the Tigers as I got the KU job a few months later. I was lucky to go out on top. The Tiger faithful was delirious in its postgame celebration and it certainly felt good to be the radio voice of the national champion. I'm sure if you went back and listened to the game as the clock counted down I was more than a little excited.

To show you how much times have changed, Bennett and Morse, who were only slight acquaintances, met for breakfast the morning of the championship game and talked basketball for a few hours. Morse was so enamored with Bennett's motion offense that he wanted to learn more about how it worked. A few years later, Morse was at the NCAA Final Four for the national coaches convention, when he was stopped in the hallway by Brad Soderberg, the point guard for that Stevens Point team. After talking about the game, Morse encouraged him to apply for an open assistant position at Fort Hays State. Soderberg accepted the job offer, and would spend the 1986-87 season looking up at an NAIA national championship banner that came at his expense.

Interestingly, Fort Hays State lost only two games that year (35-2). One was a 62-61 home loss to Emporia State, and the other an 81-64 defeat at Arizona and head coach Lute Olson. That game was known as the "Ben Lindsey Game." When Lindsey left Hays after only one day on the job, he promised Thompson he would host the Tigers for a game in Arizona in the near future. Of course, Lindsey lasted only one year and was not around to play the Tigers.

The following year, Fort Hays sweated out a 67-63 win over Athens State, then took a 65-64 decision in the semifinals over Central Washington. Fred Campbell's 12-foot, off-balance shot at the buzzer was the difference. In the title game, Morse's son Ron hit the winning shot against Wayland Baptist at the buzzer, his only points of the night, to give the Tigers back-to-back crowns. The Tigers took it the length of the court in :05 and Morse's little runner hit every portion of the rim and dropped through the net. Eason won MVP honors. Porter, who was back for another run at the title made the all-tournament second team, along with a lanky young man from Southeastern Oklahoma State by the name of Dennis Rodman.

I mentioned that the 1984 NAIA title game was my swan song as the Tigers' play-by-play voice, but I unexpectedly joined the broadcast for the last few games of the 1985 NAIA tourney. KU had finished its season, so I reached out to my KAYS successor Wyatt Thompson and told him I was coming over to watch some of the games. He was kind enough to ask me to join him and his color man Bob Templeton on the call. If you thought the three-man booth for Monday Night Football was tough, try getting three play-by-play guys to keep from stepping over each other doing basketball. But it was wonderful to be back as part of that broadcast. I knew so many of the players and of course, the coaching staff. This was a big moment for Wyatt and the last thing he needed was the old guy hanging around, but he insisted. Wyatt is one of my best friends and as voice of the Kansas State Wildcats is truly an outstanding broadcaster. I know he elevated the talent level when he took over at KAYS.

A note about Wayland Baptist. Its coach was a young 27-year-old by the name of Mark Adams. The year after I retired from KU, Adams went to Texas Tech as Chris Beard's defensive guru.

Morse also took the Tigers to the 1988 NAIA tournament, falling in the second round to eventual national champion Grand Canyon, 101-95. The Antelopes were coached by former Phoenix Suns All-Star Paul Westphal. In 2012, the NAIA celebrated its 75th anniversary of the tournament and named its 60 tournament all-stars, which included Rollins and Eason. Morse, who was 20-4 all-time in the tournament, was one of 15 all-star coaches selected.

I remember after I went on to broadcast KU games, Morse came up to see me. Tipoff was just over 20 minutes away, but I wanted Bill to meet Jayhawk head coach Larry Brown for a quick introduction. I returned to my seat and darned if they weren't talking Xs and Os up until the opening tip. There were a lot of wins between those two.

All told, Fort Hays State advanced to Kansas City eight times, finishing with a respectable 21-8 record, including two-fourth place, one third and two championship finishes. Years later, Fort Hays State completed an undefeated season in winning the 1996 NCAA Division II championship under former Missouri assistant coach Gary Garner.

The NAIA Basketball Tournament is quite an event. It began in 1937 and has had a long history in Kansas City. Fans would go to either Municipal Auditorium or Kemper Arena and watch games all day. For a brief period in the late 1990s, the event was in Tulsa. Crowds in Kansas City were good for the 32-team bracket, especially when a local team such as Fort Hays State, Rockhurst, Benedictine, Washburn, Mid-American Nazarene played. The people of Hays supported the event quite well. You didn't have to worry about the bank getting robbed because everyone was in Kansas City.

At Fort Hays State, basketball games were played in the intimate confines of Sheridan Coliseum, which was built 1915 and completed in 1922. It was intimidating for the visitors, as the floor had a pit layout with an eight foot high wall surrounding the playing surface. Only the teams were on the floor and the crowd of 1,800 was literally and physically on top of them. My broadcasting vantage point was high above the floor in the crow's nest. It could get loud and warm in there.

In 1973, basketball moved to a Gross Memorial Coliseum on the southwest corner of campus. It was an outstanding arena for any level of play, let alone an NAIA school. Seating was just under 7,000, and sellouts were a frequent occurrence after a while. It is still regularly voted the top NCAA Division II facility in the nation. The arena was part of an impressive health, physical education and recreation complex with an indoor track, four gyms, five racquetball courts, weights area, swimming pool and classrooms. It truly was ahead of its time.

The facility has been a boon to the community, attracting high school state championship events, state Special Olympics Championships, NCAA regional competitions and more. In the mid-1970s, the Kansas State High School Activities Association brought together all of the various class wrestling champions twice, and all basketball champions once for the short-lived Grand State Championships at Gross.

Fort Hays hosted a big time double-header to christen its new arena. Fort Hays beat East Central Oklahoma and then in the nightcap national powers Marymount of Salina, coached by Ken Cochran, beat Gardner Webb, which had future NBA player John Drew on the team. Marymount's Jimmy Hearns hit a baseline jumper at the buzzer for the win. It was such an electric night and community pride was on display in full force. It was a big-time environment, something Hays had never witnessed up to that point.

There was some sadness felt on that night, as well. Mike Hammerschmidt, who along with his younger brother Steve played on the first team I ever broadcast -- the American Legion -- was killed in a construction accident in building the new arena. It always took a bit out of me to hear of a player or a coach I had broadcast pass away. And, it tugged at my heart even more when it happened at a young age.

So many games stand out at Gross Memorial, but none more than a January 20, 1981 matchup between two, top-five ranked teams, Denver (14-1) and the Tigers (17-0). It was the day the hostages were released from Iran and patriotism was on full display. The Tigers won a hotly contested battle before a standing room only crowd to move to 18-0 under Rosado. Just a few weeks before I was in Lexington, Ky., filling in for a KU broadcast and I remember being somewhat in awe of the size of the building. It seats 24,000 people. I remember on the broadcast saying that Rupp had nothing on Gross that night. It was as electric an environment as I have ever witnessed.

During my last five or six years, Fort Hays State basketball was a must see event. Gross Memorial Coliseum was regularly packed and full of energy. The Tigers' fight song was the same melody as Northwestern's, a high energy, peppy beat. But the unofficial fight song was "In Heaven There is No Beer." You have to remember, you only had to be 18 to drink beer in Kansas. And whether it was true or not, many proclaimed Hays to be the beer-drinking capital of the world. Let's just say the kids enjoyed their weekends.

In football, Wayne McConnell was the coach when I took over for the last few games in 1968, then he retired. He was replaced by Tom Stromgren. A native of Osage City who had coached at the College of Emporia, Stromgren was the first coach I saw use a tower on the practice field. He had the bullhorn going full volume. He would famously deride his defense over the bullhorn for "tackling worse than Kelli and Becki Stromgren" -- his two young daughters. The echo stretched for blocks in south Hays. Stromgren would coach for three years, then go into private business creating and selling athletic support braces for knees, ankles, etc. He did quite well for himself and the company distributed products all over the world. He then re-turned to Fort Hays to serve five years as athletics director. He was inducted into the Fort Hays State Athletics Hall of Fame in 2002.

Next came Bill Giles, who played collegiately at Nebraska in the early 1950s. He was stoic and had the profile of your stereotypical football coach. Large physical stature, a square jaw, penetrating eyes and a no-nonsense approach. In his eight years he won one conference championship, the Central State Intercollegiate Conference crown in 1975. The team would have 13 players earn first, second or honorable mention team recognition. Nine of those were from small town Kansas. The biggest community represented by those 13 was Great Bend.

That season was good for local Maalox sales. The team went 5-4 overall, but 5-1 in conference play. Seven of the games were decided by 10 or fewer points, and six by six or fewer points. It was quite a turnaround after the program won a combined 10 games the previous four seasons. Giles would later become an NFL scout and stop in to visit me in Lawrence when he reviewed films of Kansas players or watched practices.

The Fort Hays football teams were regularly competitive, but never able to build consistently on periodic conference championship teams. But there were some excellent players and great people I covered in my time. Most notable was Steve Crosby, from Pawnee Rock, which had population of 250 and played 8-man football (the school eventually closed in 1972). He actually attended Kansas State for two years, was drafted into the military, then came back and finished school at Fort Hays State. He rushed for 2,780 yards and 27 touchdowns in three seasons and was an NAIA Little All-American as a senior in 1973.

Crosby was drafted by the New York Giants in 1974 -- in the 17th round! -- and played for three years before a knee injury ended his career. He returned to get a master's degree at Fort Hays and was slated to coach Scott City High School in 1978. But the summer before, the Miami Dolphins called and offered him an assistant coaching job. He would end up being an NFL assistant coach for 26 years and scout four more. He was also an assistant coach at Vanderbilt for three years.

Jerry Simmons was another Tiger who went on to enjoy a long NFL coaching career. Hailing from Elkhart, he played at Garden City Community College prior to coming to Fort Hays, where he was an all-league linebacker for the 1975 CSIC champions. He would enjoy a 23 year tenure in the league as a strength and conditioning coach. Interestingly, I would later broadcast games of his nephew, Darrin who was a punter on the victorious 1995 Kansas Jayhawk Aloha Bowl squad. Darrin himself has had a successful NFL coaching career as he is now the assistant head coach and special teams coordinator for the Cincinnati Bengals.

Interviewing Tiger Football Coach Jim Gilstrap (1981-83). Credit: Bob Davis

As a broadcaster, you generally get pretty close with the training staff. They give you the inside skinny on the injuries and know the vibe of the team. During my time, the Tigers had two pretty good ones who went on to the NFL. Steve Antonopulos was the trainer from 1973-76, and is now in his 44th year with the Denver Broncos. "Greek" as Antonopulos is known, has such respect among the Denver organization that he was selected by Pat Bowlen's family to give the induction speech for Broncos late-owner at the 2019 NFL Hall of Fame ceremonies. Brad Brown was the Fort Hays trainer from 1978-85. He joined the Antonopulos in Denver and then was named the trainer for the Houston Oilers/Tennessee Titans for 27 years. I had more than my share of fun with those guys.

Football was played in a picturesque setting on the southeast edge of campus at Lewis Field Stadium. The field received quite a workout as both high schools and Fort Hays played there. Limestone was the material of choice for almost every building on campus, including the football stadium. It was constructed in 1936 and today seats just under 6,500. The stadium was enclosed by a 10-foot limestone wall. It was a perfect location as it was a short walk from the dorms and adjacent neighborhoods.

The fortunes of the football program changed shortly after I left as former Colorado assistant and Mesa State (Colo.) head coach Bob Cortese arrived in 1990, going a respectable 55-32-3 with two league titles and three playoff berths in seven years. It was under his watch that the Tigers went from the NAIA to NCAA Division II. In 2006, Fort Hays moved to the MIAA, the most difficult Division II league in the nation. Over the past decade, the Tigers have won league titles, made the NCAA Division II playoffs and earned bowl bids. Head coach Chris Brown, a product of Liberal High School and a standout linebacker at Pitt State, has certainly rekindled excitement around the program.

Fort Hays always had a solid athletic program with Kansas kids as the base, and filling in with others from around the nation -- and even some internationally -- joining them. The Tiger cross country, and track and field programs were examples. Alex Francis was the no nonsense coach. Hailing from Oberlin, he was the brother of Nebraska football standouts, Sam and Vike. A Fort Hays grad, his teams were outstanding, winning league track titles 14 times and finishing second 14 times in his 31- year career. Francis was the distance coach for the U.S. 1968 Olympic Team and held other national coaching positions. He was not only nationally known, but you could go anywhere in the international track and field scene and the name Alex Francis was held in high esteem.

John Mason, from Phillipsburg, was a distance running contemporary of KU's Jim Ryun and Kenya's Kip Keino. Mason was a 14-time NAIA All-American and eight time NAIA champion. He was ranked in the top three in the mile in the U.S. in 1968 and 1969. He might be the most decorated athlete in school history. Not bad for a farm kid from western Kansas. The men's cross country team earned four NAIA team titles and was runner up four times. The men's program had 15 NAIA individual champions under Francis.

Fort Hays was a member of the NAIA while I was there, and later became a member of NCAA Division II. Regardless of the classification, The Tigers' various conference affiliations featured a competitive balance for as long as I was in Hays. There were league opponents from Colorado, Nebraska and Kansas - the in-state rivalries with Emporia State, Washburn and Pittsburg State were intense, yet fun. The common characteristic is that these conferences featured schools predominantly located in small cities that revolved around the universities. League titles were thought to be the pinnacle. Because of that, the coaches, administrators, media, and broadcast crews were close and friendly.

I will always look back at my days doing Fort Hays State athletics with great fondness. So many people associated with the program when I was there are still my friends today. I am also happy for them that they have had outstanding broadcasters follow me. They deserved that.

Chapter 4 Sidebar: A Rhyme for Every Season

As a broadcaster, especially when you are tied to a school or franchise, you tend to be asked to do public speaking events. It gives you a chance to interact with the fans and the people you cover in a bit of a different way. I did my share of kickoff luncheons, hall of fame award shows, postseason banquets -- and enjoyed doing them. Sometimes I was the keynote speaker and other times I was the master of ceremonies.

These events were much like broadcasting in that they were "live radio" and things did not always go as planned. You just had to go with the flow and play off the other speakers. My number one rule was to not be the "news" of the day. I really had to think about my jokes and of course make sure the "off the cuff" comments didn't come back to bite me.

The goal of these luncheons was predominantly to celebrate achievement, so the focus was positive, even if the season did not go particularly well. To accomplish this, I came up with the idea to write and share a short poem that shined the spotlight on the honorees for a Fort Hays State postseason banquet early in my career. It wasn't necessarily the plan to do it as frequently as I did, but I received so much positive feedback that I did them regularly.

1984 Fort Hays State Basketball Banquet Poem

We're back this year with another dinner; Tonight we dine with Fort Hays' all-time winner!
Blood pressure, pulse, everything's vital, our Tigers came home with the National Title.
But let's back up, let's remember a year; full of victories, excitement and perhaps a tear.
Fans talked Kansas City in early November; Last year's record was easy to remember.
Bill said all along the team could be better; but warned against expecting a records setter.
That's only logical, they were 32-4; And third in the nation,could they do more?
Well, we all know what happened. It's unbelievable, what this team did was inconceivable.
They won the conference with a mark of 13-1, of course the team knew there was more to be done.
The league finale was a victory at Kearney; at the end the Fort Hays fans were calling for Barney.
In the playoffs, Friends, Emporia and Washburn all contended, but the District 10 title was well defended.
Back again to the national tournament; two years in a row seems darn near permanent.
Taylor, Central Wesleyan and Waynesburg, a three-night chore, that carried Fort Hays back to the final four.
A pair of overtime victories, oh no time to panic; the calmest guy there was Jerry Tomanek.
When it ended we cheered in elation; the Tigers were first in the whole dang nation.
The fans loved it, the year was a hit, they yelled "Go, Fight, Win" and sometimes... "Bull Feathers."
Our special thanks to the coaches and team, you made '84 a Tiger fan's dream.

1985 Kansas Football Banquet Poem

We're glad you're here, a night where football's the word; With stories of Mike, Willie, Richard and Sylvester Byrd.

There were good and bad, highs and lows, of course; But mostly good times with the KU Air Force.

From Oahu to Florida, on to Norman and Ames, traveled soundly, Paul, Robert and John to play the games.

Rainbows, Commodores, Panthers and Sycamores, KU won four times in the non-league wars.

A Big Eight fact that needs to be told, Kansas downed the purple and white, and black and gold.

The 'Hawks were impressive topping the 'Cats; It showed on the board and in the stats.

And the season finale with Mizzou, what a jewel! I seem to recall this day was....rather cool!

The Union, the Bomb Squad, it all came alive...We had fun with the 'Hawks in 85.

Travis Hardy's bandana and Lynn Williams' muscle, and whatever the score, the 'Hawks would hustle.

But, there's more to the sport than a win or defeat, sometimes it works, sometimes you get beat.

Remember the good things football yields...guys like Skip, Arnold and Harvey Fields.

And if we might add a personal note, I'll slip it in here in this sonnet I wrote.

It was fun for us to describe the scene...that's yours truly and my friend, Mr. Falkenstien.

Ahead we'll have more good times aplenty, under the guidance of head coach Valesente.

And we hope you're there for the passes and kicks, and the tackles and blocks in '86.

Chapter 4 Friends of Bob

Bill Morse: Head Basketball Coach, Fort Hays State, 1983-91. Bob was as genuine a person there could be. He's the one who made me comfortable from the start in Hays and helped me tremendously in getting to know the people of Hays. The first day I am in town, he calls me up to go to lunch and we eat greasy french fries at Al's Chickenette. The next day he calls up the previous two coaches, Cade Suran and Chuck Brehm, and we go out for coffee. So, in two days I ended up knowing more about Fort Hays than most people who lived there. The thing about Bob is he cared so much about being a professional. He was so good at his craft. You know, when he got the job at KU, everyone in Hays was happy for him. Sure, we were going to miss him, but this was his reward. He was one of us, and we were excited for him.

John Mason: Fort Hays State University, 14-time NAIA Track & Field Champion, Third Ranked in U.S. in the Mile, 1968 & 1969. After beating Kenya's Kip Keino in Stockholm, Sweden (1968 World University Games), I returned back to the states the next day. I became very sick in Stockholm from drinking polluted water. I made it to Denver, but had to be carried off the plane to an ambulance and transported to a hospital. I was in the hospital for several weeks and then went to the Olympic Training site at Lake Tahoe where we would run the Olympic Trials. I wasn't completely recovered from my illness and had to run three races just like the Olympic Games. I came up short in the final race, where they took the top three to Mexico City. If I would not have got sick in Stockholm then I would have run much better, maybe even make the Olympic Team. Keino went on and won the gold medal at the Olympic Games after I had beat him a few months earlier. When I returned to Hays from the Olympic Trials, Bob met me at the airport and interviewed me. It was a great era for the U.S. in the mile, competing neck and neck with people like Jim Ryun and Marty Liquori.

Joe Rosado: Fort Hays State head basketball coach, 1978-81. One of the highlights of my life came on January 20, 1981. Not only were our American hostages released from captivity in Iran, but it was the day Gross Memorial Coliseum became a basketball arena.

I am not disparaging the arena or the fans, but the school went from a stadium that seated less than 2,000 to one that holds almost 7,000. That night we were hosting Denver University they had only one loss (14-1) and we were undefeated (17-0). Both of us were ranked in the top five. I'll never forget that I lived on Hillcrest Drive and noticed something strange when I drove a few blocks to 27th and Hall and saw cars backed up in all directions. There was a policeman directing traffic and I stopped and rolled down the window and asked what had happened. He did not recognize me as the coach and just said, "pregame traffic" then signalled me ahead.

All the traffic meant I got to Gross a little later than normal. I saw the lines trying to buy tickets stretching for as far as you could see. I remember our athletic staff telling us we had a problem -- we ran out of cigar boxes to hold the money as we took tickets. That is when it really hit me the night was going to be special. Bob and I recorded the pregame show and I am sure we were talking a mile a minute in anticipation. The building was juiced. I am not sure we could have squeezed another person in the building. The national anthem sent a chill down your back. I could see people with tears running down their cheeks. We got down 10 points in the first half. Denver was a very good team. But in the second half we started to play better and the crowd got behind us. It was unbelievably loud. We ended up winning by 10 (72-62) and of course went on to win the league, District 10 and go to the NAIA national tournament in Kansas City (finish at 30-4). Our crowds were near full or full the rest of the year and Gross was the place to be.

Joe Rosado, Head Basketball Coach, Fort Hays State, 1978-81. I remember meeting Bob just after I was hired. We had done some radio interviews and I spoke at a few Tiger Club events with him. I knew from the beginning he was good. What pipes! I thought to myself, "What is this guy doing in Hays, Kan.?" That is not a knock on Hays and I was definitely not complaining. We were fortunate to have him. But he was a major league talent. I was not surprised by the fact he later got the KU job and then the Royals. I became close to Bob and Linda and they would often come over to the house for coffee and just to talk. He had a great sense of humor and was just fun to be around. We still keep in contact even though I live in Florida. He usually calls when he sees on the news a hurricane hit Florida. He makes sure I didn't get blown away.

Gary Sechrist: Track/Football, Hays High, 1974-76; Track/Football, Fort Hays State, 1977-82. Sports were big in Hays and much of the reason for that was Bob. He made games fun to listen to and was the link for the fans when they could not be there in person. You knew exactly how the game was going when Bob was broadcasting. People huddled around the radio hanging on his words. I remember filling gas early one Saturday morning at the old Champlin Station at 27th and Vine. We had played the night before at home. Bob pulls in to gas up for a road trip to do a Fort Hays State game. This was early and he had been on the road the previous night to do a TMP game. But he stops me and wants to talk about how we did and get all the details. We were fortunate to have Bob broadcasting sports in Hays. He was so good.

Mark Watts: Basketball, Hays High, 1972-74; Fort Hays State, 1976-78. Because I had two other brothers who played sports at Hays High, and our family was involved in the community, we knew Bob well. We had played half the season my senior year at Fort Hays State, and Rick Covington, who was our sports information director and Bob were both trying to get me to break a record so I would have my name in the record book. The record was for the most disqualifications in a season. If my man was going in for a layup I would guard him close but not foul and get my fifth one because I sure didn't want Bob on the radio saying, "That was Mark's fifth foul and that sets a single season disqualification record of eight in one season!"

Bill Hall: Fort Hays State Baseball Letterman, 1973-74; All-American 1974; Inducted into FHSU Athletic Hall of Fame, 2019. On Christmas Day 1973, my high school sweetheart and fiance, Linda Pfeifer and I set our wedding date for the following May. It seemed like a good idea until we qualified for the NAIA World Series in St. Joseph, Mo. Our first game was to be on the same day as our wedding!

It was a no-win situation as the NAIA was not going to budge and neither could we. We had 300 invited guests. So, we had the ceremony at noon, went to the reception until 3 and then were flown by Jim Thurman (father of Fort Hays basketball player Doug Thurman) to St. Joe. Everyone was tuned into Bob Davis on the radio to make sure we made it. I actually missed the top of the first inning, but I was penciled in as the ninth batter and Dick Kohloff started in right field. I did not miss my at bat. Bob let everyone know we were finally there. We lost our first two games, so we took the bus back to Hays -- with Linda sitting up front. Some honeymoon!

There are a lot of other great Bob Davis stories but my favorite was many years later when my sons recognized Bob doing Royals games. I told them that Bob gave me my baseball nickname "Doubles" because I broke the school record for doubles my junior year and then led the nation in doubles my senior year (too slow for any triples). Of course they rolled their eyes and didn't believe it. Shortly thereafter we went to a Royals game early to watch batting practice and were standing by the dugout when Bob stuck his head out of the press box window and yelled "Hey Doubles how are you and your sons doing?" -- I suddenly had a new level of respect from my sons.

Chuck Brehm: Head Basketball Coach, Fort Hays State, 1965-77. Bob has always had such a great sense of humor. Just a lot of fun to be around. But in our return to Hays from playing Western New Mexico in 1971, he had anything but fun. There was a heck of a snowstorm and the landing was difficult. Bob was white as a sheet. It might have been the only time I saw him at a loss for words.

Bob came to Hays just a few years after I got the Fort Hays State head basketball coaching job. We hit it off right away and to this day, my wife, Jane, and I remain good friends with Bob and Linda. He had a tough job in replacing a good announcer at KAYS, but he was good in his own right. I could tell early on that he was going places. Not only because he was talented, but because he was professional and so easy to get along with.

As a coach, you do not always get to listen to the announcers that much. But you can tell how good they are by what others are saying. People in Hays loved Bob. He was very popular.

Mike Kennedy: Voice of the Wichita State Shockers, 1980 - Present; (Chanute High School [KKOY radio] 1971-73; Pittsburg State [KOAM radio] 1973-76). I first met Bob in the fall of 1973 when I broadcast Pittsburg State and he had been doing Fort Hays State for several years. The thing that stood out to me was his welcoming style and friendly attitude. He helped introduce me to the league and the various personnel, especially the radio crews. What I saw in Bob and learned from him was he was always well prepared, he was passionate about his team - but not to the point he did not acknowledge the quality of the opponent -- and of course, he had a great sense of humor.

Bonnie Lowe: Fort Hays State Women's Basketball, 1980-82; CEO Lawrence Chamber of Commerce. I grew up 30 miles west of Hays and KAYS was our radio station of choice. The sports broadcasts, especially listening to Bob Davis doing FHSU events, were a household favorite. His descriptive manner of the uniforms being worn, atmosphere, and so many other details painted a vivid picture and made you feel you were sitting in stands.

Although I certainly knew of Bob Davis long before I met him, our first encounter was when he interviewed me as a member of the FHSU women's basketball team. I was a sophomore and was flattered, and a bit surprised, when he asked to interview me after a home game. I have no idea who we played, if we won, or my stats. What

I vividly remember was his kindness. I suspect he was fully aware of how nervous I was, and handled the brief encounter as the pro he is.

Over the past few years as I have too moved to Lawrence, Bob and I have become better friends and I enjoy our conversations, usually over lunch at The Wheel, Morningstar's Pizza, or Johnny's. Bob is always gracious. He seems surprised that after a few years of being retired, he remains immensely popular and universally admired. The world is a much better place because of Bob Davis.

Growing Up in Hays, America

ONE THING THAT struck me from the beginning was how nice the people were in Hays. I had never been there before other than for a quick pit stop when driving to Denver, so I really did not know what to expect.

Being a history major in college, my hope was the days of the Wild, Wild West in Hays were long gone. Buffalo Bill Cody, Wild Bill Hickock, General Custer and Calamity Jane all spent time in Hays. Those were some pretty tough customers, And of course, Fort Hays was established to protect stage coaches and later the railroad traveling along the Smoky Hill Trail. If you ever watched the series *Gunsmoke,* you occasionally heard reference to a trip from Dodge City to Hays, and it wasn't always for peaceful purposes. I quickly found everything was up to date in Hays and I hit the ground running.

I appreciated that people felt comfortable in coming up to me and engaging in conversation. And, for someone who came from the eastern part of the state who knew nobody in the community, that was reassuring. I made a lot of friends and I did so quickly. The listeners accepted me from the get go even though I was replacing a talented broadcaster in Keith Cummings. I consider myself to this day to be a small town person, so Hays was a great fit for me. It was a perfect marriage because the radio station was good as well.

One of the smart things we did was to create the KAYS Sports Booster Club. That allowed smaller businesses to advertise and support the local team broadcasts. It got a lot of people and businesses involved that might not have been able to otherwise. As a member, you would get a mention on air with a brief one-or two-line slogan. I'll never forget Clem Hammerschmidt, who owned a refuse hauling business. He stopped me one day and asked me to not forget him for the booster club. But he told me he first needed to change his slogan. I asked him what he wanted to say. He said, "How does 'your shit is my bread and butter' sound?" We laughed about that every time we saw each other and it was a frequent joke when I did public speaking events.

Selling advertising was not what I got into the business for, but it did allow me to meet many community leaders. The quality of people in Hays was outstanding and one reason the city thrived despite being "out in western Kansas." You of course had Bob Schmidt and Ross Beach, but I also remember attorney Norman Jeter, travel agency owner Bill Aubel, Ralph Butler, a great retailer and manager of ALCO, attorney Norbert Dreiling, who was head of the Kansas Democratic Party, Don Bickle, who was in real estate and auto parts distribution, Don Volker and Russ Clark, coowners of the Village Shop Men's Clothing Store, Tommy Wiesner, owner of Wiesner's Department Store and a host of others. They were sharp people who got things done.

Schmidt and Bickle were generous philanthropists for the Hays community and Fort Hays State, and their friendship was one that went back a long way. Bob was from LaCrosse and Don was from Hoisington. I believe it was 1947 and Bob began hitch-hiking up Highway 183 to participate in a high school track meet in Hays. That wasn't a short jaunt -- about 25 miles. Well, the Hoisington High School bus comes along and stops and Bob jumps in. He takes a seat next to Don Bickle and as they say, the rest is history. Of course Bob has passed, but both have given so much to the area.

I always thought the fabric of the community was woven with people who were friendly, helpful, hard-working and fun-loving. The community celebrations were always popular, whether it was the summer sidewalk bazaar on Main Street, Oktoberfest, the county fair, parades and of course, sporting events. Hays people took a great deal of pride in their community.

For its size, Hays was a wonderful sports town. You had the two high schools, Fort Hays State and then the Legion and the Larks with baseball in the summer. In addition, there were the area high schools to cover. There were also regional and state high school competitions in wrestling, basketball, baseball and football. KAYS also carried the Royals and the Chiefs when they did not conflict with the locals. Everywhere I went, people wanted to talk about sports, and there was a lot of it to talk about.

High school sports were well-supported in Hays. There was always a great deal of energy and excitement at the games and that interest resulted in a good following on the radio. It was unusual for a town that size to have two high schools. If there would have been only one, you would have had some pretty dominant sports programs, even though both had generally successful teams on their own.

Hays High's basketball team had quite a two-year run shortly after I arrived. Don Slone was the coach, who was originally from Missouri and played collegiately at Baker University (basketball and football) in Baldwin, Kan. He had coached at Dorrance and Natoma before making the move to Hays. The 1969-70 team included Steve Clark, Kurt Watson, Dave Rentfrow, Steve Kraus, Dana Albright, Eddie Schumacher, Randy Johnson, Kevin Murphy, Pat Lee and Randy Boggs. During the regular season, the team lost only twice -- both to Russell, which had outstanding players in Greg Boxberger who went on to play at Wichita State and Hal Dumler. Ironically, that Russell team was coached by Bob Frederick, the future athletics director at Kansas. The Indians fell to a talented Junction City team in the regional finals, ending their season at 17-3.

A quick story about Bob Frederick as a college basketball recruiter. His return to KU was initially as an assistant coach to Ted Owens, where his duties included recruiting the state of Kansas. One of his targets was 6-9 Myron Schuckman from tiny McCracken, Kan., about 40 miles southwest of Hays. Frederick tells the story of driving out to McCracken from Lawrence several times with the recruiting battle finally coming down to Notre Dame and the Jayhawks. The Schuckman family were devout Catholics, so Notre Dame naturally had some appeal. But KU had the advantage in proximity and the family was comfortable with the Jayhawk coaching staff. On his last visit, Frederick was feeling pretty good until he got up to leave. Mrs. Schuckman thanked Bob and told him they would make their decision the next day after praying on it that evening. He knew that if prayer was involved, Notre Dame would be the likely winner -- and it was.

Many of the players on the Hays High team that fell to Junction City returned the following year and entered regionals with an 18-1 record -- the only loss coming to Pratt. The Indians were on a collision course with Salina Central featuring the strong and athletic Nino Samuel. He would later go on to play at KU and then transfer back home to NAIA power Marymount. Unfortunately for the Tribe, it fell 64-60 in overtime in the first round to McPherson and the Samuel matchup never materialized.

As strong as those teams were, it was odd they sent Slone's teams on the road for regional play after winning the league both seasons. It was the first time Hays High won a league title since the 1956 team featuring all-around standout athlete Jim Maska.

Hays High had moved from playing games at the high school to a new gym at Hays Junior High a few years before I arrived. That upped capacity from about 500 to five times that much. One of the more "interesting" games came in 1979-80 with the Indians hosting Salina South, coached by Hays High alum Randy Johnson (member of 1970 and 1971 teams). It was a hotly contested game throughout and the Cougars hit a shot, which appeared to give them a one point win. But, the officials ruled the clock had sounded before the shot went off and they scurried off the court to their lockerroom. It was quite a scene and a bizarre homecoming for Johnson.

Thomas More Prep had quite a run of basketball success under Al Billinger. He was full of energy and would intersperse some salty language from time to time. We joked it was a good thing he had quick access to confession. Al used a trapping 1-3-1 defense to pester opponent offenses. Playing in the fieldhouse, featuring eight-foot walls around the perimeter made the trap that much more intimidating. Later renamed after Al, the fieldhouse opened for the 1951-52 season with a capacity of just over 1,000. I loved doing games there because the ceiling was not particularly high and the sounds of the crowd, bouncing balls and yelling coaches ricocheted off the concrete walls and bleachers. The natural sound was perfect for radio.

In Al's 33 seasons, he took teams to state 11 times, with seven, top four finishes. His 1975 team finished second, defeating Wichita-Kapaun and Gardner before falling to Parsons in the title game. That team had some great shooters including Mark Bomgardner, Terry Karlin, Bill Von Lintel and Mark Wiesner, with Doug Befort on the front line.

Not that this has anything to do with basketball, but Mark Wiesner's dad, Tommy, who I mentioned earlier, was one of the great characters in the community. He was among the many fans who came up before, during or after a broadcast to say hello and offer something witty. Our KAYS radio booth was located near Wiesner's for the annual sidewalk bazaar and Tommy would have on his wide-brimmed Panama hat and held court with the shoppers. Everything was a bargain, he said.

Before business began to decentralize from Main Street to the various large discount stores and The Mall (yes, the Mall in Hays for many years was called The Mall) along Vine Street, downtown was the place to be. Wiesner's was one of the larger stores, with high ceilings and a second level in the back third of the store. The main level was clothing, while the basement was for bedding, cookware and other home goods. There was a battery-powered flour sifter at the checkout stand. I think it was placed there to keep the kids entertained while the parents shopped.

There was a grocery story off the main level, which was later changed to clothing for teenagers. Other than a phone to communicate between the basement and main level checkout stands. People just yelled across the shop if they needed something. And Tommy was the ringleader, with his bushy mustache and quick paced walk that allowed him to greet all the customers. His attire always included a cloth tape measure draped around his neck and a small bar of soap in his hand to mark alterations.

This is not to single out Wiesner's as being unique. There were dozens of other stores in the community where owners and their staffs made a visit heartwarming and fun. Main Street was the quintessential heart of the community. Heck, the high school kids spent their Friday and Saturday nights "dragging Main" - driving at a snail's pace and bumper to bumper, turning around on the north end in the police station/ library parking lot and on the south end looping around Red Wycoff's Varsity Bowl. There might have been a few beers consumed as a part of that ritual. But it was just good, clean fun. I never heard of any vandalism -- maybe a few broken beer bottles and loud car stereos, however.

But growth was inevitable and the downtown lost some of its stature. It is good to see it has undergone revitalization over the past two decades. Hays is the largest community on I-70 between Denver and Salina, so it is an important center of commerce, education, health care and entertainment. That was the case even when I arrived in the late 1960s.

Okay, sorry to digress.

Billinger closed his career strong, going to state five times in his last six years. In 1983, the Monarchs featured a strong team that included Kelly Locke, Clair Augustine, Lyle Befort and Jeff Brungardt. Locke's grandfather was the famous Natoma coaching legend John Locke, while his dad, John Jr., played at Fort Hays, as did uncles Leneal and Marlin. Clair's older brother Claude was a standout high school baseball player at Hays High. That team fell in the opening round of state to Topeka-Hayden featuring future KU guard Mark Turgeon and Washburn NAIA All-American Tom Meier. The Monarchs fell behind by 18 in the first half, but mounted a furious second-half comeback. A questionable charge on Locke late in the game wiped off a go-ahead bucket and the Monarchs fell 64-61. Hayden would go on to win state.

During my time in Hays, it was extremely difficult to qualify for state football playoffs (which began in 1969). The playoff fields were limited in number, unlike today, and it took a near-perfect season to make it. Both Hays High and SJMA/TMP had some good teams during my time in Hays, and even sent a few to players NCAA Division I programs.

TMP's most memorable season in my tenure in Hays came in 1977 when the Monarchs, coached by alum Marion Schmidt, won the Mid-State Activities Association title and qualified for state. They were 9-0 in the regular season, outscoring opponents 264-53 and ranked No. 2 in 3A. Schmidt's son Garret was the quarterback, while cousin Mark Schmidt rushed for 1,498 yards to earn all-state recognition. The season ended on a sad note as Abilene came to Hays in the blowing snow and escaped with an 18-0 win. It did not help that Garret Schmidt had to leave the game early with an injured foot. It was Schmidt's last of six seasons as head coach, going 16-3 in his final two years.

The Monarchs had another successful run in football under Eugene Flax. He was 43-20 in seven years (1980-86), with four league titles. His last five teams went 7-2 each year, but none went to state. That proved just how hard it was to qualify.

If there was one program that I felt was at a disadvantage, it was Hays High football. Many of its opponents were larger enrollment schools, and with football being a numbers game, the Indians were challenged, especially later in my time when teams like Manhattan and Junction City appeared on the schedule. When I arrived in Hays, the Indian football program was actually in the midst of a pretty good run under head coach Arlo Buller. He was 42-26-2 in eight years with the Tribe, including a 7-2 record in 1969 (his final season). Terry Claycamp, a 1967 all-conference linebacker selection for Fort Hays from WaKeeney, was fun to cover as the Indians' coach from

1972-75. He had three winning seasons. Tom Cross, a veteran high school coach, took over in 1979 and had six winning seasons in nine years, taking the team to the state playoffs in 1981 and 1984.

As I mentioned, both local schools were well supported by the fans and the rivalry between the two was strong. In 1967, both teams were undefeated after four games and met in what Kansas sports media were calling the game of the week. The stands of Lewis Field Stadium, which seat about 6,500 were overflowing. St. Joe's Chuck Schmidt would rush for over 200 yards as the Cadets won 33-6, with Buller calling Schmidt the best high school running back he had seen while at Hays High. The old-timers in the community still talk about that evening and the build-up for the game.

I do have to give special mention to two Hays High coaches who passed away at a much too young age after I left Hays but made a big impact on community athletics. Bob Kuhn is in the Fort Hays State athletics hall of fame for track and football, and his accolades include an NAIA national discus title. He graduated from Hays High in 1968, competing in football, wrestling and track. Bob was an assistant football coach and, as the head wrestling coach for the Indians, built a well-respected program with several state champions - and earned his induction into the Kansas Wrestling Hall of Fame in 2004. A gentle giant, Bob was a friend of all.

Jim Maska was an outstanding athlete who went on to compete at both Hays High and Fort Hays State. A long-time cross country and track coach at Hays High, he started the cross country program in 1969 and went on to win boys state titles in 1970-71-72-73 and 76. He was selected the National Coach of the Year in 1977. The Maska family tree has produced numerous high school and collegiate sports standouts.

The real power of high school athletics in Hays showed in its American Legion baseball teams. The combined Hays High and TMP programs, plus an occasional player from Victoria 10 miles to the east resulted in eight state titles between 1967 and 1981. I mentioned the first sporting event I ever broadcast was the American Legion state tournament in August 1968 in Hays. I had only been on the job a few days. My career got off to an exciting start as the home team took the title with a 6-4, 13-inning win over Pittsburg. That was a great squad coached by Warren Schmidt, with a roster of Rod Ruder, Ray Coupal, Jack Lietz, Dean Schueler (brother of former Major League pitcher and White Sox GM Ron Schueler) among others. They made it to the Legion regional tournament in Williston, N.D., going 2-2, beating a St. Paul, Minn. team that included Major League Baseball Hall of Famer Dave Winfield.

The first team Bob Davis broadcast - the 1968 Hays American Legion. Credit: Bob Malone.
1968 Hays American Legion Baseball State Champions
Top Row (L-R): Bob Malone, Bob Harkness, Darrell VonFelt, Dean Schueler, Rich Guffey,
Alan Dinkel, Steve Hammerschmidt, Coach Warren Schmidt.
Kneeling (L-R): Rod Ruder, Jack Urban, Jimmy Mills, Jack Lietz, Denny Staab,
Mike Hammerschmidt, Larry Sanders.
Sitting (L-R): Ray Coupal, Larry Rome

The 1971 and 1972 teams were coached by Bruno Basgall (brother of longtime Los Angeles Dodger coach Monty Basgall). Both teams dropped the first two games in the double elimination regional format (1971 in Williston, N.D., and 1972 in Hastings, Neb.). The 1971 team included Barry Boggs, Phil Groff, Dave Stecklein, Jude Stecklein and Mike Scott, among others. That team defeated a Topeka squad which featured future Kansas State all-Big Eight basketball standout Lonnie Kruger.

Mike Scott went on to win the Louisville Slugger award in the 1971 state tournament, recognizing the top hitter. I was friends of his family as a twin Pat and another brother Billy Hall were also athletes. Billy would be an NAIA Baseball All-American at Fort Hays. Mike would work in the sports industry for a while at Baylor and then the Big Eight Conference. He later moved to Lawrence and our families did much together. The Scotts were big Kansas State fans and Pat always made it a point to come see me at KU-KSU games. I gave him the nickname "Purple Pat."

In 1974, the Legion program again won state and played in the regionals at Ralston, Neb. That was a dominant Hays team coached by Rod Ruder and featured pitchers Frank Seitz, Mike Schippers and Greg Korbe, plus position players Joe Leiker,

Mark Schmidt, and Charlie Bachkora, among others. Schippers struck out 18 in a 2-0 win over Kansas City to move the Legion to 34-3 on the year and earn the right to advance. Schippers won three of the squad's four games at state. Korbe was named the Louisville Slugger of the tournament with a .500 batting average. It was a good year for baseball in Hays as TMP won the 3A-4A-5A Kansas State Baseball Tournament

At the regionals, Hays jumped to a 5-0 lead versus a Cedar Rapids, Iowa, team featuring future Boston, Baltimore and Kansas City pitcher Mike Boddicker. But after a rain delay, Cedar Rapids scored 13 runs in the final three innings to win 13-5. That tournament also included a St. Paul, Minn. team which had future Milwaukee Brewer Paul Molitor on it. Boddicker outdueled Molitor, 2-1 in a 10-inning affair, and would go on to win the regional. Years later when I was broadcasting the Royals, I mentioned to both Boddicker and Molitor that I may have been the only guy to ever broadcast both their American Legion and MLB games. Both remembered those tournaments fondly.

Two years later it was another state title and a trip to Hastings, Neb., for the regional under the direction of coach John Bollig. That was another dominant Hays team, including Kevin Koerner, Jim Mall, Claude Augustine, Mark Gerstner, Gary Sechrist, Kirk Maska, Garret Schmidt and others, The Legion lost two close games, falling 2-0 to Rapid City, S.D., and then 11-9 to Omaha. As they did in 1974, Cedar Rapids won the regional behind the arm and bat of Mike Boddicker.

Bollig was a long-time coach in Hays for the Progressive, Junior Legion and Senior Legion programs, but his claim to fame was his ownership of one of the true-epicenters of sports talk in America -- John's Barbershop. Located on Cody Avenue across the street from what was the Coachman Inn, John's was **THE** place to be on Friday afternoons and Saturday mornings. There were three barber chairs, but I don't believe two of them were ever used. They were like thrones, reserved for the royalty of the community. One always went to Dusty Glassman - the King of Hays baseball. The other would be open to only a chosen few.

There was not much hair cut during these discussions. I don't think John wanted to risk lopping off an ear during a conversation. But he did own this contraption that he would strap to the back of his hand and vibrate when switched on. The follicly-challenged gentlemen (the bald guys) loved John massaging their scalps with the unit turned up to warp speed.

The dialogue was sports. Yes, a few comments about current events, politics, religion and even local gossip would filter in -- but 99 percent of the time sports was the topic of discussion. Chairs would line the long wall, but plenty of additional metal folding chairs were available in storage. Kids loved going to John's, not so much for the haircuts, as they did for the excellent collection of comic books, sports magazines and a soda machine that was rigged to give them free drinks. These bull sessions were almost entirely for the men. It wasn't that women weren't allowed -- it was that they had better things to do with their time.

Hays won the 1978 state title and played in the regionals once again. Ironically, they were coached by John Boddicker, a cousin of 1974 Hays Legion nemesis Mike Boddicker. That squad featured power pitcher and hitter Mike Befort, who was the MVP of the state tournament and eventually went on to be drafted by the Philadelphia Phillies. Other standouts included pitcher Dave Koerner, the Schumacher brothers (Brian and Steve), Marty Newman, Brad Klaus and Len Mize. The team dropped its opener to New Ulm, Minn., which had a catcher by the name of Terry Steinbach who played for the A's and Twins in the majors. New Ulm went on to win the regional and the national championship.

The 1981 state champion team did not advance to regionals as Legion adminis-trators split the state into two divisions with the respective champions meeting. Silver Lake won the title, but Hays still had a baseball champion as TMP won the 4A-3A-2A-1A state crown. In fact, the Monarchs advanced to state four years in a row from 1980-83.

Hays has a great history of summer baseball. Community teams were organized as early as the late 1800s as many of the smaller towns around Hays had their own teams. In fact, St. Joe's Military Academy won the Kansas state high school baseball tournament in 1961 wearing uniforms of the Severin team (located north of Hays). The Larks were a semi-pro team that was primarily Hays natives. But as the sport grew and became a summer landing spot for college players, semi-pro teams expanded their rosters. Eventual pros Mitch Webster, Jack Wilson, Jason Frasor, Jim Leyritz, Albert Pujols, and Lance Berkman were Hays Larks. Frank Leo, who came to Hays in the late 1960s from Flushing, N.Y., to play for Fort Hays, has served as the Larks manager for nearly 40 years (he also coached Hays High for 33 years). They have been regular participants in the National Baseball Congress tournament in Wichita, with five runner-up finishes under Leo.

Part of the charm of summer baseball in Hays was the venue of Larks Park, not too far from the Fort Hays campus in the south part of Hays. Constructed of limestone, it was a 1940 Works Project Administration facility. It seats 1,200, with plenty of standing room down each foul line and was a great setting for baseball as tree-lined neighborhoods and parks surrounded the stadium. A foul ball sent you kids racing to find it and return for candy or change at the concession stand. While community support for baseball has always been good, the Larks program is regularly filling the stadium with overflow crowds from time to time.

I absolutely loved my time in Hays and certainly keep many friendships from those days. One moment which touches me to this day is years after I left for KU, they had a "Bob Davis Day." They had a big banquet and I had the opportunity to tell stories and see old friends. It was special. I owe much to the community.

People ask me where I grew up, and I always qualify it. I was born and spent my early years in southeast Kansas, finished grade school in Manhattan and went to junior high, high school and college in Topeka. But Hays is where I **REALLY** grew up. It is where I started my career, met my wife, our son was born there, and I met so many wonderful people. My 16 years in Hays were such a positive influence on my life.

Chapter 5 Sidebar 1: The Best of the Best

There were so many people in Hays who contributed to the success of sports and quality of life in Hays that if I were to try to identify them all, I would most certainly forget someone. But there are a few that made an impact in my mind.

Dusty Glassman was a driving force behind a popular little league baseball baseball program. Just try to get into the Dairy Queen on a summer night -- good luck -- you're competing with the Cranes, Wrens, Buffaloes, Astros and more. Laverne Schumacher was a leader of Hays baseball, organizing the many volunteers and raising funds to keep the American Legion and Larks programs strong. Paul "Busch" Gross and Cade Suran were great leaders of the Fort Hays athletic department. They gave 38 and 31 years of their lives, respectively to the school as both coaches and athletics directors.

Of course, you had solid coaches at Hays High, TMP and Fort Hays State. People at Hays High like Don Slone, Jim Maska, Terry Claycamp and Tom Cross. When I look back at TMP, guys like Al Billinger, Marion Schmidt, Jim Dinkel and Gene Flax come to mind. There were Hall of Fame coaches at Fort Hays like Chuck Brehm, Bill Morse, Joe Rosado, Alex Francis and Jim Gilstrap. They were all fun to cover and made my life easier -- well, most of the time. Postgame radio shows after losses could be difficult on occasion.

From an athlete perspective, there were certainly those who left their mark. In calling Fort Hays games over the years I marveled at the talent that stopped by middle America. They came from places ranging as small as a speck on a map in western Kansas to the bustling streets of New York City. I think of that 1971 Fort Hays State basketball team that won the league with a starting five that all came from Kansas towns with a combined population of less than 1,500.

I also think about two guys from New York, Mike Karl from Long Island, and Frank Leo from Flushing, who wandered west to Hays in 1969 and both stayed to live there. They became high school educators, with Mike a long-time Hays High athletics director, and Frank coaching Hays High and Larks baseball for nearly 40 years. Then there is John Mason, from tiny Philipsburg, who went toe-to-toe with distance running legends Jim Ryun, Marty Liquori and Kip Keino -- and beat them -- at track meets worldwide. Likewise, the diminutive Tommy Doll from Claflin, who walked on the Fort Hays football team, still remains the school's rushing leader with 4,477 yards). Fort Hays attracted so many great people who fell in love with the community (and region), and called it home, making it a wonderful place to live.

In terms of those who grew up in Hays, I am sure there could be quite a debate as to who was the best athlete the city produced. Before my days in Hays, there were several individuals who came to be revered and attained legend status. Gross, for whom the Coliseum is named, was considered to be "Mr. Athletics" at Fort Hays State. A 1917 graduate of Hays High, he went on to play football at Fort Hays. As a freshman, he quarterbacked the Tigers to their only undefeated season. He left for World War I, then returned to take the Tigers to another conference championship.

I had always heard Dusty (Glassman) was an outstanding baseball player and could have played in the majors. And in that same era, Monty Basgall from nearby Pfeifer was a standout on the diamond. He is better known for coaching all those years with the Dodgers, but he played a few years in the majors. Just before I arrived in Hays, there was quite a string of notable athletes. Larry Staab was a tremendous pitcher who made it as far as Triple A. But he was also an outstanding basketball player for the St. Joseph Military Academy Cadets, leading them to state and earning first team all-state status in 1961.

A teammate of Staab's, Larry Weigel led the state of Kansas in scoring in 1962, earning Mr. Kansas Basketball recognition and received a scholarship to play at Kansas State. It was not unusual to see Kansas State coach Tex Winter, Kansas coach Dick Harp and Wichita State coach Ralph Miller at an SJMA game to scout. Larry's a personal friend of mine, and is married to Kay Suran, the daughter of Fort Hays basketball coach and athletic director Cade Suran. It takes a pretty confident young man to turn down a coach who offered you a scholarship, but still ask for his daughter's hand in marriage.

It could be argued that Ron Schueler is the most accomplished athlete in Hays history as a former pitcher for the Twins, Phillies and White Sox over eight seasons, mainly as a reliever. He would ascend the ranks of baseball moving from a pitching coach, to scout and then, general manager. He went on to become the White Sox general manager and signed Michael Jordan to his minor league contract for the Birmingham Barons in the Chicago minor league system. The franchise won three AL Central titles under his direction and is still looked upon fondly by Southsiders for rebuilding the organization.

During my time, there were numerous Hays natives who excelled in high school and went on to college to continue their athletic careers on the Division I level. Chuck Schmidt was a bruising fullback for St. Joe's Military Academy, graduating in 1968 and earning a scholarship to play for Pepper Rodgers at KU. Two beefy lineman, Gary Geist, TMP 1971 and Doug Moeckel, Hays High 1972 also earned scholarships to Kansas State.

Hays High and coach Don Slone produced some fine basketball players in the early 1970s. The twin towers of Dana Albright and Eddie Schumacher both played collegiately. Albright first at Garden City Community College and then West Texas State as a teammate of NBA star Maurice Cheeks. Schumacher started at Western Kentucky, then finished at Fort Hays State where he is a member of Tiger Hall of Fame. There are those who might remember Chuck Faubion more because his mother Bev was the original co-host of "Party Line" on KAYS radio. But the younger Faubion excelled as Hays High quarterback, forward on the basketball team and a pitcher on the baseball team during the 1972-73 school year as a sophomore. His family would move to Arizona after that year. He completed a great high school career, went on to junior college and then started two years in basketball for Houston Baptist.

Gary Sechrist was an excellent all-around athlete at Hays High in the mid-70s. He was a state champion in the javelin (in addition to doing the high jump -- was the school record holder for 20 years - long jump, triple jump), was a linebacker on the football team and played on the 1976 state champion American Legion team. He earned a scholarship to compete in track for Nebraska, but a knee injury in the first game of his senior football season derailed those plans. He would go to Fort Hays and play football (two seasons) and compete in track and field. He was an NAIA national champion in the javelin, and placed in the top five in each of his four seasons of competition.

In the late 1970s, Hays High and Thomas More Prep had solid athletic programs, headed by multi-sport athletes Kirk Maska and Garret Schmidt, respectively. Both played quarterback in football, were members of the 1976 Hays Legion state title team, and were natural leaders. Maska, a state javelin champion, earned a scholarship to play football at Kansas, and ended his career throwing the javelin and playing football at Fort Hays. Schmidt went to Kansas State to become a veterinarian, later relocating to Kansas City where we have lunch on a periodic basis. Interesting to note, Hays could have had three of the best individual athletes in the state at that time were it not for relocation. Frank Wattelett, whose father was a manager at Travenol Labs, was a budding star. But just before high school, the family relocated to Abilene. Wattlett would later play at KU and for the NFL's New Orleans Saints.

Two TMP multisport athletes, Keith Walters and Russ Ruder, earned Division I college scholarships following their senior years in 1979 and 1980, respectively. Walters was a raw-boned defensive end who played collegiately at Baylor with NFL Hall of Fame linebacker Mike Singletary. Ruder, like his brother Rod a decade early excelled in every sport he competed. He played baseball as a freshman at Arkansas, but returned to finish at Fort Hays State after injuring his shoulder. Both Rod and Russ are in the Fort Hays State Athletics Hall of Fame.

In my opinion, the person who would be the first face on the Mt. Rushmore of Hays sports figures would be Al Billinger. He was quite a man, first starring as an all-state guard in basketball and quarterback for the Cadets. After graduating in 1941, he had several offers to play both sports in college, but opted to join the service. He was discharged in 1945 with several commendations after being on the front lines for much of that time.

Al returned to Hays and was now married and working in a meat butcher shop. My guess is he was around 26 when Fort Hays coaches for football (Red Huffman), basketball (Cade Suran) and track (Alex Francis) approached him to come to school -- and if he were to do so, play sports as well. He took them up on their offer and earned 10 varsity letters in his time. He was tremendously quick, earning him the nickname "Speedy," and achieving all-league recognition in basketball twice. It was not unusual for colleges to have athletes who were a bit older due to the war, but few excelled to the degree Billinger did. He was revered as an elder statesman and was also called "grandpappy" by his teammates. He is in both the Fort Hays State and the state of Kansas athletic halls of fame. Later in life, Billinger and Suran became fishing buddies. It was a wonderful relationship between a coach and player that lasted a lifetime.

Al would go on to teach and coach basketball at his high school alma mater. In 33 years he took teams to state 11 times, with seven top four finishes. His career record was 478-246.

I had an up close and personal view of much of this, not only as the broadcaster, but sitting in the front row of the bus on road trips. I remember Al as a gregarious, outgoing individual with an excellent sense of humor. We had great conversations. He loved to talk about sports. But he was stern and disciplined when it came to running his program. The players knew what was expected of them. His teams played hard and never gave up. They had great respect for him. He had quite a life.

I highlight these people knowing that I probably left out a dozen or so. And, there were those in other sports that I did not broadcast, who were just as accomplished. As a broadcaster you always hope you have the opportunity to witness greatness, and in Hays I did so -- on and off the field.

Chapter 5 Sidebar 2: Nick Pino's Shoe and Satchel Paige's Gun

One of the many fine retail establishments in Hays was Goodwin's Sporting Goods, located on West 11th Street. It was a beehive of activity for people buying athletic shoes, letter jackets, sport uniforms and playing equipment. The store had high ceilings where merchandise was stacked so high the help would have to climb a ladder or use a long stick with a wooden hook.

It was also the place where I bought my scorebooks for basketball, a practice I continued after moving to Lawrence. Duane Goodwin purchased the store in 1952 from Charles "Dee" Erickson who previously coached at Fort Scott Junior College, Ottawa and Washburn. Erickson was one of the early organizers of the National Association of Intercollegiate Athletics (NAIA). Goodwin sold the story to Terry Bright in 1992 who liquidated it in 2019. Goodwin was a huge supporter of sports in the community and his store was a destination for young and old.

Every community has artifacts or objects that are considered to be part of its lore. Hays had its share. There was the "Fish Within a Fish" skeleton at Sternberg Museum where a large fish swallowed a smaller fish. Both died and were fossilized. There is the ghost of Elizabeth Polly, the Blue Light Lady southwest of the Fort Hays State campus. And then there was Nick Pino's shoe.

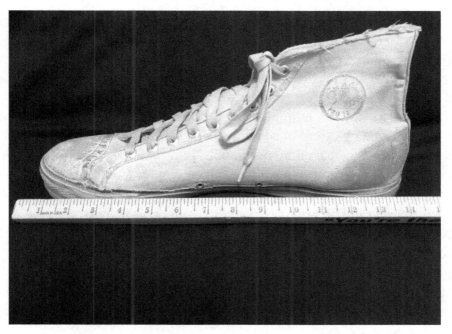

This size 20 EEEE basketball shoe sat atop the cash register at Goodwin's Sporting Goods.
Credit: Kyle Goodwin

Pino was a hulking 7-0 center from Santa Fe, N.M. who played basketball at Kansas State from 1965-68. He was a teammate of St. Joseph Military Academy standout Larry Weigel for the Wildcats. One day in the mid-1960s, a traveling sales-man passed through Hays and stopped at Goodwin's to encourage the store to sell his shoe brand - Bob Cousy Shoes. Cousy, of course, was the standout guard for the Boston Celtics and lent his name to the company. My guess is shoe contracts were a bit different back then compared to today.

The store only sold Converse's Chuck Taylor All-Star brand. To entice the store to carry the Cousys, he gave Goodwin a prototype of a shoe the company was giving to Pino - size 20 EEEE. Not knowing what to do with it, Goodwin placed it on the top of the old cash register where it sat for all to see. Over the years it became quite a conversation piece. Everyone who came into Goodwin's Sporting Goods **HAD** to hold the shoe.

While it was the topic of discussion, Goodwin never did sell the Cousy brand. As for Nick Pino? His coach, Tex Winter, was in the military with Taylor and was loyal to Converse, so the Cousys never saw the light of day in Manhattan. Although Pino never stepped foot in the shoe, he did make an appearance in Hays in 1968 for a "town team" tournament played at the Jefferson West (later Kennedy Middle School) gym. Pino was "recruited" to play for Russell and his appearance drew a decent crowd.

Perhaps the biggest celebrity to walk through the doors of Goodwin's was former Negro League and Major League pitcher Leroy "Satchel" Paige. He was a member of the Negro League's Kansas City Monarchs that would go on barnstorming tours throughout the Midwest. Hays was a favorite stop for the Monarchs, coming multiple times in a summer because of the interest in the team and the postgame barbecue for the two teams.

Paige came to Hays early in his career in the 1940s and then later in the early 1960s. A story floating around had Paige marrying his wife in Hays in 1947 at the courthouse before a justice of the peace officiating. Satchel was the star of the team and accordingly if he was to pitch at least three innings the tickets were 50 cents. If he threw two innings or fewer, or did not pitch, the price was 25 cents. Always the showman, Paige would pick an inning and have all of his fielders, with the exception of the catcher and first baseman, leave the field and he would proceed to strike out the side.

One day, the team bus pulls up to Goodwin's and Paige hops out with a shotgun. At that time, the store sold hunting and fishing supplies. An avid hunter and fisherman, Paige autographed his shotgun and traded it for a new gun according to Duane's sons Kent and Kyle.

Chapter 5 Friends of Bob

Larry Weigel: Basketball, 1960-62, St. Joseph Military Academy; Kansas State, 1963-66. "I left Hays before Bob arrived, but because I was married to (Fort Hays State Athletic Director) Cade Suran's daughter, Kay, I got to know him well. And of course, given my role at Kansas State, I always saw him when the Jayhawks came over to play in Manhattan. The Suran's treated Bob almost as if he was their son.

I can only imagine how it was for Bob to ride on the bus seated next to Al (Billinger). My guess when this started Al was about 50 and Bob was half his age. He probably learned some new words! The words weren't meant to be filthy in any way. To Al, they were just expressions -- usually in dismay or disgust. We would pray two times when we played. First, was right before tipoff. Al would say some words of encouragement, and then we say a "Hail Mary." The second time was just before we left the lockerroom before the start of the second half. He would have some choice and salty words of motivation and then transition straight to "...okay then, let's pray." It was all we could do to suppress our snickering.

Alan Billinger: Basketball, St. Joseph Military Academy,1960-63; Basketball, Fort Hays State, 1965-67. My dad (TMP basketball coach Al Billinger) and Bob had a great relationship. Dad enjoyed being around him so he had Bob travel with the team on the bus. He'd be seated in the front row next to dad. Oh, to hear those stories. Of course, my dad was known to use some colorful language from time to time. I'm sure Bob learned a few new words. I was fortunate to do some games with Bob as the color man after I graduated from college. He made it so easy for me. And his calls of the game were phenomenal. When fans weren't able to go to road games, they were excited to listen to Bob Davis. There were people who didn't go to home games because they wanted to stay at home and listen to Bob. Hays was fortunate to have him for so long.

Don Slone: Hays High Basketball Coach, 1967-73. I loved Al Billinger like a brother. He was so much fun to be around -- outgoing and loved people. He was a heck of a coach and I enjoyed our matchups more than any other games we played. They were competitive, but fun. I remember one time we were in a close game with TMP and we're both coaching our young men hard and Al yells at one of his players: "Shoot the damn ball before you throw it away!" I turn my head and look at him and smile and he gives me this sheepish grin." That was the thing about Al. He would compete like hell during the games, but he got along with all of the other coaches because he was a great guy.

Don Slone: Hays High Basketball Coach, 1967-73. Bob Davis was a fabulous broadcaster, the best I've ever heard -- and I've been around. I truly enjoyed going over to KAYS on Mondays at 5 p.m. to record our weekly update. He was so professional and made it very easy for me. I'm not surprised he went on to KU and the Royals. You could tell he was going to go far in his career. He's one of the finest people I've known in my life.

Steve Bates: Hays High School Class of 1985. My mom would drop me off at the United Methodist Church in Hays every Sunday morning for Sunday School. I was in fifth grade and our class was taught by both Bob and Linda Davis. As you could imagine, it was a big deal to be taught by Bob Davis. He was larger than life to us. I was joined by my two best friends, twins Rick and Randy Roberts. It's not that we did not like learning religion, it was just at that time in our lives, we loved talking sports. So, we'd start out with Bob talking about the game over the weekend. We would go on for quite a while. Finally Linda would reel us back in and talk about religion. But we'd go back to the sports talk a little bit later. I am sure we frustrated Linda. We just had a blast talking sports with Bob. I think he did too!

Clair Augustine: Baseball/Basketball, Thomas More Prep, 1980-83. I don't know of a person from Hays who has heard Bob Davis broadcast games who doesn't consider him to be a legend. People would stay home from games just to listen to Bob. He meant a great deal to my family because my father worked at the post office from 1 - 10 p.m. So, he could not go to my basketball games. Back in the mail sorting room he would turn up the radio and everyone would listen to Bob call the games. When he got home from work, we'd talk about the game. I gained an appreciation for how accurate and detailed Bob was when he did the games. He was so good. Other than my dad not getting to see me play, I think he might have had a better time with the guys in the sorting room listening to Bob.

Mike Leikam: Football and Track, Thomas More Prep, 1981-83. If you played sports in high school and Bob Davis broadcast your games, then you wanted a tape of it. I remember several members of the football team got some recordings. When I moved to Wichita, a few of us would get together from time to time and pull out the cassettes and listen. There's nothing better than hearing Bob Davis call your games.

Randy Johnson: Basketball, Hays High School, 1969-70; Assistant Coach Russell High School, 1975-79; Head Basketball Coach, Salina South High School, 1979-84. We'd have our parents tape the games just to hear Bob call our names. I remember Kurt Watson's dad got a tape of our last game against Junction City. We had a great team, but lost to them in the regional final and they went on a cake walk to win state. We'd listen to the game every once in a while. We'd get goose bumps! What I wouldn't do to hear that tape just one more time.

Garret Schmidt: Football, Basketball, Track, Thomas More Prep High School, 1975-78. At one of our class reunions we surprised Dad (Marion Schmidt) with a meal and the more than 40 players from the two undefeated teams he coached (assistant 1968 and head coach 1978). On short notice I contacted Bob and asked him to record a "this is your life Coach Schmidt" video for the evening. At that time Bob was still doing the play-by-play for KU and busy with travel and family. He quickly agreed and met me at Johnny's on Highway K-10 in Olathe for lunch. I had a short hand-written overview of Dad's coaching career from Dodge City, Leoti, Troy and TMP. Bob took one look at it for about 5 minutes and said "let's go." I turned on the video camera and without a hitch he recorded a perfect history of the Schmidt legacy of coaching in one take without a mistake! I should have known that would happen as he had been doing that on the fly for years and years live on the radio! That example tells you all you need to know about Bob: consummate professional and really, really nice guy.

Father Earl Befort: Instructor/Athletics Director, Thomas More Prep. I got to spend a lot of time with Bob because I kept the scorebook for the basketball games, and I also drove the bus to away games. I enjoyed his company tremendously because I was a huge sports fan and I just enjoyed listening to him. Once in a while I'd join him on air and I was in awe of just how good he was. I know people like following the team, but they also listened to the game because they liked to hear Bob. As the bus driver, my focus was on the road, but I could hear what Bob and the coaches were talking about. Al (Billinger) took a liking to Bob early on and was a huge sports fan himself. They talked about their jobs, but they talked about family, events around Hays and things like that. Bob was such a good guy. I know everyone at TMP enjoyed having him around and felt fortunate to have him broadcast the games.

Father Mike Scully: Dean of Students, Thomas More Prep-Marian High School. Two items stand out in my long association with Bob. One of the ways in which I taught was to give students a different perspective on the subject at hand -- in this case it was senior religion class.

Knowing that Bob was a church-going man, I wanted him to talk to the class about "life" from the point of view of a person pursuing a career, who was not Catholic, but still believed in God. He was famous in Hays, and I wanted to take advantage of that.

He felt at home describing what the students did on the basketball court and football and baseball fields, but he was not sure what he could say to the students that would be helpful. I must admit that I did not give him much direction, simply because I just wanted him to speak from the heart. It was a challenge for him, and later he told me that it may have been one of the most difficult things he did in his life.

However, he was definitely a hit. He talked about the difference between wants and needs. It was a tremendous message. Coming from a man who was so highly respected by the students made it more impactful. He pointed out to the students that as young people, they had many "wants" in many different circumstances of their lives, as he had in his. But those were secondary, he said. What he spent time on, and what all of us must spend time on are the different "needs" that we have.

The problem, he said, was that we begin to see the "wants" as "needs" in our lives because our feelings dictate to us what we feel would make us happy and satisfied with what we feel would be a "happy life." But the important thing in life is that we determine the "needs" that we have to make a good life.

I took what he said and applied it to the need for religion in our lives. He was a tremendous example of that—a successful man with a clear talent, but at the same time, a believer in God, a Higher Power who directs our lives. The students saw that, and I know it made a lasting impression of all of them.

I know there are a number of times that his interaction with our students was most profitable. Another one that I remember had to do with his recognizable voice that I wanted to make use of, again, in the area of religion. I wanted to put together a slideshow involving things that can roughly be described as "do good and avoid evil." And in order to do that, I wanted him to read some Scripture. As anyone who knows him, he has a tremendous voice and I wanted to make use of that, along with his successful life.

I gave him what to read, I believe, from a couple of the letters of Paul the Apostle in the Bible. It took about 20 minutes to do the reading. And after he had turned off the electronics and given me the tape (what we had to use in the 70s and 80s), I remember him pointing to all of the equipment of the recording studio where we were —microphones, recorders, etc.— and saying to me, "Those words are so much more important than all of this." I never will forget that experience because it gave me encouragement in what I was doing but more importantly, it showed the type of man that Bob Davis was.

Setting Up on the Kaw

AS MUCH AS we were sad to be leaving KAYS, Hays and the friends we made there, we were excited to be moving to Lawrence in the summer of 1984. We had numerous friends in the Topeka-Lawence-Kansas City area, so there was a comfort factor. Plus, I had done some KU games as a fill-in broadcaster, so it wasn't as if we were starting over cold.

It was also a return to my roots, so to speak. I started following Big Seven and Big Eight sports as a teenager in Manhattan and then later in Topeka. I was in college at Washburn during the Jim Ryun, Walt Wesley, JoJo White, John Riggins and Bobby Douglass era. Those are some of the all-time greats in KU athletics history.

Not only was this a time of change for the Davis family, but there was quite a transformation occurring in the Kansas athletic department. Monte Johnson, who was Wilt Chamberlain's classmate, was the athletic director and made the decision to dismiss Don Fambrough as the football coach after the 1982 season, and Ted Owens as the basketball coach after the 1982-83 basketball campaign.

Monte, who was previously an assistant athletic director at KU from 1960-71, was a successful banker with Bank IV in Wichita. He did not originally want the AD job, but he relented when the university approached him. Bob Marcum had left to become the AD at South Carolina in December 1981. A few months later, Jim Lessig was hired over former Big 12 Commissioner Steve Hatchell for the position. But Lessig's wife never moved to Lawrence, and six months later was named the Mid-American Conference commissioner.

Monte Johnson, Kansas athletics director from 1982-87 joins Larry Brown,
Calvin Thompson and Danny Manning. Credit: Kansas Athletics

Johnson told me firing Fambrough and Owens were gut-wrenching decisions. Both were loyal to KU and well-liked. "Fam" was a native Texan, but met Jayhawk all-everything Ray Evans during his military assignment and joined him to play football at Kansas after World War II. If you slit open his veins, he would bleed crimson and blue. Kansas had ended the 1981 season with an upset win over Missouri to earn a bid to the Hall of Fame Bowl. It sparked the battle cry: "Going with Fam to Birmingham!" But the team faltered in 1982, and attendance and hopes were waning.

Owens, who played collegiately at Oklahoma, was from tiny Hollis, Okla., the same hometown of legendary Texas football coach Darrell Royal and former Jayhawk broadcaster Monte Moore. Ted had taken KU to the 1971 and 1974 Final Fours and won several conference titles. But like football, attendance was falling off and a change was to be made. It took a little longer than Johnson had planned. The Jayhawks went on the road to Oklahoma for the first round of the Big Eight postseason tournament and upset the Sooners. The players carried Ted off the court.

To be fair to both coaches, they did not leave the cupboards bare for their successors. Quarterback Frank Seurer, linebacker Willie Pless, receiver Richard Estell and others provided a good nucleus for the next football coach. Owens had signed Greg Dreiling, a transfer from Wichita State, three freshmen -- Kerry Boagni, Ronnie Kellogg, Calvin Thompson -- and Carl Henry, a transfer from Oklahoma City. Owens' fingerprints were all over the 1986 Final Four team.

I remember Johnson showing me binders of what he called "hate mail" as a result of the firings. To his credit, he answered every one of those with a written response or a phone call.

There would also be a new radio analyst/color man for the network in 1983-84. Kevin Harlan, a broadcasting prodigy, graduated from KU in 1982 and became the youngest NBA play-by-play announcer at 22 years of age for the Kansas City Kings. The son of former Green Bay General Manager and President Bob Harlan, today he does television network calls for NCAA basketball, NFL football and NBA basketball. Harlan was a protege of Tom Hedrick and joined his former professor on the Jayhawk broadcasts for one season.

The 1984-85 campaign also marked the first year of Learfield Communications of Jefferson City, Mo., as the rights holder for KU games. That meant Learfield would secure stations to carry the games, produce the games, and sell sponsorships and advertising. I had experience with Learfield as a replacement for Missouri games the previous year, and I believe that had much to do with me being selected for the KU play-by-play position.

I thought it was a bit ironic that two Kansans who both were the Voice of the Jayhawks -- Harlan and me -- did Missouri sports as well. To be fair, Tiger athletics director Joe Castiglione, sports information director Bob Brendel and of course head coach Norm Stewart were good to me. I had a lot of fun doing the game and became close to my Tiger Network analyst, the late Rod Kelly - God rest his soul.

Harlan moved on to the play-by-play position for the Kansas City Chiefs in 1985 (he would also do Missouri basketball and football from 1986-89). His replacement was a familiar name and face to Jayhawk fans. Max Falkenstien had been broadcasting KU games since 1946, but ironically was never an official member of the KU Network. He did games on KTOP and WREN out of Topeka, and an FM station based in Ottawa when there were no exclusive radio rights. He went to KU and was a Beta Theta Pi fraternity member along with future Kansas Governor Robert Docking, Kansas track coach Bob Timmons and Kansas basketball player and assistant coach Jerry Waugh. Falkenstien's father Earl, was the business manager for the KU athletics department for quite a while.

It was not uncommon to not have a "true" analyst to work the broadcasts, but both Max and I had done play-by-play our whole lives. I had known of Max and met him a few times, but we really did not know each other well. I had come up to Lawrence a few times in the summer of 1984 to get to know him and talk about how we would work together. We hit it off from the start. Max had gotten out of full-time broadcasting in 1970 and became a banker for Douglas County Bank. Ironically, it was owned by Ross Beach of Hays, who owned KAYS when I worked there.

Mike Gottfried was in his second year as the head football coach as I made my

Jayhawk debut in 1984. He came to Kansas from Cincinnati after gaining a reputation as an offensive guru. He set almost all the passing records as a quarterback at Morehead (Ky.) State. Former New York Giant Phil Simms has since eclipsed most of them. Gottfried is also a cousin to Jack Harbaugh, who won an NCAA Division I-AA title at Western Kentucky. He, of course, is the father of former Baltimore Colt and current Michigan head coach Jim Harbaugh and Baltimore Raven head coach Jon Harbaugh. Georgia basketball coach Tom Crean is a brother-in-law to Jim Harbaugh. What I am saying is there are some pretty good coaching bloodlines there.

The Jayhawk athletic department gave the football program the moniker of "Air Gottfried" to market season tickets. It made sense as the Jayhawk head coach was willing to throw the ball all over the field. The school sports information staff had a busy fall keeping track of all the records being set. As one staffer said, "if we are going to lose, we might as well have fun doing it."

Gottfried was good to work with, but like any coach, had his moments -- particularly after games. One time Max asked a question that Gottfried did not necessarily like. Rather than say anything, he just waved his hand as if to say, next question. That didn't make for good radio. Mike was also known to walk home once in a while after a particularly bad practice. His home was in far west Lawrence, my guess it was at least five miles.

In Gottfried's first campaign, the team was a respectable 4-6-1, including a 26-20 win over No. 10 USC in the L.A. Coliseum. It was a fun homecoming no doubt for California Jayhawks Frank Seurer, Kerwin Bell, Dino Bell and Bill Malavasi -- son of Los Angeles Rams coach Ray Malavasi.

There was optimism mixed with intrepidation heading into 1984. KU lost several veterans on each side of the ball, however, there was slight improvement to a 5-6 record, highlighted by a 28-11 win over No. 2 Oklahoma in Lawrence. That was the game, where Sooner quarterback Danny Bradley was held out with an injury, so Barry Switzer inserted freshman and future NFL Hall-of-Famer Troy Aikman to call the plays. He completed two of 14 passes on the day for eight yards.

The day was already special as KU christened its new indoor workout facility in the morning. But Gottfried made the decision to go through pregame warmups in the new Anschutz Sports Pavilion, and not at Memorial Stadium. Our radio crew was informed of the switch well before kickoff, but you could tell the Sooner coaches, players and traveling party were a little confused. The KU busses rolled up about 30 minutes before the coin toss.

Oklahoma could not mount much offense, although the game remained close as Kansas was unable to convert field goal drives into touchdowns. The Jayhawks were leading 15-3 in the fourth quarter when Wayne Ziegler picked off an Aikman pass to score on a 63-yard touchdown return. I admit I can get excited, and I certainly did on that play. I had called some of Ziegler's high school games as the opponent of Thomas More Prep.

In 1985, the Jayhawks again improved, finishing at 6-6. A golden opportunity was missed in a 24-20 loss at No. 4 Florida State after a 3-0 start to the season. Kansas was driving for the winning score deep in Seminole territory when a fumble sealed its fate. The next week the Jayhawks defeated Eastern Illinois 44-20 as quarterback Mike Norseth outdueled Panther signal-caller and future New Orleans Saints head coach Sean Payton. NCAA rules at the time called for teams to have at least seven wins to qualify for a bowl game, but a big positive was the season ended for the third year in a row with a win over Missouri.

No one was ready for what came next. Gottfried had momentum and was signing quality players when he abruptly left after the 1985 season to go to Pittsburgh. He would later become the lead college football analyst for ESPN. That did not surprise me at all. He was always good at analyzing plays on our coaches shows and showed a natural ability. No doubt his leaving set Kansas football back, however.

The Jayhawks' basketball coach was also in his second year. Larry Brown was definitely a surprise hire by Johnson. Brown was nowhere on Johnson's radar until Spyder Reed, son of *Iola Register* publisher Clyde Reed, contacted him and said he had the perfect coach for the Jayhawks. Reed, a KU graduate, was in Denver when Brown was coaching the Nuggets. After Reed reached out, CBS analyst Billy Packer called Johnson and echoed almost exactly what Reed had said -- Larry Brown was interested.

Johnson went to Albuquerque for the 1983 Final Four and met with Packer and interviewed 10 coaching candidates. Reportedly, the other name most seriously considered was Kansan and current Arkansas head coach Eddie Sutton. Upon Johnson's return to Lawrence, he met Brown in Kansas City to seal the deal. Brown brought credibility and coaching acumen. But he also brought a long list of previous addresses. His career before, during and after Kansas always had people asking if he was leaving. No one could argue that he was an outstanding coach. And from a media perspective he was great. He was a great storyteller, respectful of history and knowledgeable of the needs of the radio crew, beat reporters and network personnel.

Brown was interested in Kansas for a few reasons. First, he had heard positive stories from North Carolina coach and Kansas alum Dean Smith. And second, when word leaked out that he was considering the move, New Jersey ownership pressured him to make an immediate decision. The owner actually asked him to leave with a few games remaining, assuming the departure was a foregone conclusion. To show you how much times have changed, Brown earned annually $55,000 plus another

$14,000 for marketing and media appearances. Johnson promised Brown he would be in the top five among NCAA coaches in terms of annual compensation if he stayed at least five years.

In his first year, Brown took Kansas to the NCAA Tournament and finished with a 22-10 record after a two-year NCAA tourney hiatus for the program. Perhaps the biggest accomplishment was a 5-0 combined record against Kansas State and Missouri, coming after an 0-9 mark combined over the previous two years. Make a mental note of the 63-61 win at Manhattan on a Carl Henry baseline jumper. It would be a sign of bigger things to come. Tickets were getting hard to come by. But not nearly as difficult as they were for Lawrence High School Chesty Lion basketball. You see, coach Ted Juneau had one Danny Manning playing for him. Manning's father Ed, who Brown coached at the Carolina Cougars of the ABA was on the Kansas staff.

Manning's freshman year lived up to preseason billing. He showed the versatility of a guard in a 6-10 frame. You could sense something was building. Dreiling was settling in after transferring and Kellogg and Thompson were making their mark as sharpshooters. Still somewhat young, the team advanced to the NCAA Tournament, but lost in the second round for the second year in a row, this time to Auburn and NBA all-star Chuck Person. Still, ranked No. 13 in the final polls at 26-8 overall and 11-3 in the BIg Eight (second), the season was a big success and momentum was building.

There was considerable anticipation for the 1985-86 season. The Jayhawks were a veteran team, balanced and deep. They began the year competing in the Preseason NIT. In the semis at Madison Square Garden they defeated Louisville, 83-78, but lost in the finals to Duke two nights later, 92-86. It would not be the last time those three teams would be playing for high stakes that year. The Jayhawks completed the regular season at 31-3 and ranked No. 2 in the polls. In addition to the loss to Duke, the Jayhawks fell in overtime at Memphis and on the road at Iowa State.

Dreiling was a force inside, while Thompson and Kellogg bombed away from the perimeter. Manning played all over the court and guard Cedric Hunter was the floor general offensively and defensively. Chris Piper, Archie Marshall and Mark Turgeon were more than capable subs. Long-time Jayhawk observers believed this might have been the best team in the program to that point.

After two wins at Dayton to begin the NCAA Tournament, the Jayhawks moved to the Sweet 16 at Kemper Arena. Iowa State was also there as was N.C. State and Michigan State. The Jayhawks downed the Spartans in overtime 96-86 to advance to the Elite Eight. The win was somewhat controversial as the clock had stopped with Kansas trying to mount a furious comeback. While those wearing Green and White claim homecourt cooking, the truth is the situation actually provided an opportunity for them to salt away the game.

Spartan head coach Jud Heathcote protested the situation to the timekeeper during live play, leaving the coaching box and questioning what had happened. Brown got in a heated discussion with referee Bobby Dibler and accidentally flipped his whistle with his rolled up program. A technical was called on Brown and the Spartans were awarded two shots and the ball. Miraculously, KU shaved a six-point lead in the final 60 seconds, punctuated by an Archie Marshall tip in with :11 left, to force overtime. With the Jayhawk crowd whipped into a frenzy, Kansas cruised in overtime to a 96-86 win.

Two days later, Kansas defeated N.C. State 75-67 to earn its first trip to the Final Four since 1974. The Wolfpack actually had a seven-point lead with over four minutes to play. After the game, their coach Jim Valvano jokingly blamed the loss on the Rock Chalk Chant emanating from the crowd that had forced his team to lose its composure.

The trip to Dallas for the Final Four was short-lived as the Jayhawks fell in the semis to Duke 71-67. It was a frustrating game to watch and broadcast because the Jayhawks fought foul problems and injury; and could never get over the hump. Archie Marshall, a junior college transfer and sixth-man extraordinaire hit a fast break layup to put the Jayhawks up three with eight minutes left. But he crumpled to the floor with a torn knee ligament and the air escaped the balloon. Duke would go on to lose to Louisville in the title game, a team KU beat twice in the regular season.

The 1986-87 campaign was a bit of a transition year with the graduation of Dreiling, Kellogg and Thompson. KU lost in the third round of the NCAA tourney to Georgetown to finish 25-11, 9-5 in the league (tie-second) and ranked No. 20. To rub salt in the wounds, the team returned from the Georgetown game only to find their hotel rooms had been broken into and items were stolen. While there was sadness among the fans, there was greater concern that Manning might go pro after the season (his junior year). He put those rumors to rest as he decided to stay after promising his mother, a teacher, that he would graduate from college.

Brown also proved to be quite a mentor as during his time at Kansas he sent numerous assistants or players to be NBA head coaches or front office personnel including John Calipari, Alvin Gentry, Bob Hill, R.C. Buford, Ed Manning, Gregg Popovich, Kevin Pritchard, Milt Newton and Mark Randall. Several others went on to be assistants or hold scouting positions.

Popovich's story might be the most interesting. He played collegiately at Air Force and after his commitment, earned a chance to try out for the 1972 U.S. Olympic Team. He was cut by Brown who was serving as a "qualifying" coach. Popovich later tried out for the NBA's Denver Nuggets, only to be cut by -- you guessed it -- Brown. Fast forward to the 1986-87 season and serving as a Jayhawk

THE DREAM IS REAL

volunteer coach was: Gregg Popovich. He was the head coach at tiny, NCAA Division III Pomona-Pitzer in California, but took the year as a sabbatical. He planned to spend the season at five schools, staying six weeks at each. He started at North Carolina and then moved on to Kansas. But Brown convinced Popovich to stay the remainder of the year.

The next season Popovich returned to Pomona-Pitzer and Brown invited the Sagehens to Allen Fieldhouse for a game. Kansas won 94-38. Popovich's pregame message to his team was: "Don't hurt Danny Manning!" Of course, Popovich made a name for himself when he moved onto the NBA, winning five titles with the San Antonio Spurs.

Gentry had a great "deadpan" sense of humor and thus was able to keep things light when the time called. He is former N.C. State All-American David Thompson's first cousin and played at Appalachian State under Press Maravich (Pistol Pete's father) and Bobby Cremins. Alvin has had a long NBA coaching career, including his recent stint as the head coach of the New Orleans Pelicans. On one of our road trips we were on a commercial flight, and Alvin was talking to a flight attendant, and he's kind of being charming -- which was his nature. He returned to his seat across the aisle from me. As he sits down, and I give him a wink, he goes, "I'm a procurer of talent — and I often recruit basketball players." We all got a good chuckle out of that.

Among those graduating off the 1986-87 team was Topeka-Hayden High School graduate Mark Turgeon, who became the first, four-time NCAA tourney qualifier at Kansas. That would never have happened had he not told Brown after his senior season at Hayden that he was better than any guard he had on the roster. Brown liked his moxie and offered him his last scholarship. As I look back, Turgeon's conversation with Brown happened just a month or so after I called a state high school game in which he played. He looked all of 100 pounds as a high school senior. He fought for everything he got.

To show you how much of a competitor Turgeon was, you only have to look back to that season when Kansas scheduled a rare back-to-back set of games versus Oklahoma State on Saturday and Notre Dame on Sunday. Brown had actually done the same thing in the 1984-85 season, but both were on the road at Colorado and at Michigan. This was done for TV purposes and certainly having Sunday afternoon to yourselves playing Notre Dame on CBS was great exposure.

Notre Dame was led by David Rivers, an outstanding guard who would go on to be an All-American. It was billed as a matchup of great point guards as Cedric Hunter was gaining quite a reputation for his play. But Hunter jammed his foot against a basket standard against the Cowboys on Saturday and his status for Notre Dame was questionable. Everyone fretted - except for Turgeon. This was his chance to step into

66

the lineup. Story has it that Turgeon told his teammates he was going to hold Rivers below double figure scoring. Things were going according to plan, however late in the game Brown got a technical and Rivers hit two free throws to get into double-digits. He got a garbage bucket later, but the Jayhawks won 70-60. Joking, but still making his point, Turgoen sarcastically noted that those last few points scored by Rivers were on Brown.

After the season, Johnson stepped down as athletic director. He had made it clear he would not be a lifer in the position and actually tried to resign earlier, but Chancellor Gene Budig asked him to wait until the basketball season was completed. It was clear that his replacement would have Jayhawk ties. The names mentioned the most in the media were Gary Hunter, a former Jayhawk football player and Johnson's right hand man; Gale Sayers, Jayhawk legendary running back and former Southern Illinois AD; and Bob Frederick, a KU alum who had previously been the director of the Jayhawk fundraising department -- the Williams Fund.

Frederick, who was the sitting AD at Illinois State, was selected for the position by Budig. I believe any of the three would have been a popular hire, but people were truly happy for "Freddy" as they called him. For me, it was a blast from the past as I broadcast high school games with him coaching the opposing Russell Broncos in the early 1970s. We both agreed we had come a long way since.

Bob Frederick, Kansas athletics director, 1987-2001. Credit: Kansas Athletics

The 1987-88 basketball campaign truly tested the thesaurus: unrealistic expectations, excitement, drama, despair, conflict, hope, determination, luck, excellence, miraculous. Any one of those terms could have been applied to the season. Unrealistic expectations because Manning was back and the Final Four was in Kansas City. Excitement due to the fact the fifth installment of Late Night with Larry Brown was becoming one of the most anticipated events on the calendar. Drama as a result of individual personalities getting in the way of team goals. Despair because the team went 1-2 at the Maui Classic and later in New York, Marshall blew out his other knee ending his season. Conflict, arising as some of the team was not getting along with each other, and at times the coaching staff. Hope that despite losing to Kansas State to end a 55-game home court winning streak, the team appeared to be coming around. Determination to prove that the Jayhawks were still a good team, despite entering the NCAA tourney at 21-11 and seeded sixth. Luck, because Murray State's Don Mann missed a shot in the lane in the second round that would have put the Racers ahead with seconds to go. Excellence in the way the team played in the final four games of the tournament. And, miraculous was the only way to describe the play of Manning and his supporting cast in the 83-79 win over Oklahoma in Kansas City's Kemper Arena.

There is little doubt that Kemper Arena and the Jayhawk fan base get an assist for the 1988 NCAA Championship. Everyone expected the Jayhawks to be well represented, but the scene was almost indescribable during the Friday open practice session when officials had to lock the doors to Kemper because there was no more room for the fans. Whether a rumor or not, it was certainly a good story going around that weekend that they wouldn't even let Mickey Krzyzewski, wife of Duke head coach Mike Krzyzewski, in for the practices. I assume she had a seat for the games.

There's a lot to unpack that could be written in a book itself about the 1987-88 season. To think at one point in the season, KU was 12-8 following four straight losses. Frederick had even instructed his staff to inquire about hosting an NIT game. The roster underwent significant change during the year. If you look at the team picture at the start of the year and one at the end of the season, there were six players lost because of grades, injuries, dismissal or redshirting. Two players, Clint Normore and Marvin Mattox, were added from the football team.

But the turning point in the season came on the road at Oklahoma State when Brown moved sophomore Kevin Pritchard to the starting point guard, inserted sophomore Jeff Gueldner as the starting off guard, gave Milt Newton freedom on the wing and let his veteran frontline players Chris Piper and Danny Manning rule the paint. KU defeated OSU, 78-68, starting a string of 14 wins in 17 games. It was obvious Brown had confidence in his sophomore backcourt. He would often remark that in preseason scrimmages, Gueldner was almost always on the winning team -- then he would say, "but that is because Danny was on his team a lot." But we got the point, Brown was looking for a group that could play together. And did they ever down the stretch.

A festive mood prevailed over the campus that spring. The football stadium was nearly half full the day after the championship for the return of the team. A parade, estimated at 100,000 rendered Massachusetts Street to a standstill. But looming were the rumors that began during the season. Would UCLA lure Brown back to coach the Bruins. There were some UCLA fans at the Final Four wearing buttons they had when he coached there previously. They said: "The Brown of Brentwood."

Brown would go to California to talk with UCLA officials. A press release had been sent to the Kansas sports information staff requesting it verify the information presented regarding Brown's coaching career. News was swirling that it was a done deal. But in a hastily called news conference, Brown sat at an empty table on the floor of Allen Fieldhouse to indicate he was staying at Kansas. People were shocked because they knew of Brown's mercurial past and the news reports that had come out. Brown truly was torn, but credit Bob Frederick for giving Brown some space to think and being there to talk the situation through.

Of course, a few weeks later Brown would be offered the head coaching job with the NBA's San Antonio Spurs. This time, he said yes. Though fans were disappointed, it is hard to blame him for taking the position as the NBA was taking off as Larry Bird, Magic Johnson, Charles Barkley and Michael Jordan were household names with a big marketing engine behind them.

Chapter 6 Sidebar 1: The Birth of the KU Network

The University of Kansas and Kansas State were somewhat ahead of their time in building radio networks.

Many people are not aware that if a radio station wanted to broadcast a football or basketball game, it would send a person/crew to the arena or stadium and they would do the game. They would order a telephone line to broadcast the game, and sell advertising. But that could be cost prohibitive when you consider paying the announcer(s), buying a phone line, covering the expense of travel and bringing in staff who would cover back at the station. There was no network to share the one broadcast.

So, three legends in the Kansas broadcast industry: Bob Schmidt (KAYS in Hays), Grover Cobb (KVGB in Great Bend), and Bob Pratt (KGGF in Coffeyville) approached KU Chancellor Franklin Murphy in 1952 to request he put together a network. The advantage would be that the stations would not have the expenses, and the university could receive some of the advertising revenues from spots aired on all of the stations. Kansas State had already established a network a year earlier with success. So, Murphy gave it his blessing and in 1952 the KU Radio Network was formed.

Former Voices of the Jayhawks (from L to R): Tom Hedrick, Bob Davis, Gary Bender, Kevin Harlan.
Credit: Kevin Harlan

Merle Harmon, who was broadcasting the minor league baseball Topeka Owls, became the first voice of the Jayhawks (1953-55). He would later move on to the Kansas City Blues, then the A's and on to network television. His first salary for the KU Radio Network was $3,500. The network grew quickly and was instantly recognized as one of the largest and best in the nation. It attracted top announcers who later went on to professional sports. Harmon was replaced by Bill Grigsby (1956-59) then Monte Moore (1959-60), who both went on to several professional announce positions. Tom Hedrick, who was at KWBW radio in Hutchinson, followed Moore from 1961 until 1967 (he became the voice of the Kansas City Chiefs in 1964 as well).

Gary Bender, a native of Ulysses, Kan., who received his master's degree from KU, held the duties from 1967-69 and of course became a popular voice of CBS Sports. Jerry Bailey shared the duties with Bender and continued until 1974. Hedrick returned for another stint in 1975-84, then I came for the 1984 football season. Of course, following the 2016 basketball season Brian Hanni took over the play-by-play duties. You might ask, but what about Max? He actually began broadcasting KU events beginning in 1947 (he did the NCAA Basketball Tournament in 1946) on various radio stations, so he was grandfathered in until 1984 when he was paired with me on the "official" network.

Chapter 6: Friends of Bob

Monte Johnson; Basketball Letterman 1956-58, Assistant Athletics Director 1960-71, Athletic Director, 1982-87, Kansas. We were in search of a new play-by-play broadcaster to start the 1984-85 academic year. Kansas had a history of outstanding broadcasters, so I knew we would attract some quality applicants. Early in the search Doug Vance, our assistant athletics director/SID, gave me an article about Bob Davis. I had known he filled in for some of our games in the past and I knew he was a substitute for some Missouri games, but I really cannot say I knew a great deal about Bob or his broadcasts.

As we went through the process, several people spoke on Bob's behalf, including the leadership at Learfield Broadcasting. They held the rights to the Missouri Network and were becoming our rightsholder in 1984. There was not one negative word spoken about Bob. His tapes were obviously very good as well. It did not matter to me that he came from small-college athletics. I wanted someone who would be professional in their representation and presentation of KU, and a broadcaster that our fans would enjoy. He checked all of those boxes.

I tell anyone who asks, that in all of my years in working at KU, Bob Davis was my best hire. He was always professional in his actions and his broadcasts were first class. And on top of that, he was just a great guy.

Larry Brown, Head Basketball Coach, Kansas, 1984-88. I have been in the pros and college each a couple of times, so I worked with some good broadcasters. I think in college you have the opportunity to get closer to them, and certainly I enjoyed being around Bob and Max. They worked so well together. And the thing I liked about them is they were caring and loyal to KU. It wasn't just a job to them. They were invested in the school, athletic department and the program. And, they were fun to be around. It seems like they were always laughing or had smiles on their faces.

In college you do a weekly radio and television show. Some coaches like doing them and for others, it's like going to the dentist. I was in the latter camp. But Bob made it so easy for me. I was comfortable because he was knowledgeable and smooth. You know, the great thing about sports is the relationships you make. During the pandemic I had the chance to watch a lot of KU games from the past being played. You see all of those people who were part of your life on the bench or in the crowd and you begin to realize just how special those days were. Certainly Bob and Max were among those.

Gary Bedore: Sports Reporter, Lawrence Journal World; Kansas City Star. Bob always had the quickest wit and knew just what to say and when. The late Chuck Woodling, the Sports Editor and my boss at the time at the *Lawrence Journal World*, provided a perfect example of this in a book documenting KU's 1988 national championship season.

The Lawrence Cosmopolitan Club had scored a major coup when it secured Indiana head coach Bob Knight to speak at its banquet October 12, 1987. Indiana had just won the 1987 NCAA title and his appearance was certain to fill the room. The agreement was made in the summer, but shortly before the event, Knight backed out. With nowhere to turn, club officials appealed to Kansas head coach Larry Brown. Just three days before the start of practice, Brown agreed to sub in for Knight. Davis served as the emcee for the evening. His opening line set the tone: With a serious look on his face and in with a deep and inquisitive delivery, Davis asked the crowd: "Who would you rather listen to tonight? The head coach of last year's national championship team? Or, the coach of this year's national championship team?" The remark elicited a loud round of applause from the crowd.

Of course, Kansas won the 1988 NCAA title.

Gary Bender: KU Network,1967-69; CBS Sports. Being on the KU Network is a real accomplishment because it had a reputation from the beginning of being one of the best in all of college sports. If you got on the network, it gave you the exposure to set you up for a professional position. Bob came from a small market in western Kansas, but don't let that fool you. If you heard him, you knew he was good. The thing that makes Bob so good is he tells the story of the game. You get a clear and vivid picture of what is happening. As a broadcaster myself, the other thing I noticed is he let his broadcast partner make his point without stepping all over him. His broadcasts were fun to listen to.

Bernie Kish: Assistant Athletics Director, Kansas, 1992-95; Executive Director College Football Hall of Fame, 1995-2005; Instructor, Kansas, 2005 - Present. I am from western Pennsylvania and a career military person. I really had no tie to the University of Kansas until I moved to Fort Leavenworth and met my wife, Judy. She just happened to be the daughter of George Bernhardt, a long-time assistant football coach under Jack Mitchell and Don Fambrough. I instantly became a Jayhawk.

In 1988 we were stationed in Germany and got to listen to the NCAA championship against Oklahoma with Bob and Max on Armed Forces Radio Network. It came on at 3 a.m. and I got so engrossed in it that I forgot to wake up my wife. Well, it was in the second half and the game was back and forth. I did not want to jinx anything, so I did not wake her up until it was over. Let's just say she was happy the Jayhawks won, but not so much with me for not waking her up.

John Baker: Football, Kansas, 1985 - 1989. I had a different relationship with Bob than most of the other athletes at KU as we both attended the Methodist church in Lawrence. I remember him taking me under his wing from the beginning and helping me get acclimated because I was from quite a distance away in Boonville, Ind. I know my parents appreciated that. And they became friends with the Davis family as well because they came to all the games. After I graduated and moved to Florida, I would meet up with Bob for lunch when the Royals would play Tampa Bay. It's then when I really came to appreciate just how funny he was. He's just a great person and friend.

I was recruited by several schools in the Midwest and it came down to Kansas and Missouri as two of the finalists. After I chose Kansas, one day during my senior year in high school, I had two NCAA investigators show up at my house. Apparently Missouri claimed that KU had given my parents free airplane trips. We showed them the paperwork and that ended the discussion, but as they left I decided to have a little fun with them and pointed to my car and told them KU did pay for that. They looked at each other and kind of smirked then left.

Mark Turgeon: Basketball, Kansas, 1984-87; Assistant Coach. Kansas, 1988-92; Current head basketball coach Maryland: Bob is so good. People loved listening to him. He had so much passion and made the game so exciting. It was so good to see him when we played the Jayhawks in the NCAA Tournament in 2016. He's just a great guy.

My first game at KU we played at Houston to open the season and they were No. 3 in the nation. We weren't any good and they were coming off a national championship game appearance the year before. They had Hakeem (Olajuwon) and a couple other guys off that team and they ended up beating us pretty bad (91-76). Two things I remember about that game. It was the first time I had flown and the flight was really bumpy going down. I got nervous. Second, I played about 15 minutes and my only interaction with Hakeem was I went to box him out and I flopped. They called a foul on him. Here I am with braces, long floppy hair and my grandmother sewed my uniform so it wouldn't fall off my shoulders. He's looking at me with a glare that said I had better not try that again. I made sure it was my last interaction with him.

I was pumped for the Notre Dame game in Allen Fieldhouse. I was a KU fan, but also a big Notre Dame fan growing up. With Ced hurt I knew I would be playing practically the whole game. I tell people we won because Danny Manning and I combined for 45 points -- he had 42 of them.

New Faces take the Jayhawks New Places

AS THE MID-1980S rolled around, college athletics was beginning to see a growing influx of cash through increasing media rights fees, donations from boosters, revenues from marketing and growing cash distributions from conference and NCAA operations.

That meant there was more pressure to win and do so right away. The days of the longstanding athletic director and tenured football and basketball coaches were waning. Such was the case for the Jayhawk football program as Bob Frederick fired head football coach Bob Valesente after going 4-17-1 in two years (1986-87). It was a difficult decision for Frederick, himself an extremely principled man. He had great respect for "Val" as he was known to everyone. Legendary UCLA basketball coach John Wooden was once asked what he thought of his recruiting class. He responded "ask me in 20 years when I see what they become and I will tell you." Val's two recruiting classes produced numerous doctors, lawyers, law enforcement officials, business executives, teachers and coaches. Val brought some tremendous young men to KU.

While there was not much to smile about those two years, there was a humorous reminder of the perils of live radio in Val's second season. The Jayhawks went to Manhattan and ended up tying the Wildcats, 17-17. Both teams squandered several scoring opportunities in the final minutes in a forgettable battle between teams that combined for a 1-19-2 mark that season. The tie was preserved when Jayhawk defensive back Marvin Mattox blocked a last second field goal attempt. When asked about it in the post game interviews, an excited Mattox proclaimed: "Well Max, Coach said to just go balls out!"

Frederick's search to replace Valesente quickly narrowed to Earle Bruce, who was fired at Ohio State with one game left on the Buckeyes' schedule. As a lame duck coach, he beat Michigan to finish 6-4-1. Frederick and Bruce agreed in principle and school officials had reserved a meeting room at the Holiday Inn in Lawrence for the announcement the following morning. In fact, one Kansas newspaper printed that Bruce would be introduced as the new Kansas football coach. But Bruce came back with some contract demands that made Frederick uncomfortable. The courtship ended at the altar.

According to the media, there were four candidates now being considered: former KU assistant John Hadl, Appalachian State's Sparky Woods, Kent State's Glen Mason and Buffalo Bills assistant Ted Tollner. Mason had an advantage in that he left a considerable impression on Frederick and Kansas fans as his Golden Flashes defeated the Jayhawks earlier in the year in Lawrence, 31-6.

Mason, a Woody Hayes and Lou Holtz disciple, had an outgoing personality and won over Frederick and the search committee. At the news conference, Frederick displayed his wonderful humility by telling of his first meeting with Mason. As was his practice, Frederick would welcome the opposing head coach on the field during pregame warmups. Unbeknownst to him, he would shake Mason's hand thinking he was an assistant coach. When he asked a Kent State representative where the head coach was, he turned and pointed to the man Freddy had just greeted. He made a beeline back to Mason to apologize and welcome him to Lawrence. Just a few months later, he was doing so again on a long-term basis.

Mason played for Woody Hayes at Ohio State and brought with him a no-nonsense, hard-nosed attitude. That being said, he had a sharp sense of humor and did not mind playful and not-so-playful banter with the media. His weekly media luncheons were often quite lively. One such session began as Mason lathered his French Fries with mustard. Pete Goering, the late sports editor of the *Topeka Capital Journal* just about had a coronary. Mason explained that in school, friends would steal food if you left or weren't looking -- and fries were among the most valuable currency. To dissuade others from taking his fries, he used mustard as his line of defense.

Mason would need a sense of humor to rebuild a program that was floundering. His first team went 1-10 in 1988 (defeating Kansas State) and improved to 4-7 in 1989. That season, he won the most important games of the year, 21-16 at Kansas State and 46-44 at Missouri. There was hope.

With Mason secured as the new football coach, Frederick would find himself in the coaching search again when Larry Brown left in the summer of 1988 for the NBA's San Antonio Spurs. Normally, the job would attract interest from all corners of the basketball world, but Kansas had received notice from the NCAA of allegations for improper benefits provided to Memphis transfer Vincent Askew. Of course, Askew never showed up to play and most of those benefits were deemed allowable a few years later due to changes in NCAA rules.

The possibility of NCAA sanctions scared away some applicants. Brown was lobbying for Ohio State head coach Gary Willams, who accepted the job and then an hour later called Frederick to rescind his acceptance. A few days later, the search committee of Frederick, Faculty Representative Del Brinkman, Galen Fiss and Associate Athletics Director Richard Konzem flew to Springfield, Mo., to talk to Southwest Missouri State head coach Charlie Spoonhour. It was a bumpy plane ride home amidst thunderstorms, which necessitated an unplanned landing in Emporia. There, the foursome huddled and reached no conclusion on Spoonhour. He was slated to leave the country for a clinic in Europe and asked for a decision either way before he left. He pulled his name having not received an offer.

Much like having Glen Mason's name in the back of his mind, Frederick considered Roy Williams, the second assistant at North Carolina (he had just moved up after Eddie Fogler went to Wichita State in 1986) to be a candidate once Gary Williams backed out. Former Kansas head coach Dick Harp, who was an administrative assistant in his retirement for Jayhawk alum Dean Smith, had actually been calling Frederick for two years, telling him that Williams was ready should Brown ever decide to leave.

On the same day Brown stepped down, Frederick called Smith to inquire about his interest in the job. There wasn't much thought that he would leave - especially since the building he was coaching in had his name on it -- but Frederick had to ask. Smith declined, but was adamant that Williams was ready. Frederick would fly to Atlanta to meet Williams at the Delta Crown Room in Hartsfield-Jackson International Airport. Williams was on his way to Bermuda for a vacation. Two days later, he cut short the vacation and was on his way to interview with the committee in Lawrence.

The day did not begin on the right foot because Williams was sick. He was picked up at Kansas City International Airport by Richard Konzem and Doug Vance and the three made a quick stop at Hardees on the Kansas Turnpike. Williams could not keep his food down. Not a great situation for a guy who later that evening would be interviewing for the biggest job in his life.

Looking back, it is no surprise that Williams spent 45 minutes of the interview laying out his plan in great detail. He even apologized to the committee for being so passionate about North Carolina. Fiss, who was a KU football standout, was also on the freshman basketball team and roomed with Smith. Nearly in tears, he stood up and impassionately told the committee that it was precisely the reason he felt Williams was the man for the job. After a brief silence, Frederick asked Williams if he would take the job if he offered it. Frederick wanted to avoid the Earle Bruce situation in the football coach search the previous year.

Williams said yes and Frederick said he would need to talk to the Chancellor Gene Budig first. With Budig's blessing, the offer was made and as they say, the rest is history. On July 8, 1988 in a ballroom at the Holiday Inn in Lawrence, Williams was introduced as only the seventh coach in the history of Kansas basketball.

Frederick knew he was taking a risk in hiring a relative unknown in Williams.

Some national media even chided him for getting the wrong Williams, a reference for not landing the Ohio State coach. Bob's personal intuition told him things would be okay, regardless of the NCAA investigation. On November 2, 1988, Kansas was sanctioned by the NCAA and would not be allowed to defend its national title. Frederick, Williams and senior Milt Newton appeared at an afternoon press conference to discuss the day's news. Immediately following, the somber team loaded a bus and headed to Salina for an intersquad scrimmage and fan reception.

After that announcement, the recruiting prospects dried up quickly. Five highly ranked prospects backed out of visits, including Harold Miner (USC) and Thomas Hill (Duke) who Williams thought were ticketed to be Jayhawks. Finally he struck paydirt when Adonis Jordan from Reseda, Calif., committed and became his first signee.

The bus ride to Salina was quiet. Blank stares looked out the window across the Kansas prairie. That night Williams wowed the crowd and the fans left depressed about the probation, but excited about the future. The pity party ended at the Bicentennial Center that night. *Salina Journal* Sports Editor Harold Bechard, who got a 20 minute one-on-one with Williams, told me at a football game shortly thereafter that the Dean Smith protege would be an instant hit with the fans. He was right.

Williams' big moment came at his first Late Night event. A bit nervous that he would not be accepted by the fans in following a national championship coach, a jam packed Allen Fieldhouse roared in approval as he was introduced. He would tell me a few days later that it was a special moment, but he felt incredible pressure not to let the fans down.

Of course, that Late Night had quite a scare. Forward Alonzo Jamison brought the goal down with a pre-scrimmage dunk that opened up a cut on his head. The place was deathly quiet for a few minutes, but trainer Mark Cairns stopped the bleeding and "Zo" played in the scrimmage. We later learned that he broke a weld of the "Y Joint" and the goal company was dispatched to check its basket standards all over the nation. Alonzo was one of the more unique basketball players at Kansas during my time. At 6-5, he was strong, had quick feet, was an excellent passer and a great defender. You might remember he had a tryout scheduled with the Kansas City Chiefs after graduation, but tore his Achilles tendon a month prior to it.

The Jayhawks jumped out to a 12-1 record to begin the 1988-89 season, but a roster with a thin bench left little margin for error and it finally succumbed to the rigors of the Big Eight Conference. Center Sean Alvarado was limited with a lower leg stress fracture and Jeff Gueldner was never the same after colliding with Kansas State's Steve Henson and injuring his leg. The season ended with a respectable 19-12 mark, but there was little doubt the best was yet to come.

Still, those outside of Lawrence were non-believers. One day prior to practice Jayhawk guard Kevin Pritchard stormed up to Williams and handed him a copy of

Inside Sports magazine. It had just come out with its preseason rankings and it had Kansas ranked last in the Big Eight. As if the Jayhawks needed any more motivation, there was definitely a firm resolve among those in the program to prove the naysayers wrong.

Kansas entered the 1989-90 season unranked, which was not unexpected given the previous campaign and for the most part, relative unknowns in the recruiting class. The new class included guard Adonis Jordan, Williams' first-ever commit, junior college sharpshooting guard Terry Brown and Finnish center Pekka Markannen. The latter was recruited off a video and the recommendations of contacts in Europe. On tape he looked 6-5, but when he arrived in Lawrence much to the pleasant surprise of the staff he was 6-10. The Jayhawks opened the season with a blowout over Alabama-Birmingham coached by Gene Bartow in the first round of the Preseason NIT.

Kansas expected to go to Chicago to meet DePaul in round two, but behind the scenes the tournament organizers were hoping for a final four in New York to feature St. John's, DePaul, LSU and UNLV. So, on Thursday morning the plans changed, Kansas found it would instead be going to Baton Rouge, La., to meet No. 2 LSU featuring Chris Jackson, Stanley Roberts and Shaquille O'Neal in a Friday evening tip. It would be a full weekend for the broadcast crew as the Jayhawk football team was in Columbia, Mo. to play the Tigers.

Max and engineer Bob Newton went straight to Columbia on Friday, and I would go to Baton Rouge and enlist Athletics Director Bob Frederick to be my analyst. The Jayhawks literally outran Dale Brown's LSU squad for an 89-83 win, which few predicted would happen. Bob and I had an early wake up call and flew to St. Louis where a representative of Learfield Communications whisked us to Columbia for the football game on Saturday.

This was the pre-cell phone era, so when the basketball team landed at KCI on Saturday afternoon, Williams went to a pay phone and called KLWN radio station in Lawrence to have them play the last few minutes of our football broadcast. He held the phone up for the travelling party which let out a roar as Charley Bowen knocked down a pass in the near dark skies to preserve a 46-44 win. Life was good on Mt. Oread. So, good in fact that Frederick and his wife Margey threw an impromptu party at their home for the coaching staff, athletics department staff -- and the radio crew.

Playing with a chip on its shoulder served Kansas well in Baton Rouge, and would do so again in New York. At the pre tournament banquet, officials introduced the Jayhawk head coach as "Ron Williams." Williams made light of it, but deep down he and his team were seething over the disrespect. Kansas upset No. 1 UNLV, 91-77 then No. 25 St. John's, 66-57 to take the title. The Jayhawks became the first team to go from unranked to No. 4 in the nation in just one week. There would be no sneaking up on opponents from that point forward. The core of the team was a veteran cast of Pritchard, Gueldner, Mark Randall and Indiana transfer Ricky Calloway, who was a senior. Brown proved to be a perfect outside shooting complement, while Jordan, Markkanen, juco transfer Freeman West and Mike Maddox were solid off the bench.

The team won 19 games to start the season before falling to Missouri on the road. Included in that streak was the amazing 150-95 homecourt win over Kentucky. I have always kept a scorebook when doing games, continuing to do so even when computerized stats became available. I remember looking at Max and producer Bob Newton and just laughing because it was so difficult keeping up with the action. What is interesting is at one point late in the first half the score was, 64-57, but it would balloon to 80-61 at intermission. The other thing that stood out about this season is the tremendous regular season the Big Eight had. Kansas, Missouri and Oklahoma were ranked among the top five most of the year and the three were part of a couple of 1 vs. 2 matchups. Kansas ended the season at 30-5, ranked No. 5, but fell in the second round of the NCAA in Atlanta to UCLA, 71-70. The Bruins snatched victory in the final minute when guard Gerald Madkins banked in a three-pointer -- the only three-point bucket UCLA would hit -- and Tracy Murray nailed two free throws.

It was truly a fantastic season, but the one takeaway I had is the team looked tired at the end of the season. It played hard for Williams and at such an uptempo pace that perhaps the legs were gone after 35 games. Plus, there were so many high-profile games -- the preseason NIT, the battles with Oklahoma and Missouri when they were both No. 1 -- that you wonder how much gas was left in the tank. Williams had clearly endeared himself to the Jayhawk faithful from the start. His respect for the program, his dogged-determination and his team's style of play made it easy for fans to get behind him.

Mason and Williams had their teams on an upward trajectory for their third seasons (1990-91 academic year). When the football team went 3-7-1 that year, there were some fears among fans that maybe things were NOT headed in the right direction. But Frederick had all the confidence in Mason and it was apparent the head coach knew how to build a program. Five of the 11 opponents were ranked at the time of kickoff in 1990, including No. 3 Miami and No. 15 Virginia; and Louisville, which was not ranked, finished No. 12 at 10-1-1 and beat Alabama in the Fiesta Bowl. Give Mason credit for not backing down from the big boys.

The 1991 season was a breakthrough for the Jayhawks. In going 6-5, they had their first winning season since the 1981 Hall of Fame Bowl Season. NCAA rules at the time required seven wins to earn a bowl bid. Today, six wins get you in a bowl and if there are not enough teams available, a 5-7 mark can qualify. Had the new rule been in play, Mason could have led the Jayhawks to five bowls in his nine seasons on Mt. Oread.

The icing on the cake in 1991 was a 53-29 win over Missouri in Lawrence to end the season. In that game, running back Tony Sands set NCAA records in rushing attempts (58) and yards gained (396 yards -- a record which stood for eight years). He had eclipsed Marshall Faulk's 386 yards for the record. The game was actually close late into the third quarter with Kansas clinging to a 32-29 lead. But the 5-6 Sands and his offensive line took matters into their own hands. There was no doubt the longer the game went on and the more carries he had, the stronger he got.

Mason was methodically building his program, recruiting the state of Kansas and athletes from Big 10 country who were overlooked or just a bit undersized for that level of competition. His staff was coaching them up as they say and the Jayhawks were gaining the reputation as a physical team that controlled the line of scrimmage. Offensive linemen Keith Loneker, Hessley Hempstead, and John Jones were opening holes. On the defensive line, few could match Dana Stubbblefield, Gilbert Brown and Chris Maumalanga. The 1992 season saw another step taken by qualifying for the Aloha Bowl with a 7-4 mark. A 23-20 win over BYU had significance because the Cougars were traditionally older and more physical than their opponents, but the Jayhawks won the rushing battle 172-142 yards.

In addition to the bowl game, two games stood out in 1992, played in back-to-back weeks in the middle of the season. On October 10 in Lawrence, Kansas thumped Kansas State 31-7, holding the Wildcats without a first down until the third quarter. In all, Kansas limited Kansas State to minus 56 yards rushing and just 69 total offensive yards. The Jayhawks recorded 20 tackles behind the line of scrimmage. The next week on October 17 in Ames Iowa, the Jayhawks stole a 50-47 win over the Cyclones. Kansas jumped to a 21-7 lead but Iowa State would score the next 40 points to lead 47-21 with two minutes left in the third quarter. The Jayhawks responded with 29 straight points, in 10 minutes of possession time for the win. A fumble recovery scooped up by LB Larry Thiel proved to be the winning score with six minutes remaining.

I am not sure if I have seen a more dominating defensive performance by a Kansas team in the win over Kansas State. The Iowa State victory was remarkable and inexplicable. There was no sign of life, and then suddenly the switch flipped.

Perhaps the most impressive thing to me was the development of recruits under Mason. Some of the players were in their fifth year at KU, having redshirted when Mason was in his first year at KU. QB Chip Hilleary, FB Maurice Douglas, RB Chaka Johnson, DT Dana Subblefield, DT Gilbert Brown, OL Keith Loneker among others. These were young men who were headed to MAC schools for the most part, but they saw the opportunity Kansas afforded them.

The Jayhawks suffered heavy graduation losses from the Aloha Bowl squad, but were a respectable 5-7 in 1993. Again, Mason dodged nobody in playing No. 1 Florida State in the kickoff classic, at Michigan State and hosted Utah in non-league games. A deeper look at the season shows how maddingly close the Jayhawks came to another bowl game. They lost a 10-9 decision at Kansas State on October 9, and then on November 6 lost a 21-20 heartbreaker at home to No. 6 Nebraska when a game-winning two-point conversion failed with :52 remaining in the game.

The 1994 campaign was a bounce back year as the Jayhawks finished 6-6, including a season-ending 31-14 win at Missouri A highlight of the season was a 17-10 win over Michigan State, led by highly-regarded quarterback Tony Banks. College football is always filled with interesting stories, and certainly those can come in handy, especially in blowouts. Kansas defeated I-AA Alabama-Birmingham 72-0 that season. The head coach was a Ph.D. by the name of Jim Hilyer, who took the program from a club sport to a 27-12-2 record in his four years there. His kicking coach was another Ph.D. -- his wife, Dr. Lynn Artz. She was a Harvard educated psychologist, and agreed to coach because her husband thought she could help with the mental side of the game. Let's just say that story helped fill air time.

Broadcasters are fortunate to get a somewhat behind-the-scenes look at the programs they cover, and that means you get the opportunity to meet some true characters. Mason's coaching staff over the years had many assistants who would fit in that category. One was defensive coordinator Bob Fello, whose squinting glare sent daggers right through you. A visit to his office revealed a library of military books and a deep affection for General George Patton. Of course that would make sense for someone in charge of the defense. He was known to occasionally salute Mason on the practice field in response to one of his directives.

Mason was not necessarily caught up in Fello's penchant for military thoughts, beliefs and mannerisms. In fact, he would occasionally chuckle at Fello's incredible focus, discipline and interest in military leadership. However, one of Mason's favorite lines he used with players, his staff and administrators to motivate was "lead, follow or get (the hell) out of the way." A quote attributed to -- you guessed it -- General Patton.

On the opposite end of the spectrum was offensive line coach Golden Pat Ruel. With a name like that, you had to have a good sense of humor. Before fall practices began, Ruel would spend the night on the practice field under the blocking cage. Mason, who brought with him some of that Woody Hayes intensity, needed someone to keep things light -- and Ruel was just the guy. On a recruiting trip to Smith Center to recruit all-stater Jeff Simoneau, Ruel joined Mason for what was going to be an admittedly tough sell. All indications were that Simoneau wanted to go somewhere warm. As the in-home visit ended, Ruel decided a little bit of humor might be their last chance. He opened his briefcase full of Monopoly money. Everyone in the room burst out laughing -- except for Mason who turned white as a sheet. Simoneau went to Arizona State.

Glen Mason served as the Jayhawks head football coach from 1988-96. Credit: Kansas Athletics

Sense of humor aside, Ruel was highly respected by his peers and loved by his offensive linemen. He would later join Pete Carroll at USC and then with the Seattle Seahawks as one of the best offensive line coaches in the NFL.

With a changing television landscape, conference realignment had become a hot topic of conversation. The Big Eight Conference originally sought to remain as is, proposing a scheduling alignment with the old Southwest Conference. But those plans deteriorated and the schools were jockeying to be part of a new league featuring schools from both the Big Eight and SWC. It was obvious not all 16 teams would be absorbed. The ultimate outcome announced on Feb. 25, 1994 was that all Big Eight schools would remain together and Texas, Texas Tech, Texas A&M and Baylor joined them. But it was made clear this was not a Big Eight expansion, it was a new league - the Big 12 Conference.

The realist in me says something had to happen. The Big Eight could not have survived on its own. But I was not a fan of the political wrangling that occurred behind the scenes that kept Kansas Athletic Director Bob Frederick from being named Big 12 commissioner and resulted in the conference office moving from Kansas City to

Dallas. It definitely had the feel of a shotgun marriage.

The Kansas football program was on strong footing heading into the 1995 season, although there were some questions at quarterback. Workman-like wins over Cincinnati, North Texas, TCU and Houston to start the season gave the Jayhawks a No. 24 ranking heading into a matchup at No. 4 Colorado. Trailing 24-23 in the third quarter, senior QB Mark Williams engineered three scoring drives to shock the patrons of Folsom Field. Williams, who played sparingly the previous year, was emerging as a playmaker, surrounded by the one-two punch of L.T. Levine and June Henley at running back, and speedy Isaac Byrd at wide receiver.

The Jayhawks climbed to No. 10 after five games and two weeks later were No. 7 when they went to Norman to face No. 15 Oklahoma. The Sooners were driving late in the second quarter, ready to make it a 21-0 lead when the Jayhawk defense stiffened and allowed the offense to mount a drive and score with 2:15 in the half to make it 14-7 at halftime. That drive totally changed the complexion of the game as it lasted more than 12 minutes, with the Jayhawks converting four, fourth-down plays, including a two-yard Williams-to-Hosea Friday pass for the score. I had never seen a team control the ball for that long on one drive -- and never missed so many commercial breaks. Kansas outscored Oklahoma 31-3 in the second half for the 38-17 win.

Kansas fell for the first time, losing 41-7 at No. 14 Kansas State, but rebounded with a win the next week 42-23, over Missouri. The only other regular-season loss was to eventual national champion Nebraska, 41-3 in Lawrence. A 9-2 regular season and No. 11 ranking set the stage for a postseason full of drama. It began with being selected to play in the Aloha Bowl against UCLA. But on Dec. 18, exactly one week before the game, Mason was introduced as Vince Dooley's replacement at Georgia.

Kansas Athletics Director Bob Frederick did not travel to the bowl game in Hawaii, opting to stay in Lawrence to search for a new football coach. Published reports indicated the finalists included defensive coordinator Mike Hankwitz and offensive coordinator Golden Pat Ruel. The search was aborted, however, when Mason told former Oklahoma quarterback and ABC sideline reporter Dean Blevins just before kickoff that he would remain at Kansas. The story has it that KU Chancellor Robert Hemenway and Mason came to terms late Christmas Eve and the team was told at breakfast the next morning.

The radio crew would learn of the news via Blevins' pregame interview, as did Frederick back in Lawrence. A comment Mason made to me when doing the pregame show suddenly had context. He said, "Bob, you know what? Christmas Day 1995 is going to be a day you will remember for a long time." A stunned fan base sat back and watched their Jayhawks run over UCLA, 51-30.

Kansas finished No. 9 in the final *Associated Press* poll, the best season-ending mark since the 1968 squad which fell to Penn State, 15-14 in the 1969 Orange Bowl. The 10 wins were the most since the 1905 team went 10-1.

There were no concerns about the Jayhawk basketball program as Roy Williams had allayed any fears that the job was too big for him. But no one knew what to expect for the 1990-91 season given the losses of veterans Pritchard, Gueldner, Markkanen and Ricky Calloway. Williams had been able to recruit off campus for nearly a year by that point, so the ability to market the Kansas name to recruits became a bit easier. But perhaps the most underrated fact was most of the roster had multiple years experience in Williams' system.

The Jayhawks actually lost their first two league games, but won 10 of the next 12 to tie for the Big Eight title at 10-4, and finished the season winning 18 of the final 22 games. Any perceived lack of talent was made up in chemistry. Randall, Mike Maddox and Jamison were all in their third year with the starting backcourt of Adonis Jordan and Terry Brown back intact. The team just got better as the year continued. It was unranked until the team came in at No. 24 in a January 29, 79-68 win at Kansas State.

Two solid wins over New Orleans and Pitt to open the NCAA Tourney sent Kansas to Charlotte, N.C. where most people had the Jayhawks ending their season in the next game versus No. 3 Indiana. KU was the lowest seed of the four teams, meaning it received the "worst" hotel property reserved by the NCAA. I remember us being located far away from the arena on the edge of town. Other than the hotel restaurant, there was nowhere to eat that was remotely close -- except for a gentlemen's club across the street from the hotel. On its sign, the club promoted two aspects that made it popular -- one of those being great food. They must not have been lying, the parking lot was continuously packed.

Williams' had his team ready from the tip against Indiana as it raced to a 49-27 halftime lead enroute to an 83-65 win. KU jumped to a 26-6 advantage, only to be cooled off by a delay in the game where a screw holding a section of the court down became loose. Hoosier coach Bobby Knight's mood changed from apoplectic to resignation when he asked the officials if that meant the game could be started over.

The run looked to be over as No. 2 Arkansas, led by Oliver Miller, Todd Day and Lee Mayberry, took a 47-35 lead at half of the regional final two nights later. But thanks to Jamison's dominating second half, the Jayhawks grabbed a 93-81 win. Jamison, the regional MVP, ran Miller ragged and finished with 26 points on 11-of-14 shooting with 9 rebounds. At the impromptu welcome home rally at Allen Fieldhouse in the wee hours of the morning, Jordan uttered his famous line: "And Arkansas...down by 12, win by 12. No problem!"

The trip to Charlotte was a special one for Williams, not only because of winning the regional, but because he had a large personal fan base. His mother was able to come to the game as did several other family members. Also in attendance was the man who Williams says had as much influence on him -- along with Dean Smith -- as anyone, his high school coach Buddy Baldwin. Williams did not make a big deal out of it to the team, but they were well ahead of the situation and were not about to let him down.

At the Final Four one week later in the semifinal game versus North Carolina, the pupil Williams beat the teacher Smith, 79-73. Two nights later, the Jayhawks fell to Duke in the NCAA title game. KU was down as much as 14, and made a furious comeback against the Blue Devils in cutting it to five at one point. As Roy Williams said, "we didn't lose, we just ran out of time."

With three Final Fours under its belt since 1986, Kansas fans were salivating in 1992. All they had to do was scan to the bottom of the schedule and see the regionals were to be played in Kansas City. The Jayhawks did their part throughout the season starting at No. 12 and slowly climbing the ladder. Jordan was an established vet, and was paired in the backcourt with Northwestern transfer Rex Walters. Jamison and Richard Scott were strong, athletic forwards and junior college transfer Eric Pauley was an effective option in the post. The bench was solid with Steve Woodberry, Patrick Richey, freshmen Greg Gurley and Greg Ostertag. A league title was secured with an 11-3 record and it was off to the NCAA tourney.

Ranked No. 2 overall and seeded No. 1 in the Midwest Regional a 100-67 blowout win over Howard in Dayton meant only UTEP stood in the way of a regional berth. Don Haskins, a Henry Iba disciple, drew up a masterful plan on both ends of the court and kept the game close throughout. Some late defensive stops and strong play in the lane gave the Miners a 66-60 upset win. UTEP had quite a collection of players that came from all over, including a short, little red head guard from a small Texas town by the name of Gym Bice. He was heady, could shoot the ball and scrapped for 40 minutes. How could you not be a good basketball player with the nickname Gym? By now, we had become accustomed to Williams' emotional season-ending postgame news conferences. We carried these live over the radio and it was some of the most raw audio I used over my career. But as much as you felt for the Jayhawks, you had to admire the old-school Haskins. The coach of the 1965-66 Texas Western "Glory Road" team that beat Kentucky for the NCAA title, he was universally respected, but worked far from the limelight in El Paso, Texas. It had been a long time since he had his moment in the sun.

A vital aspect of broadcasting is advertising and sponsorship. Without it, Max and I would be wearing headsets, talking only to each other. So, we as the broadcast crew oftentimes joined athletic department staff and coaches to interact with business partners as a means to express our appreciation. One such opportunity was the annual Kansas basketball game played in Kansas City, which typically had a sponsor.

One year, the game was known as the PowerBar Shootout. PowerBars resemble a combination of a candy bar, fruit bar and granola bar and are said to be high in protein. I have to admit, I have never had one.

One of the promotional elements was a news conference held a day or two prior to the event to pump the game and the sponsor. For this particular contest, Kansas officials decided to use its weekly media gathering as the platform. In addition to the media, KU marketing staff, radio network administrators and PowerBar representatives were also on hand. There was a nice PowerBar banner and samples were shared with those in attendance. So prior to practice, Coach Williams comes to the media room -- and my guess is either did not remember or had no idea that PowerBar would have such a presence.

A member of the media asked Roy if he had ever had a PowerBar. His immediate response was "they're awful!" There was a snicker from the media, but just as the color began to leave the faces of the KU staff and PowerBar marketing representatives, Williams made the save of the century by saying a particular flavor was not his favorite, but he did like the others. Not that this had anything to do with it, but there was a new sponsor the next year.

With the basketball program on strong footing, Kansas rarely featured a depleted roster from one year to the next because of the staff's excellent recruiting -- and the fact that players were not leaving for the NBA early. In 1993, seniors Jordan and Walters formed arguably one of the best backcourts in the nation, while Pauley was a steady veteran as well. High-flying Garden City Community College transfer Darrin Hancock gave Wiliams an athlete he had never had before at Kansas. Richard Scott, Woodberry and Richey were seasoned juniors. It was a squad that had potential written all over it.

The team spent much of the season ranked in the top five, and would go on to finish 29-7 and win the Big Eight with an 11-3 record. Without a doubt, the highlight of the year was a sweep of Indiana, with the first win a 74-69 win at the Hoosier Dome in the second game of the year. The next one would be for much higher stakes. Kansas took care of Ball State and BYU in the first round of the NCAA Tournament in Chicago and advanced to the Sweet 16 at the old Checkerdome in St. Louis. The tournament had a similar feel to the 1991 Charlotte regional with high profile teams and a Goliath that stood in the way of the Jayhawks.

But first, Kansas would need to get by a talented California team that featured future NBA stars Jason Kidd and Lamond Murray, and a freshman by the name of Jerod Haase. The Jayhawks whipped the Bears, 93-76, setting the stage for a regional final matchup against No. 1 Indiana and head coach Bobby Knight. But after the Cal game, Williams was approached by Haase about the possibility of transferring. It had been a challenging year for Haase, whose father passed away during the season. An outstanding young man, Haase would be a perfect fit for Williams' program and he ultimately ended up in Lawrence.

The Hoosiers were a veteran team with standouts like Alan Henderson, Calbert Cheaney, Damon Bailey and Greg Graham. But a steal and bucket by freshman Calvin Rayford midway through the second half turned a tight game in the Jayhawks' favor. All five starters would score in double figures and the team would shoot 59.6 percent in the win. It meant the Jayhawks were heading to the Final Four in New Orleans and a second matchup for Williams against his mentor Dean Smith. The Tar Heels were the better team that night, out rebounding the Jayhawks by 10 and shooting 10 percent better in a 78-68 win.

This was a fun team to follow as it was among Williams' most consistent teams. It never lost more than one game in a row, primarily because the senior guard tandem of Jordan and Walters would not let them. Jordan, Williams's first recruit at Kansas, was considered a level below the other top point guards coming out of high school. But he's among the most beloved by Jayhawk fans for his faith placed in a program on probation. Two Final Fours are not too shabby, either. Walters was an intense, fiery and confident performer. He was the wild horse Williams had to tame over two years.

A few months later, the Kansas baseball team was putting the finishing touches on a magical season under head coach Dave Bingham. A highly successful coach on the NAIA level at Emporia State, Bingham made a big impact at KU. In 1993, the squad went 45-18, and 17-9 in the Big Eight. Kansas was awarded the third seed in the six-team NCAA Mideast Regional in Knoxville. Fighting its way back through the loser's bracket after a 4-3 opening round loss to Fresno State, the Jayhawks beat in order the top-seeded host Tennessee, then Rutgers, Clemson and in an extra-inning affair, a 3-2 win over Fresno State to earn the trip to the school's first-ever NCAA College World Series.

It was a bit of an unusual team composition in that it was senior laden -- in baseball, players are eligible for the MLB draft after their junior seasons. Guys like Jeff Berblinger, Jimmy Walker, David Soult and Jeff Neimeier were solid, and dependable, but certainly not first round picks. There was also a freshman by the name of Jamie Splittorff, son of my future Royals broadcast partner Paul Splittorff, who pitched 8 ⅓ innings to get the win over Tennessee. The Jayhawks' stay in Omaha was short, losing to Texas A&M and Long Beach State, but it allowed Kansas to accomplish a feat no other school had done to that point in time. Kansas was the first school ever to win a bowl game, go to the Final Four and advance to the College World Series in the same academic year.

As the final few seconds ran off the clock in the win over Indiana in the 1993 NCAA Tournament, CBS basketball analyst Bill Raftery proclaimed that Roy Williams had arrived. The following season, another arrival had Jayhawk fans full of optimism.

Jacque Vaughn, a top-rated point guard from Pasadena, Calif., chose KU over a host of suitors and instantly etched his name in the history books. In a December 22 matchup against Indiana in Allen Fieldhouse, the Jayhawks and Hoosiers waged a battle for the ages. Damon Bailey was phenomenal for Indiana. But it was Vaughn, standing what seemed to be a few feet from our broadcast position, who sank a three pointer at the buzzer to give the Crimson & Blue an 86-83 win in overtime. Greg Ostertag carried Vaughn around the court like a rag doll with the young freshman beaming from ear-to-ear. I am often asked about the best games I've ever witnessed. I tell people it is a long list, but that Indiana game is on it.

The season ended in the Sweet 16 in Knoxville as Kansas simply got beat by a better team in Purdue, 83-78. It was an uphill battle all night as Glen Robinson went off for 44 points. The Jayhawks would have been able to withstand that - the problem was future Missouri coach Cuonzo Martin had 29 points in hitting eight three point buckets. It was also the swan song for a productive group of seniors in Richey, Scott and Woodberry. That class will always be remembered for what could have been. Chris Lindley, a high school All-American from Raytown South High School in Kansas City injured his leg in a "train jumping" game his senior year in high school. He would later have the lower portion amputated. Lindley gave it his all and with a prosthesis worked towards playing in organized competition again, but it wasn't to be. He later became a health care worker in Lawrence and passed away in 2007 at the age of 34.

The Jayhawks were relatively young in 1994-95, but you could tell Williams was now making inroads with the top recruits in the nation. The prior year he got Vaughn over UCLA and Scot Pollard over Arizona. This year, he bested Duke and Iowa for Raef LaFrentz. The recruiting of LaFrentz was heated. All of the top programs were after him, and it was not easy to get to tiny Monona, Iowa, (population 1,500) in the far northeastern corner of the state. Williams would fly into Prairie du Chien, Wisc., on a university jet, then walk to a local car dealership to rent a car for the 15-minute drive across the border to Iowa. He was such a frequent visitor that later airport workers had the car and a sub sandwich waiting for him at the airport.

Add to that class Haase, who would be a sophomore after sitting out a season, and the future looked bright. But the present wasn't too shabby either. That team went 25-6, won the Big Eight at 11-3 and finished No. 5 in the *Associated Press* poll. Without a doubt, the high point of the season was an 88-59 win over No. 2 Connecticut in a bit of an unusual doubleheader at Kemper Arena. The women's teams met in the opener, followed by the men. The Jayhawks jumped out to a 47-27 lead and never looked back. The other big news that day was Paul Pierce committed to be a Jayhawk.

They say that success in the NCAA Tournament is a mixture of good play, luck and favorable matchups. Kansas was playing well and was fortunate to advance to the Sweet 16 in Kansas City, but there was nothing favorable about the matchup with No. 13 Virginia. The Cavaliers were a more veteran and physical team and they pushed the Jayhawks around enroute to a 67-58 win. Roy Williams probably had nightmares about the burly Junior Burrough for a month after the season ended.

The final year of the Big Eight was a bit nostalgic for me. As I had said before, I knew change was necessary, but this was a big cultural change. It was a new conference, not an expansion of the Big Eight. There was much hype for the future, but the Jayhawks had eyes on the present. The 1995-96 campaign began with three straight wins over ranked non-league opponents: No. 8 Utah, No. 15 Virginia (somewhat of a revenge game) and No. 23 UCLA. That moved the Jayhawks from No. 2 to No. 1 in the polls. They would not be ranked lower than No. 5 the rest of the way.

One of the wins that season was a 91-83 decision over an unranked Indiana team. Because of NCAA Tournament pairings, the two schools met six times from 1990-91 to 1995-96, with Kansas winning five times. This was a veteran Jayhawk squad, with every member of the starting five of Haase, Vaughn, Pierce, Pollard and LaFrentz averaging in double figures. They won the final Big Eight league title with a 12-2 mark and headed to the NCAA tournament on a roll. A Sweet Sixteen matchup against No. 11 Arizona in Denver was nip and tuck with Kansas pulling out an 83-80 victory. That meant all that stood between Kansas and the Final Four was the No. 15 Syracuse Orangemen and its match up zone.

The game was not a work of art as Syracuse shot 35.7 percent and Kansas a meager 34.4 percent, including a 4-25 clip for three point range. Kansas shot only 16 percent in the second half in falling 60-57. It ended the season at 29-5 and No. 4 in the AP poll. The loss stung, but even more so by the way they shot the ball. The silver lining was practically everyone would be back for the inaugural season of the Big 12 Conference.

Chapter 7 Sidebar 1: Tuxedo Tony Sands

If you've ever heard an athlete or coach speak at a retirement ceremony, hall of fame induction or jersey retirement, you'll notice they rarely talk about their statistics or win-loss records. Their focus is almost always on the relationships they have established.

While the national championships, bowl wins and record setting performances are certainly fun and rewarding, the best part of a career in sports is the people you meet: the coaches, athletes, support personnel, media, officials, etc. That is probably the one aspect fans do not see or appreciate. People often ask me who my favorite people in sports are and I tell them it would take a month of Sundays to go through the list. There are just too many.

But that doesn't mean there aren't some people who made quite an impression on me during my 48 years of broadcasting. One person who comes to mind is Tony Sands, the young man who on November 23, 1991 in his final game as a Jayhawk set NCAA records with 396 yards on 58 carries in a 53-29 win over Missouri. KU's all-time leading rusher with 3,877 yards, Sands was the man with a great personality, a million dollar smile and was a friend to all -- and according to Glen Mason, the toughest person he has ever coached. Tony Sands never had a bad day - he would not allow it to happen.

Sands grew up in humble surroundings in Ft. Lauderdale, Fla., and graduated from St. Thomas Aquinas High School as Broward County's all-time leading rusher. But at 5-6, he was not highly recruited. He turned down an opportunity to walk on at his dream school, Florida State, because he did not want to put the financial burden on his parents. The only power school option was Kansas.

So he packed up his belongings, and moved to Lawrence in the summer of 1988, leaving his wife and young son Maxie at home. He said he did that, rather than going to a smaller school near his home, to help toughen him and grow up. He impressed coaches from the beginning and on the first day of pads, sent a teammate to the hospital for observation after colliding with him in a tackling drill. And while Sands' teams never went to a bowl game, he was part of a class that set the foundation for future bowl teams.

Sands earned the nickname "Tuxedo Tony" from a member of the media because Mason required the team to wear a suit on the bus to home and road games. These were business trips and that meant dressing for success. Tony did not own a suit, but his aunt made tuxedos. So she made him one and several cummerbunds to rotate throughout the year. When his wife and son Maxie moved to Lawrence to begin Tony's junior year, his aunt made Maxie a tuxedo that he would wear to games as well.

Everyone was smitten with Sands. How could you not be? Among those was Kansas Chancellor Gene Budig. In fact, after Sands was cut following a tryout with the Arizona Cardinals in 1994, it was Budig who helped Sands deliver on a promise to his parents by getting his criminal justice degree. When Budig went to work for Major League Baseball and Sands returned to Florida, the two remained in touch.

As talented and hard-working as Sands was, what impressed me the most was his character. After breaking the NCAA record, in each interview he talked about the contributions of every player on the team. He broke down in tears, talking about what his teammates meant to him. It truly was a team record in his eyes.

After serving as a graduate assistant for Kansas and earning his degree, the Sands family returned to Florida where Tony worked in various security positions and then became a personal trainer. Today, he and his wife Clandra (married 32 years) have three children and eight grandchildren. A remarkable testament to two people who met as juniors in high school and made it work through the distance, time spent in football, lack of money -- and raising young kids.

Of his time at Kansas, Sands says it was the key to his success and becoming a good husband and parent. He is thankful for all the people who touched his life. And we are thankful for Tony Sands.

Chapter 7 Sidebar 2: We'll Play Anyone, Anytime, Anywhere

Roy Williams had an element of "corny" in his lexicon and would put it on display periodically during our interactions on the air: pregame, postgame, coach's shows, and so on. When the Jayhawks had a performance not meeting the head coach's expectations, he would lament that his team "could not beat Alvamar Tech."

If you haven't heard of Alvamar Tech, don't feel bad. Such a school did not exist. Alvamar is the development in west Lawrence that was the brainchild of the late Bob Billings. The name was derived from Billings' parents' first names - Alva and Margaret. Williams lived at Alvamar and played golf there regularly. A native of Russell (the same hometown of my wife, Linda) and a teammate of Wilt Chamberlain at Kansas, Billings was a prominent businessman and personality in Lawrence. He also had a great sense of humor.

So, after Williams offered the critique on a postgame report, Billings decided to have tee-shirts and sweatshirts made that said "Alvamar Tech Athletic Department" on the front. There was also a university seal created and prominently placed on the front. On the back, it said "We'll Play Anyone, Anytime, Anywhere. Billy Bob Williams, AD." Of course, that name refers to a combination of Bob Billings and Roy Williams.

Billings had shirts made for his staff and they were displayed for Willaims to see when he showed up to play golf one day. He got a big kick out of it, and made sure they became a part of his wardrobe.

Chapter 7 Friends of Bob

Danny Manning: Kansas Basketball, 1985-88; Assistant Basketball Coach 2006-12. I remember as a player going to our basketball banquets and being amazed at how good Bob was. He was the emcee. He did it so smoothly, with great humor and personality. And then, when they played the highlight film, they used clips of his broadcasts over the footage. I was thinking, how does he know to say the right thing at the right time all the time? I can see why fans enjoyed listening to him. He was definitely into his work.

As I have gotten older and been a coach, I've gained an even greater appreciation for what it means to be a voice of a team. As a player, you get to know the broadcasters because they are part of the family. They are with you on road trips, in the locker-room, on the bus and so on. But you really do not get to listen to them much. When you are a coach, you see how they become your link to the fans and the program. You get a feel for how they broadcast. You do coaches shows and speaking engagements with them. You're just around them more. Bob was such an asset to our program and the athletic department.

When I say it was family, with Bob it was truly that. His family would be around a lot so I got to know Linda and Steven. I remember carrying and tossing Steven around as a young kid. Now he's grown up and a broadcaster doing a great job himself. Coach Brown always used to say "there is no place like Kansas." He's right. And Bob was part of the reason it felt that way.

Dean Buchan: Sports Information Director, Kansas 1993-2000. Because most of the Big Eight Conference – and later Big 12 – was within driving distance, Bob, Max, Bob Newton and sometimes Richard Konzem and/or Doug Vance packed into a van and made those trips to Columbia, Ames, Manhattan, and often Stillwater and Norman. Now and then I would ride with those guys instead of the team and I just remember: A) hearing the same hilarious stories over and over, and B) laughing until my stomach hurt. The chemistry between Bob and Max off the radio -- well, that should have been a reality TV show.

One of my first memories of Bob came in the fall of 1990, my first year at KU, when the Jayhawks played at Miami in football. There was a pregame scuffle on the field that ignited an otherwise sleepy Miami team and the Hurricanes won 34-0. On the charter flight home, I sat next to Bob. The radio guys and SIDs sat somewhere near the back – behind the players but in front of the student trainers and managers. Back then the charter flights were relaxed and Bob Newton, who had his pilot's license, spent part of the flight in the cockpit. In mid-flight we lost an engine and they told Newton to go back to his seat, where he caused a mild panic by telling everyone within earshot that "I'm not supposed to say anything, but we lost an engine."

We had to make an emergency landing in St. Louis and on our approach, Bob elbowed me and said, "Look at Max." Max had found a way to sit next to our team priest, Father Vince Krische. About that time the flight attendant announced over the public address that we would need to assume the emergency landing position. Bob whispers to me: "You know what that is, right? You put your hands behind your head. You put your head between your knees. And you kiss your ass good-bye." We landed perfectly fine, although emergency vehicles were lined up along the runway. After landing, Bob said, "First touchdown we had all day." Then waited for another plane to come get us and take us to Topeka, where we got home the next morning.

Glen Mason: Head Football Coach, Kansas, 1988-96. The 1995 season began terribly, even though we got off to a 4-0 start. In the season opener, we beat Cincinnati, but we had to deflect a pass on the final play in the endzone to win 23-18. We then beat North Texas, but did not play well. We beat TCU and then came home to play Houston. It took a tipped pass and an interception for us to win. So we go to Colorado and they are ranked fourth in the nation. We're behind in the fourth quarter, but not playing all that bad. All of a sudden we score three times and boom, we win 40-24. That game and the Oklahoma game where we outscored them 31-3 in the second half in Norman built our confidence and gave us momentum for the rest of the year.

What people don't know is a few years before that season, I told all of the assistant coaches to reach out to their sources to see if there might be a quarterback out there we could get and develop for a season or two down the road. Our assistant coach Mitch Browning contacted Bill Rees, the recruiting coordinator at UCLA, whose son Tommy later played at Notre Dame. He was actually glad we called because they had a guy at San Francisco City College who they liked, but were going to offer a scholarship to someone else. But he said if we could offer him immediately after UCLA declined, we would have a chance to get him. That player was Mark Williams and that is exactly what happened. So, in 1995 we went on to beat UCLA 51-30 in the Aloha Bowl in (former Kansas assistant coach) Terry Donohue's last game. At the postgame handshake he asked me where we found our quarterback. I didn't have the guts to tell him, but I sure did laugh.

Glen Mason: Head Football Coach, Kansas, 1988-96. My relationship with Bob at KU was great from start to finish. We went from a program that was a joke to a top 10 team. Bob was there through the bad times as well as the good. The one constant was Bob Davis. Totally supportive and always professional.

One story that sticks out is doing my TV show in 1995 from Hawaii just before we played UCLA. I had agreed to the University of Georgia offer, but was going to coach the Jayhawks in the bowl game. This was supposed to be my final show. The show was being filmed on the beach for effect. There were two live parrots on the set as well. During the filming, one of the birds decided to fly and landed right on top of my head. Bob did not miss a beat and continued on. I was startled, but reacted to Bob and just kept going as Mr. Parrot was perched on top of my head. Bob commented at the end of the show that "it seemed like an omen!" Two days later I changed my mind and remained at KU. Oh, by the way, KU 51, UCLA 30!

Richard Konzem: Associate Athletics Director, Kansas, 1981-2003. You learned the first time that you stepped on the bus for a Kansas basketball road trip that Roy Williams was in charge on and off the court. The bus left on time or even earlier.

Team dinners had specific menus. Only certain people other than the players and coaches rode on the bus. And who was to argue? It was all part of Williams creating a successful structure.

We were scheduled to eat at the Angus Barn in Raleigh, N.C. and the head coach was already fidgeting as our flight was late. I called ahead to make sure our reserved tables would be available when we arrived. We walked in the door, only to find some of the tables had been given away. The restaurant staff worked to find room for the team, but it was not at the urgency Williams desired. His glare was burning a hole in the wall. As he made his way to what appeared to be the manager, Bob Davis grabbed my arm, pulled me aside and whispered: "take cover, and watch out for flying shrapnel."

Richard Konzem: Associate Athletics Director, Kansas, 1981-2003. Following the 23-20, victory over BYU in the 1992 Aloha Bowl, Kansas was selected to play in the Eddie Robinson Kickoff Classic, August 28 against preseason No. 1 and eventual national champion Florida State at Giants Stadium in East Rutherford, N.J., to begin the 1993 season. ABC Sports broadcast the game with Keith Jackson and Bob Griese on the call. The guarantee payment to KU for appearing in the game was used to purchase the furniture in the newly completed Wagnon Athletic Center. The football coaches would later refer to them as their "42 to nothing" desks.

Media day for the season opener was the day before, at 1 p.m., on the artificial turf field. The temperature topped out at 94 degrees with 95 percent humidity. Temperature on the field was at least 110. About 30 minutes of that was about all a man wanted. Bob, Doug Vance and I headed into the tunnel past the goal posts to get in the shade and cool off. Once in the shade in the bowels of the stadium, Bob found a box to sit on while the sweat dripped off his forehead. After cooling down and recovering somewhat, we decided it was time to head back to the field. Bob put his hands down on the box to push himself up to stand. "Oh shit," he bellowed as he looked at his hands with blue paint on both palms. You see, the Meadowlands staff had painted the boxes blue in preparation for the start of the season. The paint hadn't dried, before Bob sat down.

When he finally stood up, you could see the imprint of Bob's rear end on the box. His new denim shorts had N.Y. Giants blue paint on the backside. "Linda's gonna kill me," he moaned. We wandered back onto the field for the rest of the media day events with Doug pointing out to everyone that Bob had sat in wet paint. On game day, we taped signs on the boxes "Reserved for Bob Davis."

Later in September, I was watching a Sunday NFL game with the Giants playing at the Meadowlands. Lawrence Taylor was injured and headed to the locker room. The cameras followed him up the tunnel and he ran past Bob Davis' box. I immediately called him. Apparently, he was watching the same game because as soon as he heard my voice, he responded, "You SOB."

Roy Williams: Head Basketball Coach, Kansas, 1989-2003. I have a special place in my heart for radio broadcasters because as a youngster who loved baseball, I listened to the games as much as I could. Growing up in the mountains of Asheville, N.C. we'd be able to get KMOX out of St. Louis, so I followed the Cardinals. Then, I started to follow the Yankees because I was a Mickey Mantle fan. I remember one time we had one of those big old radios at my grandparents and I actually broke the dial and we couldn't get the games. I was devastated. When I got to North Carolina hardly any of the games were on television, so I would listen to Bill Curry, the Mouth of the South, do the games.

Coach Smith treated the radio crew like family. On our bus rides we had only the team ride, but also had space for the athletic director, the SID and the radio guys. I did that at Kansas and do that at North Carolina today. They are an important part of our program. And at Kansas, I could tell how much both Bob and Max meant to the program and to the fans. They had so much respect. I relied on Bob to tell me how it was done when it came to interacting on air. I was prepared to coach, but I knew nothing about the media side. He was so good at making me feel comfortable. I trusted him to lead me in the right direction.

There were two things that stand out to me about Bob. First, he was so professional. I admire that about people. He was committed to representing himself, the broadcast and the school in a first-class manner. Obviously, that was a benefit to our program. And second, he was so passionate about the University of Kansas. I guess those two things kind of go hand in hand. His commitment was so strong. But as dedicated and focused as he was, he had such a great sense of humor. He could get you laughing just like that. Because of all of that, I just felt comfortable around him. He's a great friend.

Tony Sands: Football, Kansas, 1988-91. The Missouri game in which I broke the NCAA record was not on TV, so I have had to search for some clips of game film on the internet. Bob's voice is over the video. I get the chills when I listen to how excited he got as I got closer to the record. But my wife is the one who really got excited. She was at the game with my sons Maxie and DeShaun. They were little guys, ages five and three. But it was so cold and when it was clear we were going to win, she decided to leave with the boys and get them warm. So she gets in her car and drives away and turns on the radio. She hears Bob getting excited and talking about me getting close to the record. So, she turns the car around and talks her way back in the stadium and gets to see me break the record.

Doug Vance: Associate Athletic Director/Media Relations, University of Kansas 1983-2007. The scene was the 1992 Aloha Bowl in Hawaii and a pre-game hospitality room. Access to the room included the media and there was an impressive breakfast buffet for everyone to enjoy. Bob and Max rarely missed any media meals. After making their way through the buffet line, they were seated next to each other in a line of chairs against a wall with paper plates nearly overflowing on their laps. Miss Aloha Bowl – outfitted in a grass skirt - was wandering around the room greeting the VIPs.

Richard Konzem (Associate Athletic Director) and I never missed an opportunity to have a little fun at the expense of Max and seeing Miss Aloha Bowl triggered an idea. After introducing ourselves and engaging her in friendly conversation, we pointed to where Max and Bob were seated. We told her about Max and that she would make his day if she went over and sat on his lap. She wanted to make sure she had the right person before being sent on the mission and we pointed their direction with the simple instruction – "he's the older one of the two." Richard and I nearly fell to the floor with laughter as we watched her arrive where Bob and Max were seated and proceed to sit on Bob's lap!

Alonzo Jamison: Basketball, Kansas, 1990-92. As a player, you do not get to listen to the radio announcers other than a highlight here and there. When I was playing, I knew Bob and Max were well-respected. But after I graduated and got to listen to them, you understood why people loved listening to them. Bob had so much passion and got so excited. You always knew how the Jayhawks were doing when he was broadcasting.

Bob Newton: Radio Engineer, Jayhawk Network, 1984 - 2018. Bob and Max and I started together on the Jayhawk Radio Network when it became a separate entity in 1984. I was Bob's press box, courtside, and travel partner as producer/engineer for his entire 32-year career with the network. In September, 1984, we embarked on our first football road trip to Nashville, Tenn., to play Vanderbilt. The night before the game, we and our sports information staff were invited to dinner with the Vanderbilt sports information staff and radio announcers. I ended up seated next to their play-by-play announcer Charlie McAlexander. Bob, my safety net in such situations, was seated a few chairs away.

It was no secret among the network family that I wasn't a sports guy -- I was a radio guy. The conversation all around the table, naturally, was all about football. Having nothing to contribute regarding the game, I proceeded to attempt dinner conversation with Charlie Mac (McAlexander) by asking him how he uplinked his broadcast from the stadium to their radio affiliates. Charlie stopped his fork in midair, paused, turned to me and said, "Shit, man, they point at me and I talk!" It got a good laugh, but Bob was mortified. Many times after that, when we went to dinner with the other team's announcers, Bob would caution me on the way into the restaurant, "Now, don't ask them about their uplink!" And then, during dinner, he would tell that story and get a big laugh.

Chris Piper: Basketball, Kansas, 1984-88; Jayhawk Television Network, ESPN+, Jayhawk Radio Network, 2007-12. We respected Oklahoma, but we weren't intimidated by them. We only lost by eight points in both games during the year. It's true that Coach Brown didn't want us to run with them, but he also told us whenever we had the advantage we needed to attack the basket. We beat the press so much we just kept attacking. But I think both teams felt they had to try something different because both had played great, and yet it was tied at halftime. My basket that put us ahead by six late in the game wasn't a result of any great strategy. I wasn't being guarded and I could see the shot clock winding down so when the ball was passed to me I had to throw it up from the baseline.

CHAPTER **8**

Eight is Not Enough

JAYHAWK ATHLETICS WAS on a roll heading into inaugural Big 12 Conference season 1996-97. The football team was coming off a bowl win and the basketball team was looking to build off an Elite Eight appearance with a veteran and highly-regarded squad.

Even though he changed his mind, Glen Mason's original acceptance of the Georgia job just prior to the 1995 Aloha Bowl was not entirely surprising. Obviously, the Bulldogs had a top program playing in what many consider to be the best football conference. There also had been rumors of Mason's name being tied to other jobs in recent years. So, when the 1996 season came around, there was widespread media speculation that just because he spurned Georgia, it did not mean he would remain at Kansas for another eight years.

The first football season for Kansas in the Big 12 started well, with three wins in the first four games, including a 52-24 shellacking of Oklahoma in Norman. The Jayhawks climbed to No. 20 in the *Associated Press* poll. But six losses in the final seven games sunk any chances for a return to a bowl game and left the Jayhawks at 4-7. For the second year in a row, Mason said yes to a new job offer -- this time to Minnesota. But unlike his experience with Georgia, he did not change his mind. Mason had strong ties to the Big 10, so it did not catch people totally off guard.

Now some 25 years removed from the Glen Mason era, there is no question he made Kansas a competitive program, providing a structure for consistent success. The program won bowl games, spent several weeks in the rankings, and sent many letter-winners to the pros. Kansas went from a laughingstock to a steady, if not strong, program. But the constant rumors of Mason's departure -- not to mention his accepting the Georgia job -- began to chip away at the program's fragile ego. Opposing coaches used it against Kansas in the recruiting process. From a pure broadcast perspective, he was interesting to cover and made for good content.

When I was broadcasting the Royals, I met up with Glen on the Minnesota campus for lunch during spring practice. Afterward, he asked me to address the team and introduced me as his "dear friend." My guess is my words of wisdom were not very inspirational. He never had me back in future visits. I do chuckle a bit that Mason has become somewhat of a media star in the Twin Cities. Not that he doesn't have the talent, just the opposite. He will go out on a limb, he knows his subject matter, and he is talkative. I just did not see him becoming one of "us." He is a regular on a talk sports station and does analysis for the BigTen Network.

Frederick's trial run in a coaching search the previous year prepared him to expedite the process to find a replacement for Mason. One of the candidates that immediately rose to the top was Northern Iowa coach Terry Allen. The collegiate coach of NFL Hall of Famer Kurt Warner, Allen perennially had the Panthers in the I-AA playoffs. He was also highly recommended by Big 12 Commissioner-to-be Bob Bowlsby, who was the Northern Iowa AD who hired Allen. In the tangled web of coaching searches, Allen was also a candidate and interviewed for the Minnesota job that went to Mason.

The other published candidates who were either contacted or interviewed for the job were native Kansan and New Mexico State coach Dennis Franchione, Ruel, Hankwitz, Matt Simon of North Texas, and another native Kansan, Charlie Weatherbie, who played at Oklahoma State and was the head coach at Navy. Franchione had support from several boosters given his success at Southwestern and Pittsburg State, but you could tell Frederick liked Allen from the beginning. On December 28, 1996, Allen was introduced as the Jayhawks' new football coach.

Allen was personable, approachable and likeable. He and his wife, Lynn, were a great cultural fit in the athletic department and with the fans. A native Iowan and former Northern Iowa quarterback, everyone in the Hawkeye State, with the exclusion of the Cyclones, wanted him to succeed. From a broadcaster perspective, he gave good access and was glib. He brought with him a wide open offensive philosophy and the fans were hopeful that meant the Jayhawks would be lighting up the scoreboard.

Allen started off on the right foot, winning his first three games against UAB, TCU (remember, they were not one of the Big 12's original chosen ones) and Missouri all at home. The Missouri game was moved up from the traditional last game of the year by the Big 12 to create some early-season drama. Kansas defensive end Ron Warner was a sack machine, causing Missouri's Corby Jones to fumble deep in Kansas territory late in the game to preserve a 15-7 win. Two weeks later, KU defeated Oklahoma 20-17, its third straight win over the Sooners. The Jayhawks would finish 5-6, however, dropping five of their final six contests.

After two seasons in the Big 12 Conference, two things were evident. First, the four Texas schools were giddy. They felt the Southwest Conference was dying and they were being left behind in terms of the national picture. Second, football was going to be a much tougher proposition than in the Big Eight. The Texas schools felt the SWC weakness made it hard to keep top talent home. That would no longer be the case. It was going to be more difficult for the old Big Eight schools, perhaps with the exception of Oklahoma, to get the players they had in the past.

Kansas went 4-7, 5-7 and 4-7 in 1998, 1999 and 2000. There were some solid wins in that period, including a 33-17 defeat of No. 17 Colorado (1998), a 21-0 win over Missouri (1999) and a 23-15 win against Colorado and 38-17 victory over Missouri (2000). The problem was there were just not enough wins. The pressure to win in 2001 was ramped up for two reasons. First, Frederick, the man who hired Allen, announced his retirement, April 26, 2001. And second, the natives (fans) were getting restless.

I am sure most people think success on the Division I level rests purely with the head football and men's basketball coaches, but without a good athletics director that success cannot be sustained. It is a difficult job that requires stamina, political savvy, great people skills and vision. I give Bob Frederick a tremendous amount of credit for what KU was able to accomplish during his tenure from 1987 - 2001. But he was also giving to his school. Many probably are not aware that Bob signed with the Air Force Academy out of Kirkwood (Mo.) High School where the assistant coach was former Jayhawk Dean Smith. But he was denied entry because of an eye condition, so Smith worked to have him get admitted to KU. He played freshman basketball in 1960-61, but tore his knee up and his career was over.

Frederick represented himself, the department and the university with integrity and class. The NCAA awards a sportsmanship award to a coach, administrator or staff member in Bob's honor each year. I was sorry to see him leave. I thought his final statement at his press conference was telling: "I haven't had a weekend (off) since I graduated from college. I'm going to be reading the Sunday paper out on my deck, and I'm going to be smiling."

Chancellor Bob Hemenway's focus for a new athletics director was to attract someone who could help turn the football program around. The finalists for the position were Al Bohl, Toledo AD; Doug Woolard, St. Louis AD; Mike Hamrick, former KU staffer and current Marshall AD; and Kathy DeBoer, Senior Associate AD at Kentucky. The committee was attracted to Bohl's experience in hiring winning football coaches in Pat Hill at Fresno State, and Nick Saban and Gary Pinkel at Toledo. He was awarded the job and began in August of 2001.

I think it's fair to say that Bohl was much different than Frederick. Bob was much more reserved and quieter. Bohl did not mind being the life of the party or injecting himself into the setting. At basketball games he would sit in the student section and engage in organized chants. He would wave the wheat with students at football games after Jayhawk scores. He was full of energy and tried to exude it whenever and wherever he could.

Allen's Jayhawks were off to a respectable 2-2 start in 2001, including a thrilling 34-31 overtime win at Texas Tech. The next week Kansas fell to Oklahoma, setting up crucial back-to-back meetings with archrivals Missouri and Kansas State. The Tigers won a back-and-forth contest, 38-34, while the Wildcats took a 40-6 decision. At 2-5 and Nebraska up next, rumors were growing that Allen was on the hot seat. The Jayhawks fell to the No. 2 Huskers, 51-7 and it was announced after the game that Allen had been fired. Defensive coordinator Tom Hayes would fill in for the last three games, going 1-2 to give the Jayawks a 3-8 record for the campaign.

To Allen's credit, he handled his departure with dignity and class. He appeared at a Sunday press conference and apologized for not being able to complete the job but thanked the university for the opportunity. "They have been just absolutely wonderful to us, to Lynn and I and our family. Our two boys (Chase, 3, and Alex, 1) were both born here in Kansas. They're Jayhawkers and Lynn and (5-year-old daughter) Angie and myself and those two boys, we'll always be Jayhawkers."

The removal of Allen before the end of the season was somewhat controversial. Should a coach be able to finish out the season with his team? How much can actually be done in terms of a coaching hire during a season? On the collegiate level, most coaches fired in the middle of the year had the opportunity to stay. Bohl felt the program needed to move as quickly as possible to find a replacement.

The committee reached out to several people to gauge their interest including former Jayhawk standout and then-assistant with the Seattle Seahawks Nolan Cromwell; Kansan Bill Miller, Michigan State defensive coordinator; former Oklahoma head coach Gary Gibbs, who was with the San Francisco 49ers; Jim Chaney, Purdue, offensive coordinator; Gary Darnell, Western Michigan head coach; Charlie Strong, Florida defensive coordinator; former Kansas State and Oklahoma assistant coach Mark Mangino and interim coach Hayes.

Hayes, Strong and Mangino were the finalists, but Mangino pulled his name out of the running. He would later say he felt there were some elements the program needed in order to be successful. After receiving promises those would come, he changed his mind and on December 4, was named Kansas' next football coach. Among the happiest of people with that selection was Jayhawk sports information department student assistant Samantha Mangino.

Mangino preached a similar message of his former mentors Bill Snyder and Bob Stoops. Namely, Rome was not built in a day. The focus would be on getting better each day. The Jayhawks went 2-10 in 2002 and 0-8 in the Big 12. The only wins would be over Southwest Missouri State and Tulsa. Mangino said the only means to improve was to "Keep Sawing Wood," a refrain he would use frequently throughout his stay in Lawrence.

While the Texas schools had much to gain in football with the formation of the Big 12, the reality is they had even more opportunity in basketball. The joke in Texas is that basketball season was to bide the time between football and spring football. But Texas high school basketball produces outstanding players. It's just that they never stayed home. That was about to change.

In basketball, Kansas began the Big 12 like it ended the Big Eight -- by winning the league title and doing so in dominating fashion, outpacing runner-up Colorado by four games. This was to be the year for the Jayhawks as Raef LaFrentz, Jacque Vaughn, Scot Pollard, Jerod Haase and Paul Pierce were all back for a run at the national title. They won their first 22 games before falling 96-94 in double overtime at Missouri. But if you look closely at the team, some red flags began to pop up in the form of injuries. Pollard suffered a stress fracture in his foot and was never the same the rest of the year. Haase injured his right wrist and because of his willingness to get on the floor for every play, he only aggravated it as the year went on.

Despite that, the team breezed through the rest of the season and the first two games of the NCAA Tournament without a loss. A Sweet Sixteen matchup with Arizona was not advantageous in the least for Kansas. The Wildcats had an extremely athletic and deep team, but had underachieved all season. Once the NCAA tournament began, they were a new team. The Wildcats were a cat-quick team with scorers at all positions. Perhaps the most telling stats were those of Haase and Pollard. In 14 minutes, Haase was 1-3 shooting and had two points, while Pollard was 0-1 in 20 minutes. Their injuries hampered them significantly and Kansas fell 85-82.

It was an emotional scene postgame in the lockerroom. Williams naturally took the final loss of the year hard, but this one even more so because Pollard and Vaughn would depart Lawrence without a Final Four appearance between them. But credit Arizona, the win over Kansas was no fluke. The Wildcats became the first team to beat three No. 1 seeds in an NCAA tourney, also taking down North Carolina and in the title game, Kentucky. In my opinion, when this team was healthy it was as good as any Kansas team I can remember to that point, perhaps challenged only by the 1986 Final Four team.

In 1997-98 the Jayhawks were the dominant team in the league once again, starting the season ranked No. 2 nationally and never falling below No. 5. They would go 35-4 overall and 15-1 in the Big 12. Without a doubt, one of the best stories of the season was the return of Wilt Chamberlain for the Kansas State game on January 17. He was honored in an emotional halftime ceremony featuring his assistant coach Jerry Waugh, and ended his speech with the words: "Rock Chalk." Ironically, Paul Pierce passed Chamberlain on the all-time KU scoring list in that game.

I had the opportunity to spend some time at the various functions Wilt attended. You could tell he truly enjoyed connecting with people he had not seen in a while, especially Max. Chamberlain hosted a radio show called "Flippin' with the Dipper" on the campus station KANU and also broadcast on WREN, where Falkenstien was the station manager. Chamberlain loved and knew music, and would often invite guests to join him. One was teammate and future KU athletics director Monte Johnson who could play the spoons. Monte was so proficient at the spoons that he joined country music star Roy Clark on stage for the 1983 homecoming concert.

Chamberlain was much larger than life. He was charismatic and talented. He acted in movies, played pro volleyball and was even in discussions to box Muhammad Ali. No player impacted the game in terms of rules changes like Wilt the Stilt. He was also among the first college athletes I began to follow when we moved to Topeka in 1957. Unfortunately, he passed away about 19 months after visiting on October 12, 1999.

As accomplished as the season was, the ending came abruptly. Kansas ran into an extremely quick Rhode Island team with future NBA players Cutino Mobley and Tyson Wheeler. The Jayhawks shooting let them down, hitting only 42.5 percent overall and a 27.8 percent from three-point range in falling 80-75. It would be the final game for seniors LaFrentz and Billy Thomas, and junior Paul Pierce.

The next two campaigns were transition years for Williams and Company. It says a great deal about your program when you record 47 wins over two years and they are considered to be "down." The departure of Vaughn, Pollard, Haase, Pierce and LaFrentz over the previous two years was a loss of considerable firepower. The leadership fell on the shoulders of senior Ryan Robertson, who I feel was one of the more underappreciated Jayhawks over time. Despite coming in a losing effort, his 31 points in a 92-88 overtime loss to Kentucky in the second round of the 1999 NCAA tournament was truly a gutsy performance.

The 1999-2000 season looked similar to the previous year on paper. A 24-10 record, fifth-place finish in the Big 12 and a 69-64 loss in the second round of the NCAA tourney to Duke. The Jayhawks were unranked at the finish of the season, the last week they would be unranked in the Roy Williams era. But there was a tinge of optimism as three highly regarded freshmen in Drew Gooden, Nick Collison and Kirk Hinrich made their debut in Lawrence. You could sense good things lie ahead.

What you could not sense, however, is that North Carolina head coach, and Parsons, Kan., native Bill Guthridge was going to retire in the summer of 2000 one-week before the opening of off-campus recruiting. Naturally, all eyes turned towards Williams as the next Tar Heel coach. North Carolina Athletics Director Dick Baddour and the Carolina Blue family came hard after WIlliams. It was a surreal week as Williams was tugged in every direction. Finally, on a hot and steamy July 7 evening, Williams announced at a press conference in Memorial Stadium - with 16,300 in attendance -- "I'm staying."

At the time of the announcement, Williams looked relieved. He said he was leaning towards leaving at one point in the week. But in the end, he did not feel he could turn his back on his promise to Nick Collison that he would be there for the entirety of his career. A shocked North Carolina basketball family turned to one of their own, a former KU assistant and Notre Dame coach for one season, Matt Doherty.

In retrospect, you cannot underestimate the role Bob Frederick played in Williams' decision. Roy was extremely loyal to Bob and throughout the week, he never pushed Williams. He made himself available to talk at all hours of the day. Certainly Roy's commitment to his players was the major factor, but if there was an ace in the hole, it was Bob. I also have to think how different the situation would have been today. There was no Facebook or Twitter to create a continuous news feed or offer theories. I can only imagine the frenzy that would have caused.

Sadly, Bob passed away June 12, 2009, at the age of 69 as the result of a bicycle accident. As Roy Williams said, "he was as fine a man as there was."

Everyone knew the upcoming Late Night with Roy Willams event to kickoff the 2000-01 season would be festive -- and it was. There were also the prospects of the young talent being a year older. The Jayhawks improved to 26-7, tied for second in the Big 12 and advanced to the NCAA Sweet Sixteen. The season ended on the San Antonio Riverwalk as a more veteran and physical Illinois team, coached by Bill Self, advanced 80-64. Nonetheless, the campaign proved the Jayhawks were not going away as long as Williams was the coach.

A year older, a year wiser and a year stronger. The Jayhawks were on a mission in 2002. An inexplicable loss to a talented Ball State team at the Maui Invitational to start the season was a head scratcher. The gym was so hot that everyone was cramping. Heck, Max and I had lockjaw a few times. Kansas would reel off 13 wins before another loss (at UCLA), then another 16 before falling to No. 4 Oklahoma 64-55 in the Big 12 Tournament title game. Following a December 1, 105-97 win over No. 4 Arizona, the Jayhawks never dropped out of the top five in the AP poll.

This was a fun team to follow. The junior class was drawing rave reviews, but the freshman signees of Wayne Simien, Keith Langford, Aaron Miles and Michael Lee had fans peeking ahead just a bit. They were going to be good. Drew Gooden was an absolute double-double machine and would go on to earn national player-of-the-year honors.

The NCAA Tournament began with a call for a defibrillator for the Jayhawk broadcast crew as a fiesty No. 16-seed Holy Cross had Kansas on the ropes with the potential for history in a No. 16 defeating a No. 1 seed. Guard Kirk Hinrich went out with an ankle sprain that looked like someone wrapped a grapefruit round his leg. The Jayhawks prevailed late and pulled out a 70-58 win. Survive and advance they say, but this was taking it to the extreme.

If I were a betting man, I would have been on the first plane to Vegas and lay down money that Hinrich would not play two nights later against Stanford. There wasn't much hope among the Kansas staff either. But play he did. The Jayhawks jumped to a 15-0 lead enroute to an 86-63 win enroute to a Sweet 16 rematch with Illinois. Hinich did not start, but scored 15 points in 21 minutes with the heavily braced right ankle. If any of you are old enough to remember Willis Reed of the 1970 New York Knicks, you'll understand when I say Hinrich's performance was "Reed-esque." Not one to show much emotion, I am not sure there was a tougher basketball player in my time at Kansas.

The Jayhawks exacted revenge against Illinois and Bill Self in Madison, out-toughing the No. 13 Illini 75-69. It set up a match-up with Oregon, who like Kansas, got up and down the court. Collison and Gooden combined for 43 points and 35 rebounds in a 104-86 win, earning the Jayhawks a Final Four meeting in Atlanta with No. 4 Maryland.

Roy Williams led the Jayhawks to four NCAA Final Four berths during his tenure at Kansas (1989-2003). Credit: Kansas Athletics

In a battle of veteran teams, Maryland won 97-88 in a game of runs. Counting the Jayhawks' 13-2 start and 25-14 finish, they outscored the Terrapins, 38-16. It was 81-50 run by the victors in the middle that sealed the deal. Valiant in defeat, it ended the career of senior sharpshooter Jeff Boschee, who was told by more than one coach out of high school that he would ride the pine at Kansas. Boschee owns the school three-point-made record at 338.

The Jayhawks were primed for another successful season in 2002-03. Gooden had left for the NBA, but Simien and Jeff Graves were there to pick up the slack. Things did not start out so well, however. Preseason ranked No. 2, Kansas was 3-3 after six games, with losses to North Carolina and Florida in New York, and Oregon in Portland, resulting in a fall in the polls to No. 20. The ship was righted somewhat with 10 straight wins, including an 87-70 blowout of UCLA in Lawrence. However, all was not bright as Simien separated his shoulder in a January 4 win over UMKC and suddenly front line depth was an issue.

The winning streak ended with a 60-59 loss at No. 6 Colorado followed by a 91-74 loss to No. 1 Arizona at home. In that game, the Jayhawks had a 20-point lead in the first half and scored 52 points in the first stanza. But the Wildcats stormed back and the Jayhawks went ice cold. In 48 hours, Kansas at 13-5 and confidence waning, would host No. 4 Texas on ESPN's Big Monday. It was not the best set of circumstances, but playing at home gave Kansas a chance against the Longhorns, led by T.J. Ford.

The game was back and forth, and the Jayhawks avoided their first three-game losing streak in nine years with a 90-87 win. Hinrich had 25 points, while Collison was masterful with 24 points and 23 rebounds. I am not sure I have personally witnessed a better performance. Neither had Dick Vitale who was in attendance. He gave Collison a standing ovation.

The win seemed to ignite Kansas as it went on to win 12 of 14 entering the NCAA Tournament. An opening round 64-61 win over a well-coached Utah State team was followed by a 108-76 blowout of Arizona State. It would be on to Anaheim for the Sweet 16 and a matchup with No. 7 Duke. The Jayhawks made all the plays, including a 33-point, 19-rebound performance by Collison for a 69-65 win to earn a rematch with Arizona. Hinrich would come up big with 28 points and a big block of a Jason Gardner three-point attempt to preserve a 78-75 victory. The Jayhawks were making a return trip to the Final Four.

Then on Wednesday of Final Four week, Matt Doherty stepped down as the head coach at North Carolina, and as Yogi Berra would say, "it was deja vu all over again." Williams, Kansas officials and North Carolina did their best to divert the attention of the open coaching position. But you could not go anywhere in New Orleans without it being the topic of discussion. I felt for Williams as he focused so much on the elusive NCAA title. I also felt for the Jayhawk fans.

If there was a distraction, it did not show in the semis as Kansas trounced Dwyane Wade and Marquette, 94-61. Syracuse and its 2-3 zone was up next in the title game. The Orangemen, behind freshmen Gerry McNamara and Carmelo Anthony bombed their way to a 52-43 halftime lead. The Jayhawks fought back, thanks to a 49-34 rebound advantage for the game. But a frigid 4-of-20 from three and an uncharacteristic 12-of-30 from the line kept them from finishing the comeback. Hakeem Warrick blocked Michael Lee's three and an off-balance attempt by Hinrich in the final four seconds went awry and Kansas fell, 81-78.

A tearful and worn out Roy Willaims told CBS' Bonnie Bernstein in the post game, "I could give a shit about North Carolina right now." The question had to be asked, and the answer was perfect for live television. It would be an interesting next week for two blue bloods of college basketball.

Chapter 8 Sidebar: Larger than Life

Having been around high-profile personalities for the better part of five decades, I am long past being star-struck when in their presence. But I have to say even I was taken back a bit by the presence of Wilton Norman Chamberlain upon his return to Kansas on January 17, 1998 as part of the season's celebration of 100 years of Jayhawk basketball. Wilt spent the weekend reconnecting with old friends and exorcising past disappointment. He was with the current edition of the Jayhawks a considerable amount of time and made quite an impact on everyone with whom he came in contact.

For me, it was like going back in time because Chamberlain played at Kansas when I was a teenager in Manhattan and Topeka. He was larger than life back then and that was no different upon his return to Lawrence.

Wearing the same letterman's jacket he donned as a student, Chamberlain delivered an emotional halftime speech to the crowd. He expressed his feelings for the school in a way he had never done before. There were more than a few tears flowing. The plan was for Wilt to depart the game at the final media timeout to escape from being engulfed by admiring fans. However, he told Kansas officials he would not only stay for the rest of the game, but would sit at a table and talk with anyone who wanted to do so afterward. The line went all the way around Allen Fieldhouse, several people deep, and for two hours he conversed, took photos and signed autographs.

It would be Chamberlain's last visit as he passed away just 19 months later, as a result of heart failure. Here is that halftime speech:

"A little over 40 years ago, I lost the toughest battle in sports in losing to the North Carolina Tar Heels by one point in triple overtime (national championship game). It was a devastating thing to me because I let the University of Kansas down and my teammates down.

"But when I come back here today and realize not a simple loss of a game, but how many people have shown such appreciation and warmth, I'm humbled and deeply honored."

"I've learned in life that you have to take the bitter with the sweet and how sweet this is, right here! I'm a Jayhawk and I know now why there is so much tradition here and why so many wonderful things have come from here and I am now very much a part of it by being there (pointing to his jersey hanging from the rafters) and very proud of it."

"Rock Chalk, Jayhawk!"

Chamberlain had a huge personality and at times his bravado overshadowed his contributions and remarkable intellect. Generous and thoughtful, he took pride in breaking down racial barriers faced at movie theaters, restaurants and on campus. When he arrived at Kansas, he became active in the community and on campus. Popular among the students, he gained a following for his efforts and as a host of a radio show. Chamberlain's 30-minute weekly radio show on the student radio station KUOK "Flippin' with Dipper" featured popular music and his commentary. He would invite his teammates to join him on occasion. His co-host was Max Falkenstien.

Many wondered why Chamberlain never returned. There were stories of an occasional visit to friends, but no one knew until his halftime speech that his absence was because he felt he let the fans down with the loss in the 1957 NCAA title game to North Carolina. But, Chamberlain clearly was enjoying his time at Mt. Oread. He used the opportunity to make new friends and rekindle old relationships. He was also in demand by the local media. A press conference went one hour, and was followed by more than another session of one-one one media conferences. He made it a point to dispel thoughts of any ill will towards Kansas.

"A lot of people thought there was something missing between me and the University of Kansas in a negative way," said Chamberlain to a packed room of media types and fans. "But it was a great building block for me. It helped prepare me for life. I'm negligent in not being here sooner."

Former Kansas athletics director Monte Johnson and the late Bob Billings, both teammates of Chamberlain's, were key in his return. Though Johnson knew Chamberlain was not healthy, Johnson told me his teammate was energized by the experience. In fact, Chamberlain told Johnson and Billings before he left to return back to Los Angeles, the weekend was one of the most meaningful experiences of his life.

Chamberlain's legacy is large and one of benevolence. One of his final acts was to give something that could help those who needed it most. He gave his letterman's jacket that he wore during his visit back to the university. Additionally, his estate donated $650,000 to assist KU in conducting an annual clinic for Special Olympians.

Chapter 8: Friends of Bob

Bill Self: Head Basketball Coach, Kansas, 2004 - Present. The decision to come to Kansas was difficult because we were going to be really good the next year with the guys we had coming back at Illinois. The day of our banquet at Illinois it was announced Roy was going to North Carolina so the media and everyone was asking me about Kansas. I had not been contacted, so there was nothing to say. We decided to go on a vacation two days later on a Wednesday to Fisher Island near Miami and my cell phone was blowing up with the media and others calling. That was in the day when your cell phone could not store many voicemail recordings. I kept on having to delete them so I could get more.

After two days we decided it really wasn't a vacation so we went back home. Eventually I was contacted and had a decision to make. I talked to Jay Bilas, who told me Kansas was a place where you win championships. Dick Vitale said it was a mistake to follow Roy Williams. I talked to Coach Owens, Coach Brown and Coach Williams, and some former players, so I felt I knew about as much as you could about the program. I also leaned on my Dad. He told me if I was a competitor, then I shouldn't worry about the success they had before. It was a hard decision, but obviously I made the right one.

Mark Mangino: Head Football Coach, Kansas, 2002-09. I did not know Bob Davis before coming to Kansas, but I knew of him by watching him and listening to him do the Royals. I grew up listening to the Indians and the Pirates on radio, so I thought that it was pretty cool that our broadcaster also did the Royals. Several things stand out about Bob. First, he has a wonderful sense of humor. I appreciated that, especially early on when we weren't very good. Second, he was a true professional. He put a lot into his job and he took pride in what he did. He was so good at calling the game. And third, he was trusted. I felt comfortable giving him information he could use for the broadcast that we did not need getting out until the game. Bob respected our team and players, and he was vested in its success and failure. This was not something he did just because it was a job. He was really engaged and lived it.

Our players loved Bob's calls of the game. We would do those hype videos played just before the games to get fired up. We'd set them to music and to Bob's radio broadcast. He would get so excited and the descriptions were so vivid. The guys got fired up listening to Bob -- and so did I.

Mark Mangino: Head Football Coach, Kansas, 2002-09. We weren't going to get the five-star recruits, so we had to find those diamonds in the rough and develop them once they got here. We had to go beyond the standard height, weight and 40-time. We'd watch kids do other sports, we'd talk to their coaches, we'd look at how they handled themselves, and we'd look for intelligence in how they played the game....anything to learn more about them that might give us a better picture. Kevin Kane is a perfect example. He played for a great program in Rockhurst, so you knew he was well-coached. He wasn't big at all, but his pad level was good and his angle of pursuit was almost perfect. You knew he had a chance to be good if he put in the time in the weight room.

Our defensive coordinator Bill Young brought us a film of Chris Harris that he got through a contact. The only school that had shown interest other than us was Tulsa. All of the sudden word got out on him and Wisconsin offered, but he stuck with us. Everyone told me that Brandon McAnderson was too slow, too short and too fat. But I watched him play with my son in high school and I knew how tough he was and how hard he worked. All it would take is work with the strength coach. Todd Reesing only visited Kansas State and us. So, you see we had to go about it a bit differently. Everyone talks about how good our Orange Bowl team was because we had developed them into good football players. That may be true, but it was also a very intelligent team. They played smart.

Mark Mangino led the Jayhawks to the 2008 Orange Bowl title, finishing 12-1 for the season. Credit: Kansas Athletics.

David Lawrence: Kansas Football Letterman, 1978-81; Graduate Assistant, 1982; Jayhawk Radio Network, 1994 - Present. Road trips with Bob and Max were special. Almost immediately after getting in the car, Bob would start: "Have you heard the one about?" Even if I had, you wanted to hear it again. There was no better storyteller than Bob Davis. Incredibly funny. The jokes would continue into the night as we found our favorite mom and pop restaurant. No chains for those guys. They wanted barbecue, mashed potatoes, green beans and some dessert with a caloric intake that would be enough to tide you over for the rest of the week. Bob and Max played off each other so well. I think they had a competition to see if they could make each other laugh harder. The thing I did not realize at first is how many people they knew and knew them. I could not go anywhere without other media, administrators, even fans coming up to them. And, being so humble and gracious, Bob would treat them like they were best friends.

Mike Leas: Former Hays High School Instructor and Coach. Bob had the ability to be incredibly descriptive and quite witty on his broadcasts -- and amazingly could do it at the same time. I remember listening to him do a KU game with Chris Piper, when Bob said with a hint of disgust, "There's an AT&T foul." Piper, not catching on, asked Bob what an AT&T foul was. Without missing a beat, he said, "that's when you reach out and touch someone."

Doug Vance: Assistant Athletic Director, Kansas 1983-2003. Not all of my fun memories of Bob involved a football field or basketball court.

Bob, Linda and Steven joined me, Sue (my wife), along with our two sons, Cory and Stuart, one summer for a family vacation trip to the Lake of the Ozarks in Missouri. Our wives had mustered up the courage to experience their first-ever massage. Bob and I remained back in the rooms, content on keeping the beds from rising up and hitting the ceiling (a common phrase you heard from Bob on road trips).

When the ladies returned, they proclaimed the massage one of the most relaxing experiences of their lives and encouraged Bob and I book our own appointments. 'Reluctant' is probably the best word to describe our response.

What our wives described, stripping down and laying on a table covered only by a towel with a stranger – female at that – exploring our back sides with their hands, left us both intrigued and terrified at the same time. Plus, factoring into the decision, was an inflated cost that would leave a hefty dent in the wallets. But, somewhere we found the courage to do it. I think Linda and Sue were more surprised than we were. The appointment was booked and off we went.

We arrived for the appointment, uncertain of what to expect in terms of the process, and were directed into a small room with two padded tables. We were told to undress, lay face down on the table, with the rather small towel covering the appropriate part on the back side of our bodies.

All I can remember from that moment on is Bob and I reporting back to our wives that it was, indeed, one of the best experiences we could remember in some time. Bob offered one final description of the experience that I'll always remember.

"The only thing that bothered me was that while lying unclothed and face down on the table, those girls hands went rather deep into my back pockets."

Chris Theisen: Assistant Athletics Director for Communications, Kansas 2004-Present. When I think of Bob Davis, I think of a great friend to all and an incredible storyteller. His storytelling resonated in his broadcasts of Kansas athletics, painting the picture for the fans when describing a play or scene. And it goes beyond calling KU football and basketball contests. During my Big Eight Conference days, it was the weekly football and men's basketball briefings held at the office. At Kansas, we host 15 or so weekly press conferences each season, known as pressers, with head basketball coach Bill Self. They run around 20 minutes with some 30-plus media present. Coach Self will then eat lunch with the media following the presser.

There are no formal assigned seats at the large rectangular table. Upon arrival for the presser, media members will place a coat or something near Coach Self's chair in trying to save a seat. Bob would never try to save a seat, it was always assumed that he gets one of the two chairs next to Coach Self. These conversations amongst Coach Self and the media present will go as long as an hour and are quite entertaining discussing anything and everything - national and local news, all sports, telling old stories about games, events, etc. Bob and Coach Self would make the lunch a must-see-and-listen experience, a time the media who stayed for the meal looked forward to every week. It was about 10 or so years ago that Bob didn't get one of the chairs next to coach for a presser lunch. Afterwards, Coach Self pulled me to the side and said don't let that happen again. In my 16 years at KU, that is the only time Coach Self has singled out someone to make sure he or she sits by him for a presser lunch.

Changing of the Guard

AFTER THE 2003 NCAA basketball title game, the team returned to an informal pep rally at Allen Fieldhouse. But there weren't many in the mood to celebrate. Although North Carolina was indicating it had a list of candidates to replace Doherty, its aim was squarely on Williams. Chancellor Robert Hemenway said earlier the university would do all it could to retain Williams, and that meant the first step was removing Athletics Director Al Bohl.

On Wednesday, April 9, Bohl conducted the now-famous "crushed like a dove" press conference on his driveway, blaming Williams for his demise. But the truth be told, Bohl's relationship with much of the athletics department coaches and staff had significantly deteriorated. Although successful in previous jobs, he just wasn't the right fit on Mt. Oread. Even with Bohl no longer around, keeping Williams would be difficult.

Over the weekend, Williams, Nick Collison and other Kansas officials headed to Los Angeles for the John R. Wooden Awards. Williams would receive a national coaching award and Collison was up for national player of the year. The group would spend the weekend at the home of Kansas alum Dana Anderson, but the Tar Heels matched the lobbying effort as James Worthy was the emcee for the banquet and UNC alum and Los Angeles Laker General Manager Mitch Kupchak appeared at Bel Air Country Club on Sunday as the Jayhawk group got in a round of golf. And of course, Dean Smith was more forceful in his desire to have Williams back in Chapel Hill compared to 2000.

Monday, April 14 was "Decision Day" as a teary-eyed Williams met with the team in the Kansas basketball lockerroom and told the players that he was headed to North Carolina. He thanked the media for treating him well during his stay, then headed to the Lawrence airport for a University of North Carolina jet that would take him back home. That evening he was announced as the next Tar Heel coach. He clearly looked and sounded tired, and somewhat conflicted in his feelings (he wore a red and blue tie). He later called the moment he walked out of the Kansas lockerroom one of the lowest times of his life and that he felt worthless. I often wondered what influence Bob Frederick would have had if he were still the AD. Perhaps the outcome would have been the same, but there was no denying the environment in the department the last two years made the decision easier for Williams.

There was no doubt the Jayhawk season-ending basketball banquet on April 17 would exhibit a wide range of emotions. It was conducted at the Lied Center on west campus and I served as the emcee. Williams and staff members who went to Carolina were on stage with the rest of the team. The former Jayhawk head coach knew his return would be met with mixed reactions, but he wanted to be there for the players. Many players from his previous teams were in attendance as well. The reaction to Williams was overwhelmingly positive, although one catcall of "traitor" incurred the wrath of Collison's father, Dave. For those players who had eligibility remaining, there was sadness their coach was gone, but also a strong resolve to return and finish what they could not get done this year.

Personally, you grow attached to some coaches more than others. It was not hard to be a Roy Williams fan. He was wonderful to work with and professional in our interactions. Our son Steven was a manager for the last two years of Roy's tenure, and he could not have treated him better. You couldn't fault him for going home. He had family members who were aging and some were not healthy. Few of us would not have made the same decision. What he did for the Kansas program was amazing on and off the court.

Williams continues to speak well of his time at Kansas, calling Allen Fieldhouse the best arena in college basketball. He created a stir among the Carolina faithful when two nights after being drubbed by Kansas in the 2008 NCAA tourney semifinals, was in the stands for the KU-Memphis title game with a Jayhawk sticker on his sweater. In 2014 he returned for a wonderful 60th anniversary celebration of Allen Fieldhouse with previous Kansas coaches Larry Brown and Ted Owens. It was the first time he stepped foot in Allen Fieldhouse since he left. And, in my opinion, it offered some closure for him.

In 2014, former Kansas basketball coaches Ted Owens, Larry Brown and Roy Williams joined current coach Bill Self to celebrate 60 years of Allen Fieldhouse. Credit: Kansas Athletics

While all of the Williams-to-UNC talk was going on, Kansas officials wasted no time in identifying its next basketball coach. Drue Jennings, a retired Kansas City business executive and former KU football player, was appointed interim athletics director the day Bohl was relieved of his duties. He would be ably assisted by assistant athletics directors Doug Vance and Richard Konzem. The goal was to move quickly as possible.

There was a groundswell of support for Illinois head coach Bill Self, who was a graduate assistant for Larry Brown at Kansas in 1985-86. Also interviewed were Oregon's Ernie Kent, who had a win over Kansas in Portland earlier in the season, Marquette's Tom Crean and Kansas alum and Wichita State coach Mark Turgeon. Crean was going to be tough to swallow after his Eagles were blitzed by KU in the NCAA semis. Turgeon actually pulled his name, saying the timing was not right for him.

Still, Self was not a slam-dunk hire. He had much going for him at Illinois, winning two Big Ten titles and three NCAA appearances in three years. Meanwhile, Kansas did not have an athletic director and the prospects of following the wildly successful Williams would mean the honeymoon would be measured in hours, if not minutes. Credit Vance and Konzem for being the familiar faces and voices who helped convince Self Kansas was the place for him. Self agreed to be the next Jayhawk coach on April 21, just two weeks after Kansas fell in the NCAA title game to Syracuse.

Self and his family flew into Lawrence on Easter Sunday and after meeting with school officials, took his family on a tour of Lawrence. That included a trip down Naismith Drive and it was at that point the magnitude of the opportunity hit him. He would work in the building named after the "Father of Basketball Coaching" on the street named after the "Inventor of the Game of Basketball."

You don't get points for winning the press conference, but Self was no doubt overjoyed to be in Lawrence. And so were the smiling faces in the packed John Hadl Auditorium in the Wagnon Center. He was just the person needed to keep the juggernaut program trending in the right direction. It was almost as if he had rehearsed what he was going to say. Who knows, maybe he had. You could tell Kansas was special to him. There would be big shoes to fill, but Self would be up to the task.

The next step for the chancellor was to fill the vacant athletics director position. Hemenway conducted the search on his own and interviewed Konzem, a loyal and long-time department staffer, Lew Perkins, Connecticut AD, and Oral Roberts AD Mike Carter, an attorney who was considered an up-and-comer in college athletics. In somewhat of a surprise, Carter was offered and accepted the job. Assistant Athletics Director Doug Vance was on the verge of calling the media for a news conference when the call of "hold the presses" went out. Carter called Jennings 24 hours later saying family issues had caused him to reverse course.

With Hemenway under pressure to meet his self-imposed deadline of having an AD within a week, negotiations began with Perkins and he was announced as the new Kansas AD, June 10, 2003. He was not totally unfamiliar with KU and the state of Kansas. He had previously served as the AD at Wichita State (1983-87) and played basketball at Iowa for Jayhawk star and Chanute native Ralph Miller.

With those pieces in place, the attention turned to football in the fall of 2003 and hopes for improvement from a 2-10 mark in Mangino's first season. Those were realized early on as the Jayhawks bounced back from a 28-20 season-opening home loss to Northwestern to reel off four straight wins, including a 35-14 victory over Missouri. Among the fans carrying the goal posts to Potter Lake was one Russell Robinson. In Lawrence for a recruiting visit, he would commit to Bill Self's basketball program days after his eventful weekend. It was not the first time a Jayhawk hoops recruit committed after watching a Jayhawk football win over a rival. Some 40 years earlier, young Joseph (JoJo) White was in the stands watching Kansas upset Oklahoma, 15-14, behind the exploits of Gale Sayers.

The Jayhawks entered the final game of the 2003 campaign versus Iowa State at 5-6 needing a win to qualify for a bowl. The Jayhawks were down 7-6 after the first quarter, but outscored the Cyclones by a 30-0 count the rest of the way to win 36-7.

For the first time since 1995, Kansas was going bowling. It would meet heavily favored North Carolina State in the Tangerine Bowl in Orlando, featuring the lethal pass-combination of quarterback Philip Rivers and receiver Torry Holt. The Wolfpack prevailed in a high scoring matchup, 56-26. The plus-four win improvement for Kansas was one of the best in the nation in Division I. Offensively, quarterback Bill Whittemore, running back Clark Green and receiver Charles Gordon provided play-making ability. Young linebackers Banks Floodman and Nick Reid showed they were two Kansas high school products who could play on this level.

I remember that first year working with Mark -- the losses were so draining for him. He had all of this success at Kansas State and Oklahoma. I would tape our pre-game show for Saturday in his office during the week. I would come with some of my best jokes just to give him a laugh and take his mind off the losses, if only for a short while. He was grinding so hard. You could tell he had a plan. He had a winning pedigree and he knew what it took to build a winning program.

Mark was driven and had high expectations of himself and those around him. But the truth is tensions can rise within athletic departments and within teams from time to time. People are focused on winning and anything that is perceived as not aligned with that is called into question. That was not specific to Mark, it applies to almost every coach I have been around. I've seen it at radio stations, as well.

Mark and I developed a rapport from the start because we were both baseball fans and grew up following the game by listening to it on the radio. He was a Cleveland Indians fan, despite growing up 45 miles west of Pittsburgh. With the Royals and the Indians both in the American League Central, we talked frequently about the pennant race. The trust level between us was extremely high and I appreciated that Mark would confide in me information that would help the broadcast, but also not make us look uninformed or ill-prepared.

The next season (2004) was a bit of a mixed bag, best remembered for what could have been. After winning their first two games, the Jayhawks entered their final game with Missouri having lost seven of their last eight games. The high point of that stretch was a 31-28 win over Kansas State, ending an 11-game losing streak to the Wildcats. The low point was a 27-23 loss to No. 6 Texas. In that game, Kansas held a 23-20 lead late when a Brian Luke to Charles Gordon pass gave the Crimson & Blue a first down and would allow them to run out the clock. But officials ruled Gordon pushed off the and the Jayhawks were penalized and had to punt the ball away. Vince Young would rally the Longhorns for the win.

Afterward, Mangino was none too happy and he let it be known: "You know what this is all about, don't you? BCS. That's what made a difference today in the game. That's what made the difference in a call in front of their bench. Dollar signs." It made for high drama in the postgame news conference and reinforced what I tell the listeners: You always want to stay around for the postgame shows because you never know what you are going to get on live radio.

The Jayhawks rebounded the next week to win on the road at Missouri, 31-14, giving them their eighth win in the last 12 meetings versus their bitter rivals. Kansas finished at 4-7, with five losses by six or fewer points.

Mangino's fourth season (2005) would result in his second bowl game at Kansas, but it did not come easy. After winning its first three games against non-league foes, the Crimson & Blue dropped four consecutive league games and the season was at a crossroads. A 13-3 win over Missouri began a strong finish of four wins in five games. The last being a bowl-qualifying 24-21 home win over Iowa State. With starting quarterback Jason Swanson injured earlier in the game, Brian Luke came in and hit Dexton Fields for a 15-yard game-tying touchdown pass with 1:05 left in regulation. Scott Webb's field goal won it in overtime. The Jayhawks marched into Texas, defeating Houston, 42-13 in the Fort Worth Bowl.

The football program clearly had momentum. It also sent my partner Max Falkenstien out a winner as he broadcast his final KU football game. We enjoyed our time at the bowl, eating some of the greasiest food around, including some wonderful barbecue. And the season also saw the Jayawks finally topple their nemesis, the Nebraska Cornhuskers 40-15. It ended a 36-game losing streak to its rival to the north and in the process released decades of pent up frustration.

The 2006 season was one of change as graduation losses from the previous campaign were significant, including DEs Charlton Keith and Jermail Ashley, QBs Brian Luke and Jason Swanson, RB Clark Green, and an overachieving group of LBs Banks Floodman, Kevin Kane and Nick Reid. The latter, who committed to KU out of Derby, Kan., as a QB and with no head coach, ended up winning Big 12 Defensive Player-of-the-Year honors over Texas standout and future Kansas City Chief LB Derrick Johnson.

After winning three of four non-league games to open the season, the Jayhawks dropped four straight conference outings and appeared to be headed to a disaster of a finish. But in game eight, Mangino pulled the redshirt of freshman Todd Reesing whose Division I offers were only Kansas and Kansas State. Playing at home and down 9-0 at halftime to the Buffs, the young, Austin, Texas native lived up to his "Sparky" nickname by engineering a 20-15 come-from-behind victory. Reesing was 11 of 16 for 106 yards and rushed for 90 yards. He was aided by two, second-half interceptions by an unheralded two-star recruit by the name of Aqib Talib. Kansas defeated Iowa State and Kansas State in its next two outings, before falling to Missouri, 42-17 to end the season at 6-6.

It was obvious the Kansas program was making strides, and doing so without the three- or four-star recruits. Mangino and his staff focused on toughness, character and a pinch of swagger. He would often say he did not mind a hint of cockiness in his players. That showed they believed in themselves and took pride in getting better. He also looked for players who were smart and understood the game of football.

David Lawrence moved from the sideline up to the booth to call the action with me, taking the seat held by Max. You cannot replace a character like Max, but I will say no one, including Don Fambrough, God rest his soul, is more passionate about KU football than David. A 1981 first team all-Big Eight selection, he has made himself an astute football analyst. Not to mention that he is just a great person.

Jayhawk football letterwinner David Lawrence moved from the sideline to the booth in replacing Max Falkenstien in 2006. Credit: Bob Newton

For the first time in quite a while, Kansas would enter a season with the feeling that it could compete for the league title - even if no one else thought it could. The Jayhawks began the 2007 campaign by blitzing four non-league opponents to the tune of a 214-23 margin. But that start wouldn't matter if they couldn't take care of No. 24 Kansas State the next week. The Jayhawks won at Manhattan, 30-24 for the first time since 1989 and suddenly they were ranked No. 20 heading into a meeting with Baylor. It was the first time in the polls for KU football since September 28, 1996.

The win over Kansas State was huge for the program and Mangino. He returned to the place where his coaching career took off. Plus, to end the losing streak in Manhattan was important for fans and recruiting. The Jayhawks dispatched Baylor, 58-10, the next week, then headed to Colorado ranked No. 15. A hard-fought 19-14 win moved Kansas to 7-0 and No. 12 with the formidable task of playing at Texas

A&M in front of 85,000-plus fans. The Jayhawks jumped to a 19-0 lead and hung on for a 19-11 win to move to 8-0 for the first time since 1909. That's no typo -- 1909.

Up to No. 8 in the polls and hosting Nebraska, the Jayhawks were not really in the discussion of a BCS bowl because they weren't blowing conference teams out. Nebraska was not ranked, but that did not matter. The Big Red had inflicted so much pain on the Jayhawk football program that a one point win would be reason enough to send the goalposts to Potter Lake.

With a win and an overtime loss in its last two games versus the Big Red, the players and staff were not intimidated, but the fans were pensive after the Huskers jumped to 7-0 and 14-7 leads. The Jayhawks struck for three quick scores to go up 28-14 in the second quarter, however the Huskers got back into the game midway through the period making it 28-21. Then the Red Sea parted. Reesing threw his third TD of the game and fullback Brandon McAnderson scored his third rushing TD to make it 42-21. A fourth Reesing touchdown pass offset a Nebraska field goal and the halftime score stood at 48-24.

The rout was on and the only question was how much of a defense Kansas officials would put up in protecting the goal posts. Kansas scored its 76th point with 11:12 left in the game and took the foot off the gas in securing a 76-39 win. Reesing set a school record with six passing TDs on 30-of-41 passing for 354 yards, and McAnderson rushed for four scores. I don't really rank all-time wins, but in my lifetime it has to rank in the top 10 for Jayhawk football victories. The Huskers were by no means dominant, but I think that game convinced the rest of the nation the Jayhawks were for real.

Wins over Oklahoma State and Iowa State moved the Jayhawks to 11-0 and No. 2 in the nation heading into a matchup with No. 4 Missouri at Arrowhead Stadium. Mangino would say that it was the 43-28 win at Stillwater that told him the team had a chance to be pretty darn good. The Cowboys had a physically imposing team with wide receiver Dez Bryant and cornerback Adarius Bowman among others. Every time Oklahoma State threatened to take control, the Jayhawks responded with a score. The win meant a great deal to Mangino because he was coming back home to Oklahoma and several Jayhawks were native Oklahomans bypassed by both the Sooners and the Cowboys.

ESPN's College GameDay would be on hand for the epic battle against Missouri in a rivalry that has had more than its share of outstanding battles. It was a cold evening, but the stadium was full. Missouri had an outstanding team with the cagey Chase Daniel at quarterback and a host of outstanding receivers in Chase Coffman, son of Kansas State standout Paul Coffman, Martin Rucker, Danario Alexander, Jeremy Maclin and Rockhurst's Tony Temple at running back. The Jayhawks were game, but fell short, 36-28.

That meant Missouri would head to the Big 12 title game in an attempt to gain revenge against Oklahoma, who was responsible for the Tigers' only loss of the season. Missouri lost the second matchup as well, creating for an interesting few days of sports talk radio in Kansas City. The loss dropped Missouri to No. 7 in the rankings, one spot ahead of Kansas. With one berth open in the Bowl Championship Series, the lobbying began. Missouri owned the win over Kansas, but had one more loss and was coming off a big defeat to Oklahoma. Lew Perkins convinced Orange Bowl officials that the Jayhawks would travel well and that was good enough for them. The Jayhawks would meet the No. 5 Virginia Tech Hokies, while Missouri faced No. 25 Arkansas in the Cotton Bowl.

It would be Kansas' first visit to the Orange Bowl since the John Riggins-Bobby Douglass-John Zook-Donnie Shanklin led Jayhawks fell to Penn State, 15-14, following the 1968 season. Going in as underdogs, the Jayhawks threw the first haymaker when Talib picked off a pass and went 60 yards for a score. They made it 17-0 on a Scott Webb field goal and a Reesing-to-Marcus Henry touchdown pass.

The Hokies narrowed the gap 17-7 right before half and then made things interesting with a punt return for a score after the Jayhawks' first series of the second half. After that, it became a game of field position, key plays to extend drives and an exchange of turnovers that kept the momentum on the side of the Jayhawks. The Jayhawks used a time-consuming drive to run out the clock, ending inside the Tech five-yard line, finishing out a 24-21 win.

When there are not great expectations, good teams tend to play more loose and that is what Kansas did all season. This was a team of good players and good depth. As we found out based on what they accomplished in the NFL, the players were probably better than we gave them credit for, especially defensive backs Talib, Chris Harris and Darrell Stuckey, and offensive lineman Anthony Collins. It was an incredibly fun team to be around and the bowl win was certainly the cherry on the top.

With Jayhawk football rolling, Bill Self was busy putting his fingerprints on the Jayhawk hoops program. When you are only the eighth coach all-time, and following the lineage of Naismith, Allen, Owens, Brown and Williams, there is no easing into the job. Expectations are always high. But if there was a person who understood that and had the temperament for it, that would be Bill Self. Fiery, competitive, focused -- Self had his teams hang their hats on toughness. He would often joke that the other team could not win if it didn't score. He wasn't totally serious, but his point was clear.

Self's past experience at Kansas, plus his knowledge of the school and its constituents obviously helped in his transition. He was well aware of the following Jayhawk basketball had and as such was active in attending University events in every corner of the Sunflower State. He has been a great representative of the program, athletics department and the university -- and he has fun doing it. He's approachable, charismatic, engaging and once he meets you -- you're a friend for life and he'll never forget your name. Personally, we meshed well and understood each other. Plus, he was always up for a good joke.

While following in Williams' footsteps from a performance standpoint was not going to be easy in itself, Self also had to convince the veterans on the team that a new style of play would be as or more successful for a program that was coming off back-to-back Final Fours. It wasn't as if Self hadn't experienced success himself, but sometimes it takes more cajoling for youngsters to accept. He had the perfect personality and charisma to make it happen.

Bill Self was hired as only the eighth basketball coach in Kansas history on April 21, 2003.
Credit: Kansas Athletics

Self's tenure got off on the right foot as in his second game of his KU career and the 2003-04 season, the No. 6-rated Jayhawks downed No. 3 Michigan State, 81-74 in Allen Fieldhouse. I remember his postgame interview, his voice tinged with excitement bordering on giddiness as he shared what the evening meant to him. He was nervous during the day in anticipation of meeting a Spartan team that had been to the Elite Eight the previous season. The fieldhouse was juiced, led by a raucous student section. Simien led the Jayhawks with 28 points in what Self called "a confidence builder and a money game for his squad."

Self also endeared himself to the fans by going 5-0 against Kansas State and Missouri combined his first year -- including an 84-82 win over the Tigers in the final game played at the Hearnes Center, thanks to freshman David Padgett's baseline jumper at the buzzer. Seeded No. 4 in the NCAA Tournament, the Jayhawks had a relatively short road if they were to make the Final Four. They picked up wins over Illinois-Chicago and Pacific in Kansas City, then traveled to St. Louis for the regional. Kansas defeated UAB, 100-74 after the Blazers upset No. 1 seed Kentucky, setting up a regional final with third-seed Georgia Tech.

The game was one of runs as each team would create separation, only to give it up. Georgia Tech went on a 7-0 scoring spree to lead 65-58 with just under four minutes left, but Kansas sent the game to overtime by outscoring the Yellow Jackets 8-1 the rest of the way. The momentum changed in Tech's favor big time with 3:44 left and the game tied at 68. Jayhawk Keith Langford came slashing down the court and was called for a charge that left KU fans more than a little exasperated. Replays showed the play was a clear flop, but referee Jim Burr saw it differently. The Jackets outscored the Jayhawks 11-3 the rest of the way to win 79-71 and advance to the Final Four.

By all accounts, it was a successful first campaign for Self and Company, finishing at 24-9 overall, 12-4 in the Big 12 (for a second place tie) and a No. 16 final ranking. From the radio crew's perspective, Self was easy to work with, however given his quick wit, the postgame interviewer had to be on his toes. Personally, the season was great fun as our son Steven served his third season as a KU basketball manager. I've always told him that his splitting his college career by being a manager for two years for Roy Williams and two years for Bill Self would provide memories for a lifetime.

Because the coaching change was rather late in the recruiting process, Self's first Jayhawk team was largely upper class holdovers and recruits signed by Williams. The next two years would be a transition period and give us a glimpse of what the future would look like in terms of style of play. In many ways, they would be Self's most challenging campaigns at KU. I say that fully aware that the Jayhawks would tie for the league title in both seasons (2005 - Oklahoma; 2006 - Texas).

Year two under Self began with a 14-0 win streak, including a New Year's Day 70-68 overtime win over No. 9 Georgia Tech at Allen Fieldhouse. It was sweet revenge for the Jayhawks and Keith Langford from the regional final of the previous year. Langford's fade-away in the lane in the final seconds was the winner. A week later Kansas went to Rupp Arena and defeated No. 8 Kentucky, 66-59. The unbeaten streak ended in Philadelphia with an 83-62 loss to Villanova. It was a snowy day and the team had difficulty getting to the arena. Villanova could not miss, hitting 12-of-19 from three as the Jayhawks played from behind the entire game.

Three weeks later Kansas would uncharacteristically drop three consecutive games. And, there was a real potential for a fourth consecutive loss as No. 4

Oklahoma State came to town for a late February nationally-televised game. The Jayhawks rode the 32-point, 13-rebound performance of Simien for an 81-79 win. It was an incredibly well-played game by both teams as they were efficient offensively. Self is usually even keel at the final buzzer, win or lose, but on occasion he will let out a fist pump and a big yell. This was a top five postgame celebration for him.

The Jayhawks would go on to be a No. 3 seed for the NCAA Tournament and pitted against No. 14 seed Bucknell in Oklahoma City. But all was not right. Langford hurt is anke in a season-ending loss to Missouri and had done nothing for two weeks. He was not expected to play and while he gave it a try, he was significantly hampered against the Bison. Without Langford, Simien and Michael Lee carried the load with 24 and 18 points, respectively. In the end, Bucknell took a 64-63 win, a result that surprised everyone, but the Jayhawks. Bucknell was underseeded and Kansas was tired and limited. In the second round versus Wisconsin, Bucknell held a lead with eight minutes left in the game and pushed the Badgers until the final two minutes. Kansas, meanwhile, had lost three of its last four games to finish 23-7 and tied for first in the Big 12 with Oklahoma at 12-4. Self called it a "good" season, which shows you how high his and the program's standards are.

The 2005-06 season was truly a changing of the guard. Gone were seniors Simien, Langford, Miles and Lee, and J.R. Giddens, who left later in the summer. This would be a new team. The sophomore class was headlined by Russell Robinson, Darnell Jackson and Sasha Kaun, while a talented group of freshmen included Mario Chalmers, Julian Wright, Micah Downs and the late addition of Brandon Rush. I remember talking with Bill prior to the season and he said this team was going to be good, he just did not know if it was going to be this year. He expected some struggles.

Self was prophetic as the Jayhawks began the season unranked and limped to a 3-4 start. A modest seven game winning streak followed, including a 73-46 beat down of No. 19 Kentucky at home. But the vagaries of youth surfaced and Kansas fell to Kansas State at home 59-55, (ending a 31-game winning streak over the Wildcats) and at Missouri 89-86 in overtime in consecutive games. The Jayhawks bounced back to win 12 of their final 13 regular-season games to tie Texas for the Big 12 title. That was followed by a Big 12 Tournament title in Dallas, earning Kansas a No. 4 seed in the NCAA Tournament.

The tourney organizers did the Jayhawks no favors, pitting them against No. 13 seed Bradley, a physical and veteran team from the Missouri Valley Conference. With a lottery pick at center in 7-0 Patrick O'Bryant and burly 6-8 forward Marcellus Sommerville ruling the paint, the young Jayhawks panicked and fell behind by 10 at half and 14 in the second. A late comeback fell short and the season ended with a

25-8 mark, including a 13-3 league co-championship.

There are those who put the Bucknell and Bradley games in the same category, but really there were much different circumstances. Against Bucknell, the Jayhawks were a veteran team that fell apart at the wrong time. Versus Bradley, the stage was just a little too big for a very young team. People forget the Braves won their next game against Pitt to advance to the Sweet 16.

As soon as one season ends, there is always great anticipation for Late Night -- the unveiling of the team and the start of practice. I will admit as the years went on, my attendance was more sporadic. Some might call that aging, but I say that is showing my wisdom. Truthfully, it was an event for the college kids and they made it an energetic evening of fun. Late Night was actually the brainchild of Maryland coach Lefty Driesell in 1971 that began as a team run and evolved into a scrimmage. Larry Brown instituted it his first year at KU in 1983-84 and it was embraced by both Williams and Self.

There have been some funny, entertaining, unusual and let's say, "interesting" activities as part of the evening over the years. In 1985, Larry "Bud" Melman, a member of David Letterman's Late Night cast, participated in the skits. One of those had the players mixing a variety of ingredients in a blender and then daring assistant coach Mark Freidinger to down it. It included soda, corn and other as-sorted foods and liquids. "Dinger" took the challenge and downed it, but nearly gagged in the process. In 1988, Williams' first Late Night, Alonzo Jamison caused a delay in the action when his dunk brought down the basketball goal and opened a slight gash on his head.

The 2006 Late Night had plenty of energy because the team was preseason ranked No. 3. The kids were growing up and had plenty of promise -- and a young guard from Chicago by the name of Sherron Collins and a center from Dallas by the name of Darrell Arthur would be joining them. The pre conference schedule included one of the most mind-numbing games that I can remember. In the second game of the year, Kansas fell -- at home -- to Oral Roberts, 78-71. In that game, Golden Eagle forward Marchello Vealy hit seven of eight three pointers and fin-ished with 22 points. In the remaining 31 games that year, he only hit 15 more three-point shots.

A few weeks later, Kansas met No. 1 Florida in a highly-anticipated showdown. That Gator team won the NCAA the year prior -- and would do so in 2006-07. Self was worried about getting blown out because his squad looked lackadaisical the previous night in beating Ball State. He called a team meeting and read the team the riot act. He asked assistant coach Tim Jankovich, who had the scout, what he thought of Florida. He said they could beat the Lakers. Whether or not that was motivation, the night would belong to the Jayhawks. Kansas took a hard-fought 82-80 overtime win against a team that featured Al Horford, Joakim Noah and Corey Brewer. Julian Wright had one of the best games a Jayhawk has had under Self, scoring 30 points on 9-of-12 shooting and collecting 10 rebounds. I believe Self would call Julian a "stud" after that performance.

The Jayhawks completed the hat-trick, winning their third straight league title, finishing 14-2, with only losses at Texas Tech and at home to No. 10 Texas A&M. The title was preserved by beating No. 15 Texas in Allen Fieldhouse in the final regular season game, 90-86. It was an absolute shootout as Texas led at half 54-42 behind a sensational 25-point performance by the Longhorns' Kevin Durant. The Jayhawks turned the momentum with a 29-11 start to lead 71-65. Then something happened that showed how much Kansas fans understand and respect the game. Durant injured his ankle and lay on the floor for a while. When he got up, he received an ovation from the fans. He came back from the lockerroom later and the crowd roared its approval.

Kansas also won the Big 12 postseason trophy, defeating No. 15 Texas 88-84 in overtime in Oklahoma City. The game matched all of the intensity of the matchup in Lawrence a week earlier. Durant (37 points) and A.J. Abrams combined for 58 points, while Rush, Collins, Wright and Chalmers totaled 75. The Jayhawks would head to the NCAA Tournament as a No. 1 seed. Wins over Niagara, Kentucky and Southern Illinois put Kansas in the regional final for the second time in four years, this time meeting second seeded UCLA. It was a bit of an unusual bracketing to put the No. 1 seed playing a lower seeded team in its backyard of San Jose. Still, KU jumped to a 29-23 lead, but UCLA gained a 35-31 lead at intermission behind guards Aaron Afflalo and Darren Collison. UCLA pulled away late for a 68-55 win. The Jayhawks, with no seniors on the team, finished 33-5 and No. 2 in the final *Associated Press* poll.

It was also a successful season for the radio crew in my opinion as former Jayhawk Chris Piper filled the shoes of the retired Max Falkenstien. Chris had done television for Kansas, the Big 12 and the Missouri Valley Conference in the past, so there was little adjustment from what I could tell. He was such a cerebral player and that came across in his analysis. I thought he and my former Royals television partner, the late Paul Splittorff were cut much from the same cloth in that nothing irritated them more than selfish play and a lack of effort.

Piper, of course, was a senior on the 1988 national championship team and truly an unsung player. I still contend his fall-away baseline jumper as the shot clock expired to give KU a 77-71 lead with three minutes left in the win over Oklahoma may have been the biggest shot of the game. If you ever want to win a bet, ask someone which Lawrence High School team won a state title - the one with Chris Piper or Danny Manning. The correct answer is Piper.

Chris Piper, a captain on the Kansas 1988 national title team replaced Max Falkenstien as color analyst in 2006-07. Credit: Kansas Athletics

By the time the 2007 football season was completed, the Kansas basketball team was well on its way to another strong season under Bill Self. The only personnel loss from the previous year was Julian Wright, who declared for the NBA Draft and was selected as the No. 13 pick of the New Orleans Pelicans. Lanky Cole Aldrich headlined the incoming freshman class. By the end of December, KU was 13-0, ranked No. 3 nationally and had wins over Arizona, USC and Georgia Tech. The streak would grow to 20-0 heading into a matchup with No. 22 Kansas State in Manhattan. The Wildcats under Frank Martin, and featuring freshman phenom Michael Beasley, ended a 24-game homecourt losing streak to the Jayhawks, 84-75. During that time, KU had a 56-8 advantage over its rival to the west.

The Jayhawks would lose two more times during the regular season, both road contests at No. 11 Texas and at Oklahoma State, 61-60. That earned the Jayhawks their fourth straight league title. They followed that with a sweep of the Big 12 Tournament in Kansas City, avenging the loss to Texas, 88-74 in the championship game. It was also good enough to give the Jayhawks a No. 1 seed in the Midwest regional. They dispatched Portland State and UNLV in Omaha and advanced to Detroit for the Elite Eight. A 72-57 win over Villanova meant a date with Davidson, destiny's darling, for a trip to the Final Four.

All of the pressure was on Kansas -- and it played like it for much of the game. Led by Steph Curry, the 10th-seeded Wildcats upset Gonzaga, Georgetown and Wisconsin enroute to the meeting with the Jayhawks. Davidson, playing its patterned offense, slowed the game down. But the Jayhawk defense was up to the task, limiting the Wildcats to 38.6

percent shooting, including 29 percent from three. Curry had 25 points, but was only 9-25 from the field. Senior Sasha Kaun came up big for the Jayhawks with 13 points on 6-of-6 shooting and six rebounds in 20 minutes. The game was not secured until a 25-foot shot by Davidson guard Jason Richards was wide left. Self, who was on one knee for the final play, exhaled a big sigh of relief as he bowed his head and lowered his palms to the floor. It was his first Final Four berth as a head coach.

The Final Four would be played in San Antonio and for the first time, all four No. 1 seeds advanced: Kansas, UCLA, Memphis, North Carolina. The Jayhawks were the lowest of the four, No. 1 seeds and they drew the Tar Heels, led by former Jayhawk coach Roy Williams. The story line was clear, but unfortunately Williams could not shoot or defend for his squad. In an absolutely shocking development, Kansas blitzed Carolina from that start, building a 40-12 lead with 6:49 left in the first half. The Jayhawks took a 46-27 lead at halftime. Kansas was so dominant the CBS analys Billy Packer said the game was "over" midway through the first half.

To this day, Self calls it the most fun he has had in a game. Never has he had a team play better. It came out like a thoroughbred in pounding the Tar Heels. You might remember Self called time out twice in the first half. But it was not for strategic purposes. His team had started so fast and played at such a pace that it was exhausted. Halftime could not come soon enough. The Tar Heels came out strong in the second half and eventually whittled the lead down to 64-59 with 5:41 remaining. The run appeared to expend North Carolina's energy and Kansas responded with a 20-7 streak to make the final 84-66.

The win set up the championship game between Larry Brown disciples John Calipari and Bill Self. The Tigers were installed as a slight favorite, thanks mainly to the presence of All-American guard Derek Rose. The game would be nip and tuck throughout, played with great intensity on both ends. The Jayhawks closed on a 5-0 run over the last five minutes of the first half to lead 33-28 at the half. The Tigers closed the gap immediately and took a 39-38 lead on a Joey Dorsey dunk three and a half minutes into the second half. From the 8:50 to the 2:12 mark Rose went to work and the Tigers turned a 47-46 deficit in a 60-51 lead. Rose accounted for eight of those points and things were looking bleak for the good guys.

But momentum turned when the Jayhawks forced turnovers and took advantage of missed Memphis free throws by converting them into points. The biggest, of course, came when Rose missed a free throw and then Kansas ran its patented "chop" play, resulting in a Mario Chalmers three-point shot with :03.6 remaining in regulation to tie the game at 63. Kansas had new life. In the overtime, the Jayhawks scored the first six points, and Memphis went even colder from the field. The final of 75-68 was Kansas' largest lead. Chalmers was the MVP, but a case could have been made for Arthur who had 22 points and 10 rebounds. Eight of his points were in the last 3:36 and overtime.

Other than the Davidson game, I thought Kansas played loose throughout the tournament. The entire North Carolina game and the overtime of Memphis might have been the time when it played with the most "free mind" as Self would say. And while I was happy for the players, I was most pleased for Bill. He had the pressure of following two eventual hall of famers and one could argue he elevated the program. He had been so close to the Final Four, and on that night he knocked the door down.

The win also erased some bad memories for the senior class that had the albatross of the Bucknell and Bradley losses around their collective necks. And while it was the underclassmen of Rush, Chalmers, Collins and Arthur who received the accolades, Self said the title was won because of the toughness Robinson, Kaun and Jackson brought to the team He called it KU's first "foundational" class and Robinson the most unheralded standout in program history.

Lawrence and the KU campus were certainly in a celebratory mood. From San Antonio, we saw on social media scenes of a packed Mass Street after the semifinal win over North Carolina and then again after the title game win over Memphis. It was a sea of humanity. That was followed by a welcome home celebration at Memorial Stadium and then a parade that finished with the awards banquet that night. It was estimated 80,000 people lined Mass Street for the parade.

The 2007-08 school year was one to remember with the Orange Bowl Championship and the NCAA title. T-shirt, book and souvenir sales were at an all-time high.

Chapter 9 Sidebar: My Offices: Stadiums, Arenas, Ballparks and More

I have yet to come across a broadcaster who doesn't have an interest in the architecture of the arenas, stadiums and ballparks in which they do games. They are truly part of the story and their character -- or lack of it -- invariably work their way into the broadcast.

When you broadcast 48 years and do baseball, basketball and football, you get to experience quite a variety of venues. I've done games from the position of a card table doing a high school baseball game to the plush press box of the new Yankee Stadium. They are all snowflakes, no two are alike. One arena that we made a special effort to work in was the Palestra in Philadelphia. It is on the campus of Pennsylvania and was the place where the Big 5 -- LaSalle, Temple, Penn, Villanova and St. Joseph's -- would play. I had seen it on television numerous times. Everyone who has seen both facilities, tells me it was a "mini" Allen Fieldhouse.

So, one day, Max and I got to talking with Roy Williams about the Palestra and asked him if he had ever played there. He had not and we had not broadcast a game there. So an idea was hatched and in the second game of the 1998-99 season, the No. 8 Jayhawks nipped Penn at the Palestra, 61-56 after trailing much of the game. It was the last game a head coach ever let the broadcast team schedule.

Memorial Stadium at the base of Campanile Hill has quite a storied history. In 1920, the Jayhawks tied Nebraska 20-20 at McCook Field which was essentially located where Memorial Stadium is today. Phog Allen was the football coach, his only season in that position, and the athletic director. Fortified by the win, Chancellor Lindley started a fund drive for a new stadium and put Allen in charge of the project. In the spring of the next year, the students were encouraged to come to McCook Field and help tear the wooden bleachers down. That was accomplished in no time at all as the event was made to be a carnival-like celebration with lunch, speeches and games.

Games began being played at Memorial Stadium in 1921 and today it is the seventh-oldest stadium in Division I. Allen wanted it designed like Penn's horseshoe stadium with a track. The sides were completed first and then a few years later the bowl was added. Interestingly, former UCLA coach John Wooden helped construct the stadium. Allen was recruiting Wooden from Indiana to play basketball, and encouraged him to come to Kansas for a summer to harvest crops to earn money. When he got here, the crops were not ready, but Allen offered him a chance to make money by working on the stadium. So in 1927, between his junior and senior years of high school, the future Wizard of Westwood helped construct Memorial Stadium.

The setting of Memorial Stadium is wonderful, and sitting high above the field you can see for miles. It was a great vantage point for the games. Tucked on the northeast side of campus, it is surrounded by neighborhoods full of tailgaters on game day. The change of colors in the fall creates an idyllic setting. In the days when the scoreboard was smaller and there were no end zone stands, fans would sit on the hill to watch the game. Games versus Kansas State and Missouri drew large crowds on the hill.

Bob Davis served as the Grand Marshal of the 2016 KU Homecoming Parade. Credit: Steve Puppe

Allen Fieldhouse has been called the best college basketball arena and I would argue not only is that true, but it is in rarified company with legendary venues such as Lambeau Field, Fenway Park, Yankee Stadium and Augusta National Golf Course. Trying to describe the game atmosphere does not do the experience justice. Tradition oozes out of the building. Not only in terms of the great basketball, but also because of the total experience. From the camping out by the students hours (sometimes days) before the game, the mad rush of fans when the doors open, the pregame music of the band, the Rock Chalk Chant and the entrance of the team. It's all done according to a schedule, yet not choreographed by anyone.

Every move has meaning and it rises to a crescendo when head coach Bill Self walks out onto the court with just over a minute until tipoff. You'll notice that Self will blow on his hands as he walks through the tunnel into the main arena. That all began when there was only one set of doors and the cold winter air would work its way into the bottom concourse. Renovations have eliminated that problem, but because of habit and tradition, Self still blows on his hands.

Working a game there is truly an experience, regardless of how close the outcome is. But when there is a big-time matchup with a big-time atmosphere, you get goosebumps. The sounds, the colors, the smells capture you. It is almost as if you are suspended from reality as you enjoy a special atmosphere. And even though there are always new bells and whistles, there is also a tie to the past. I mean, there's always few sightings each year of the Dancing Nachos graphic from the 1980s.

Bill Self has lost 14 games in Allen Fieldhouse in his 17 years as the Jayhawks head coach (278 games total). But he has often said if it weren't for the energy of the fans, the losses would be more than double. The atmosphere is indeed second to none.

The Davis family has several ties to Allen Fieldhouse. In addition to my 32 years of calling the Jayhawks, our son Steven served as a basketball manager for four years -- two years under Roy Williams and two years under Bill Self. My grandfather Edwin Davis, who was a carpenter, was involved in the construction of the fieldhouse in the mid-1950s. While there will always be a need for upgrades. I hope the character never changes.

Thanks to KU's proximity to Kansas City and the fact that the Big Eight/12 Postseason Tournaments (including the now-defunct Holiday Tournament) are held there, the Jayhawks have played numerous games in Kansas City. I have broadcast games in Municipal Auditorium, Kemper Arena and the Sprint Center (now T-Mobile Center). Because of Kansas' success in those venues, they were often referred to as "Allen Fieldhouse East." Municipal is still in use and is a grand old arena at 13th and Central in downtown Kansas City. There have been more NCAA Final Fours played in the building than anywhere else. In addition to the Big Eight Holiday Tournament, the league also used to host its indoor track championships there.

Kemper Arena was ahead of its time in many regards as it was built in 1974 with suites when others of that time did not. It also had the unusual design of renowned architect Frank Lloyd Wright where outside trusses allowed for no internal columns. Of course, no one could have predicted that a huge snowstorm in the late 1970s would cause the roof to collapse. From a sentimental standpoint, Kemper Arena was the venue where I called two basketball championships in five years: Fort Hays State winning the 1984 NAIA title and KU the NCAA crown in 1988. Kemper also served to help develop the West Bottoms area of downtown Kansas City.

Big Eight Tournament weekend was quite a spectacle in the West Bottoms. Always sold out, the area was buzzing with fans from all over the Big Eight region. Also buzzing around were the birds. Perhaps it was the large canopy over the tunnel door that attracted them and served to funnel them in the arena proper. It always seemed like a couple of birds would be flying around during a game.

The Sprint Center, and as of 2020 the T-Mobile Center, was an upgrade from Kemper Arena and had another interesting architectural design. It looks like a fishbowl with the glass exterior. As part of the Power and Light District, it served as an anchor and helped to spur impressive development of that part of downtown. It opened in 2007 and 13 years later it looks as good as new. And, like Municipal and Kemper, it was the scene of many Jayhawk victories.

One fact that is just another tie between the broadcasting careers of our son Steven and me is the fact that both of us are just a few of a handful to broadcast games in Municipal Auditorium, Kemper Arena and the Sprint Center.

With so many outstanding architectural firms in Kansas City, it is not surprising to see the diversity and quality of design throughout the region. Consider that in the early 70s, the forward-thinking design firm of McKivett and Myers opened Kansas City International Airport (1972), Arrowhead Stadium (1972) and Royals (now Kauffman) Stadium in 1973. It is a credit to all involved that those structures are functional today with minor renovations along the way.

Kauffman Stadium was impressive at its opening with the large, crown-themed scoreboard in centerfield and the outfield fountains. Compared to what it looks like today, photos of the past look somewhat stark. The renovations during my time added a great look, color and fan amenities. I always thought it was fun to go to the ballpark, but from a fan perspective, the changes only enhanced the experience. If you look closely at the symmetrical design, you will notice it has a similar layout to that of Dodger Stadium. Lore has it that Muriel Kauffman, wife of the Royals owner, liked the look of Dodger Stadium so much that she wanted a design that replicated it.

Chapter 9: Friends of Bob

Tom Dore: Radio Announcer 1991-93; Missouri, Basketball Letterman, 1978-80. When I came back to the Big Eight as Missouri's radio announcer, one of the first guys I met was Bob. We shared a lot of laughs, but what I liked the most was that we'd try to listen to each other doing football or basketball games when we weren't doing our own games. Mostly to make fun of each other.

I was easily the world's worst football analyst, and he was always happy to confirm my fears.

But there was a day when MU was playing a home game in scenic Columbia, Mo. Bob is likely already nodding his head, or was he already asleep? Tough to tell, I know. Our radio booth was next to the MU coaches booth, and MU tried a pass over the middle to a soon to be former tight end. The guy on the field developed a case of alligator arms on the pass play. This result brought a string of profanities from the coaches that was picked up on our crowd mic.

The Missouri offensive coordinator at the time was a vindictive SOB. So he called the same formation and the same play, designed to go to the same guy on the next play. I believe he had a death wish for the soon to be former Tiger. This time, the player almost put his arms behind him so he could be assured that, even if the ball hit him in the chest, he could not possibly catch the damn thing. As the play was over, the Tiger assistant seemed upset as he yelled directly into our (quite poorly placed) crowd mic, "Get that WORTHLESS EXPLETIVE EXPLETIVE off the field FOR EXPLETIVE EVER".

As I was driving home after the game, my brand new cell phone rings, with a call from Davis' also brand new cell phone. He was laughing so hard, I thought it was a bad connection. Finally he managed to say the same line as the MU coach, and then laughed like hell. I arrived home and my wife greeted me. Her first words weren't hello honey or good job or great to have you home. She looked at me and deadpanned, "well, just who was the worthless EXPLETIVE anyway?"

Bob said it was MU's finest radio broadcast ever.

I had to agree.

Dick Vitale: ESPN college basketball analyst. I always looked forward to going to Allen Fieldhouse. I love Rock Chalk Jayhawk, baby! Great talent on the court, outstanding coaching, it has always been a treat and thrill. It is one of my favorite sites to call a game. One of the great moments broadcasting Kansas games was visiting with Hall of Fame sportscaster Bob Davis. Sharing time and having great conversations with him have been so special.

Davis is known for his brilliant calls of Kansas basketball and football games, as well as his time with the Kansas City Royals. That whetted my appetite big time as I am a big baseball fan and I had feelings for the Royals as my neighbor was Hal McRae! His son Brian also starred in the majors.

Bob and I shared many conversations about Kansas hoops and the Royals and their great players over the years. I remember talking about George Brett with him. I loved Bob's passion, his pride, his love for what he was doing. That made him so special. He was multi-talented, doing different sports. Whether it was football, basketball or baseball, he always shined.

He was always prepared. Davis showed his enthusiasm calling games. He had the energy calling the action. It was a thrill to get a moment to chat with him. I enjoyed seeing Bob and the late Max Falkenstien. Yes, it was also nice to see so many great games there!

That duo was together for 22 years and they were as good as it gets. Kansas fans were blessed to have such an exceptional duo.

The spirit there was so special. Bob is a special talent.

Jeff Hawkins: Kansas Basketball, 2003-06; Jayhawk Television post game analyst. The thing that stands out to me about Bob Davis is "that" voice. It's just so powerful and distinctive. It gets your attention right away. I've been friends with his son Steven since he was a team manager when I played at KU. Now, I do some post game shows with him for the Jayhawk Network. You can tell the apple doesn't fall far from the tree. They both have their own styles, but you see many mannerisms in Steven that come from Bob. Steven is destined to get a big time broadcasting job, I believe.

In 2010 I moved to Hays and was the junior varsity basketball coach and assistant varsity coach at Ellis High School a few miles just to the west. Everyone wanted to talk about Kansas basketball. I grew up in Kansas City so I knew just how popular the Jayhawks were in that part of the state. But they love KU out west as much. What I also found out is just how popular Bob Davis still is in the Hays area. He's been gone more than 35 years and people still talk about him like he is one of theirs. They are very proud of him.

Eric Heft: Basketball, Iowa State 1971-74; Cyclone Radio Network, 1979 - Present. I guess I am the old man of the Big 12 now because I have been doing this 41 years. In that time, Bob is truly one of the finest gentlemen I have met. I think the one thing that stands out for me was senior night in 2016 in Lawrence. It was actually Bob's last home game and it was great to see him recognized. The fans gave him a wonderful ovation. Bob also served as the emcee for the Jayhawks' senior celebration after the game. Right before it began, Georges Niang came out to do a postgame interview for the Cyclone Network. I was sitting with Georges waiting for a commercial break to end, and the first thing Bob did is to ask the crowd to recognize Georges for his night and good career. Georges got a quite a nice ovation and I remember him being impressed by that. It just shows you the type of person Bob is. He always had great respect for the game and recognizing the opponent.

The other aspect I just love about Bob is whenever you saw him for the first time in a while, he's ready with a joke. And, I mean it's a good one. I probably hadn't heard 90 percent of them. We started getting together as conference broadcasters the night before the postseason tournament and had a big dinner. We call it the "Bob Davis Memorial Dinner" because he can really hold court. I love it that he still joins us.

I enjoyed the Kansas rivalry, both as a player and as a broadcaster. Kansas has been so good for so long. But Iowa State has won its share and of course Hilton Coliseum gets fired up for the Jayhawks. It's amazing to think that neither Larry Brown or Danny Manning won there.

Big 12 Conference basketball radio crews meet annually at the postseason tournament for dinner.
Credit: Bob Newton

Blair Kerkhoff: Sports Reporter, Kansas City Star, 1989 - Present. More than anything, I just liked to hang around Bob. He was fun, knew a lot of people and could tell the best stories and jokes. Bob's son, Steven, was in his early years as UMKC's broadcaster, and I was doing a doubleheader, covering a Kansas game in the afternoon and a UMKC game that night. When Bob found out, he asked to join me. We drove together to Kansas City and he grabbed a seat in the stands, just a spectator. I found him sneaking glances over at his son throughout the game. He was rightly proud.

When I covered Kansas as a beat writer (1989-97), if I didn't stay at the team hotel during road games, I often made it a point to drop in at some point during the trip because Bob, Max Falkenstien, Richard Konzem and Doug Vance (athletic department staff) would be sitting in the lobby, drinking coffee and telling wonderful stories about Kansas athletics. I learned more about KU sports history crashing those conversations than in any book.

When Kansas played in Hawaii, Bob made sure to mention during a broadcast the names of the media there to cover the event. Acknowledging those who had made the long trip was always a nice gesture on his part.

Tim Allen: Big Eight/Big 12 Conference Associate Commissioner, 1983 - 2020. I have been blessed to know and work with some great radio play-by-play guys. Growing up in an era where the numbers of games on television were limited, you relied on them to do more than just provide name, number, stats and accolades -- they painted the picture for your mind's eye. Even when television became more prevalent, you still were dependent on them to fill in the blanks because they travel, eat, sleep and drink with the team. They are part of the program and the best ones were the Rembrandts of the radio. Master artists who use words, inside knowledge and golden voices instead of a brush.

The best thing about Bob was his sense of humor. It came through on the air, but away from the microphone he is a great storyteller and laugher. The best ones are, of course. Dev Nelson was a great play-by-play man at K-State and had the most infectious laugh ever. Big smile, a chortle and head thrown back. Bob Barry was another great artist behind the mic with a knack for laughing at the start, in the middle and before the end of any story or joke. He never made it through any humorous story without laugh breaks. Bob Davis was kind of a combination of both -- but every tale, every joke, every story came off as a serious topic until he decided it was time to let you in on the "rest of the story" with a smile, snort and then short laugh.

Jim Marchiony: Former NCAA Staff, Former Associate Athletic Director, Kansas, 2004 - 19. We all know about Bob's prowess as a play-by-play announcer, but I enjoyed him most as the host of coaches' weekly radio shows. I constantly marveled at his innate ability to keep those shows moving, and keep the coaches and guests comfortable, regardless of how well or poorly the previous week had gone. He achieved this by using his encyclopedic knowledge of Kansas Athletics, his ability to recall names and incidents from generations ago, and his terrific sense of humor.

I remember Bob using all those attributes when I worked with him during my NCAA days when he annually hosted the hours-long NCAA Selection Show on radio with the great Dave Gavitt. He impressed all of us back then with his ability to prepare mountains of information, conduct interviews with coaches around the country, and make the show a must-listen part of Selection Sunday.

Waving the Wheat and Waving Goodbye

RARELY ARE THE words "rebuilding" and "Kansas basketball" used in the same sentence, but there was some re-tooling going on for Bill Self as he had to replace Robinson, Kaun, Jackson, Rush, Chalmers and Arthur from the 2008 national championship team. Aldrich, Collins and Brady Morningstar and Tyrel Reed were the returning foundation, and they were joined by talented freshmen Tyshawn Taylor and the Morris twins - Marcus and Markieff. This team had the added burden of being the defending national champions, even though Collins was the only one who saw appreciable playing time. The Jayhawks went from being one of the most experienced to least experienced teams in the nation.

Anyone who has spent time with Bill Self knows there are no excuses in his lexicon. He was going to have this team ready to play and not back down from the expectation of a fifth straight conference title. The pollsters knew this all too well. Despite the talent drain, the Jayhawks were ranked No. 24 in the preseason polls.

We've come to expect that struggling is relative when it comes to Kansas basketball. Following a 66-61 win over Colorado on January 31, 2008 in Lawrence, the Jayhawks were a fairly nondescript 17-4, with a 1-1 record against ranked foes (92-85 win over No. 14 Tennessee and a 75-62 loss at No. 8 Michigan State). What is so notable about the Colorado game is it is last time a Bill Self team would be unranked. Following the Michigan State loss, the Jayhawks closed out the regular season on a 14-3 run (including an uncharacteristic loss to Baylor in the first round of the Big 12 Tournament). They "won one for the thumb" in getting their fifth Big 12 title in a row, and were seeded No. 3 in the NCAA Tournament Midwest Regional.

Victories over North Dakota State and Dayton meant a rematch of a regular season loss to Michigan State in the round of 16 in Indianapolis. The Jayhawks jumped out to a 32-19 lead with 3:26 left in the first half. Then the Spartans began to grind away, taking their first lead at 51-49 at 8:46. Tied 60-60 with 1:50 remaining, Michigan State went on a 7-2 run to win the game. It masked an outstanding game by Collins, who had 20 points in going 9-of-13 from the field. The year ended with a 27-8 record and No. 14 *Associated Press* rating. After starting five seniors the previous season, this squad started two freshmen, two sophomores and a junior. The outlook for next season was bright.

If you've been a follower of Kansas football for a long time, you know that there have been several occasions when very good to outstanding seasons have been followed by less than stellar campaigns. It was going to be hard to replicate the 2007 Orange Bowl championship season, but Mangino and his staff had coached up his squad and there were quality returners back for another run at a bowl. Remember, up to that point, the Jayhawks had never been to back-to-back bowl games. Reesing, Kerry Meier, Jake Sharp, Dezmon Briscoe and Dexton Fields were back on offense, while Joe Mortensen, Mike Riviera, Harris, Stuckey, Justin Thornton and James Holt returned on defense.

The squad got off to a good start, going 5-1 with the only loss at No. 19 South Florida, on a field goal at the final gun. The third and fourth wins were over Iowa State and Colorado and put the squad at No. 16 in the national polls heading into a matchup at No. 4 Oklahoma. The Hawks hung tough in losing 45-31. It was the start of a skid of four losses in five games, the win coming in a 52-21 shellacking of Kansas State. Standing at 6-5, the Jayhawks' obstacle to a better bowl bid was a heated rival - the Missouri Tigers. The game would be a rematch of last year's battle, again in Arrowhead Stadium, in weather conditions that started bad and got worse.

The Jayhawks held the upper hand for most of the game, but Missouri's quick strike with 1:50 left gave it a 37-33 lead. It set up a wild finish where the Jayhawks would score with :27 remaining on a fourth-down touchdown pass from Reesing to Meier. It was somewhat of a broken play as Reesing was flushed from the pocket and saw Meier break off his route to the endzone. Reesing lofted the pass through the large snowflakes and Meier cradled it for the score. Safety Philip Strozier's blocked field goal preserved the 40-37 win. The two teams combined for 28 points in the final seven minutes. The 7-5 mark guaranteed history with the first back-to-back bowl seasons for Jayhawk football.

While there were many individuals who contributed to the success of the Jayhawk program during the unprecedented run, the one person I felt most happy for was Meier. A native Kansan from Pittsburg, he came to KU with high hopes to be its next quarterback. But he underwent a procedure for a heart ailment as a freshman and there was some question if he would ever suit up again. He was cleared to play, but after losing the QB battle to Reesing, he was moved to a slot receiver position. He never complained about the situation he was dealt, he just went about his business. Mangino would call Meier the most important player when it came to changing the culture of the Kansas football program. His willingness to change positions for the good of the team, his leadership and intelligence were contagious.

The Jayhawks were ticketed to meet Minnesota in the Insight Bowl following the win over Missouri. After falling behind the Gophers 14-7, the Jayhawks outscored them 35-7 the rest of the way behind Reesing's four touchdown passes. The season ended at 8-5 and more hardware was added to the trophy case.

Mangino clearly had the program on strong footing, but he faced the prospects of replacing key personnel losses from the previous two years. Nobody would be surprised if 2009 was to be a rebuilding year. The Jayhawks were preseason ranked No. 25. Wins over Northern Colorado, UTEP, Duke, Southern Mississippi and Iowa State allowed them to climb to No. 16 facing a road trip to Colorado. The Jayhawks fell behind 24-3, but mounted a comeback, scoring on their next five possessions to take a 30-27 lead with 13:02 left in the game. Colorado responded with a touchdown to make it 34-30. Then, in one of the more bizarre circumstances in memory, Reesing drove the Jayhawks down the field for the apparent lead with 5:36 left. The Jayhawks were called for offensive pass interference on a pick play where there was no contact. The score was nullified and Colorado hung on when a last gasp-pass to Briscoe was knocked away.

The scene after the Colorado game was eerily familiar to the 2004 loss to Texas in the infamous "dollar signs" game. The interference was called on a play that every team runs with never a flag being thrown. And it came as such a crucial point in the game. The loss was certainly disappointing and slowed the momentum from the great start. It started a spiral of losses that continued with a 35-15 loss to No. 25 Oklahoma and continued to the final 41-39 heartbreaking loss to Missouri (field goal on the last play). You normally don't say one play turned a season around, but that one at Colorado might just have broken that rule.

The Jayhawks would finish 5-7 and miss out on a bowl game. The Colorado defeat was painful, but a 17-10 loss at Kansas State was the killer. The Jayhawks had three turnovers compared to Kansas State's zero, and they missed two short field goals as well. In Mangino's eight seasons, this is the only one that could be called disappointing. Key injuries played a part, especially a leg ailment for running back Jake Sharp that limited him to only 429 yards rushing on the year.

But there was more happening in the athletic department. A rift had grown between Perkins and Mangino and it was obvious they were not on the same page. Perkins did not hire Mangino and that factored into the situation. Distractions mounted and whether they were the cause of the losing streak is up for debate. But one thing is for certain, they did not help. Rumors mounted in the final weeks of the season and on December 3, 2009, Perkins announced that Mangino and the school "mutually agreed to part ways."

It was a sad way to end what might have been the best era in Kansas football. As someone who was on the outside of the program, but had inside access, it is my opinion it did not have to end this way. Perkins and Mangino both had strong personalities, and that complicated matters. If there were issues, then they should have been worked out. I enjoyed my time with Mark. He was professional in all interactions. The turnaround he engineered at KU was amazing -- and it took energy, discipline and patience. You had to admire what he and his staff accomplished. In the end, I felt he deserved better -- or at least the opportunity to continue.

Mangino returned to Memorial Stadium in 2014 as the offensive coordinator at Iowa State, and then again in 2017 as part of the ceremonies to induct the 2007 Orange Bowl team into the athletic hall of fame. He received a strong ovation, recognizing his contributions to the program.

There surely wasn't a shortage of names being thrown around to succeed Mangino. The program was elevated to the point where people like Stanford's Jim Harbaugh, Southern Mississippi's Larry Fedora, East Carolina's Skip Holtz, and even Tommy Tuberville, who had just been fired at Auburn were under consideration. There was much excitement generated by Harbaugh's candidacy because he had relatives in the Kansas City region, but ultimately Turner Gill was the choice. Harbaugh would later intimate on radio shows in Kansas City that he would have taken the job, but Perkins was not going to allow him to coach the Cardinal in its bowl game that year.

Gill had terrorized Kansas fans as the quarterback at Nebraska under Tom Osborne and there was hope he would be able to return the favor to those in Lincoln and other locales. He was coming off a four year run at Buffalo, where he had a 20-30 record, but was 13-13 in his last two campaigns including a 2008 Mid-American Conference East Division championship. He came with a great reputation for his character and integrity. But the Big 12 Conference was definitely a step up.

This was also a different environment for the hiring of a new head coach at Kansas. Fans and media had been conditioned to a multi-year rebuilding process in past hires. But given the success under Mangino, there was the expectation that any step back would be small. Fans were of the opinion there could be sustained success for Kansas football.

Before Gill's inaugural Kansas football season, Self and his squad were poised for another championship campaign in 2009-10. The Jayhawks would begin the season preseason ranked No. 1 and fall to no lower than No. 3 the remainder of the season. Kansas reeled off 14 wins before falling at No. 16 Tennessee, 76-68. It would then win the next 13 before losing 85-77 at Oklahoma State. That would be the only Big 12 Conference loss, giving the Jayhawks their sixth straight title. Throw in another conference tourney title and the team entered the NCAA Tournament as a No. 1 seed for the first/second rounds at Oklahoma City. That was built on a strength of schedule which saw them go 8-1 against ranked opponents.

The Jayhawks dispatched Lehigh in the opening round and would meet ninth-seeded

Northern Iowa in round two. The Panthers were no slouch. They would finish 30-5 that year and win the Missouri Valley Conference. And early on, you had the feeling this just might be their day. After falling behind 2-0, the Panthers would not relinquish the lead the rest of the way. Behemoth center Jordan Eglseder hit a three-point bucket to make it 3-2 and later a second one to make it 25-19 (he scored 10 of his 14 points to that point). In 31 other games, he hit one three-point shot. Of course, the killer was an unguarded three-point bucket by Ali Farokhmanesh with :45 left to seal the 69-67 win. And if you thought Northern Iowa wasn't for real, in the next round, the Panthers fell to Michigan State, but the game was tied at 51 with three minutes left before UNI lost by seven.

The loss was shocking no doubt, but it is also the reason why the NCAA Basketball Tournament is one of the best sporting events going. Self would later say that he had a bad feeling coming out of the lockerroom for the second half. It wasn't just that Kansas was trailing 36-28. He did not sense an urgency or energy level needed for a game in the NCAA tournament. The team had trailed at other points in the year, but this was a different animal. Still a 33-3 record, 15-1 league record and No. 1 *Associated Press* final ranking ain't all bad.

If you are a Division I football coach, it is important to have the athletic director in your corner because building a program is resource intensive -- and requires patience of the leadership. Gill had to be the most shocked person around when Perkins announced the following June that he would be stepping down after the 2010-11 school year. My guess is that shock gave way to bewilderment when Perkins moved up his departure to September 7, 2010.

In Gill's debut, Kansas fell 6-3 to North Dakota State, a perennial I-AA power who would also go on to own Big 12 wins over Kansas State and Iowa State in later years. But the next week the Jayhawks upset No. 15 Georgia Tech at home, and then followed a loss at Southern Miss with a 42-16 win over New Mexico State. The proverbial damn burst and the squad lost seven of its next eight. But the one win was memorable. On November 6, Colorado came to Lawrence and was up 45-17 after the first play of the fourth quarter. Suddenly the Jayhawks could do no wrong, outscoring the Buffs 35-0 the rest of the way thanks to three James Sims rushing touchdowns. It would be the largest comeback in school history.

I have to give credit to my partner David Lawrence. He noted that it was a high possession game and with a change in momentum, strange things can happen. In this case, with 9:26 remaining, defensive end Toben Opurum forced a fumble and Tyler Patmon picked it up and ran it in for 28 yards and a score. Suddenly it was 45-37 and the prospects of a win were real. The broadcast booth went from sounding like a morgue to that of a postgame celebration at Allen Fieldhouse after a win over Missouri.

Self and company were more than ready to put the 2009-10 campaign behind them and had plenty of talent returning, but there would be some holes to fill: Aldrich and freshman Xavier Henry had declared for the draft and Collins graduated. The team now belonged to a trio of juniors -- the Morris twins and Tyshawn Taylor. They were more than up to the task, leading the team to a 15-0 non-conference record through early January.

That was also the time when Kansas settled on a new athletics director. All indications were that Tulsa's Bubba Cunningham would be the choice, but North Carolina got to him first. Jayhawk officials turned to Sheahon Zenger, who was the AD at Illinois State. Zenger had connections to Lawrence and KU as he spent some of his childhood in the community and received his doctorate here. I had a connection as well, broadcasting his play as a member of the Hays High School football team.

The second half of the 2010-11 basketball season continued to go well as the Jayhawks eventually moved from No. 7 to No. 1 in the polls. Their first loss came at home to No. 10 Texas, 74-63 under the most tragic of circumstances. Kansas was 18-0 and No. 2 in the polls, and had a school-record 69 straight wins at Allen Fieldhouse. Late the evening before the game, the team was informed that the mother of sophomore Thomas Robinson had died of a heart attack. Robinson played in that game and with the support of his team jumped to a 35-23 halftime lead. But the energy and emotion waned and the Longhorns outscored the Jayhawks 51-28 in the second period. Five days later, the team joined Robinson in Washington D.C., as his mother was laid to rest.

It was a lot to go through for Thomas and his younger sister. His teammates, coaching staff and school were his support system. It was heartening to see the reaction and how he was supported.

Kansas closed the regular season strong with only one more loss the rest of the way, an 84-68 loss to Kansas State on the day the Jayhawks were announced No. 1 in the polls. A seventh straight league title and a conference tournament championship earned the Jayhawks the No. 1 NCAA Tournament seed. Wins over Boston University and Illinois in Oklahoma City advanced the Jayhawks to the scene of the 2008 title -- San Antonio. They put away Richmond and only Virginia Commonwealth stood between them and a Final Four.

VCU had been the tournament darlings, winning a play-in game to start the tourney. The Rams were a completely different team than Northern Iowa, but this game had the same type of feel. They were confident from the start and jumped to a lead of 17 points in the first half, before KU narrowed it to 46-44 in the second. Ultimately, the Rams held on to win 71-61 and advance to the Final Four. The killer was a 2-for-21 shooting performance from three-point distance. Kansas would end the season at 35-3, ranked No. 2.

Bill Self has been quoted as saying the Bucknell, Northern Iowa and VCU losses have been the toughest in his career. No doubt his squad would win probably nine out of 10 matchups with those teams, but in a one-and-done setting, you only need to have the magic on that day. It also begs for one to keep some perspective. The "blue bloods" of college basketball are not immune to the upset. In the time Self has been at Kansas, Duke has had three first-round losses, Kentucky has had a first-round loss and missed the tournament twice altogether (one of which they lost a first round NIT game), and North Carolina has three second-round losses and missed the tournament once.

The 2011 football season began with two wins, but the wheels came off in game No. 3, a 66-24 loss at Georgia Tech as the Yellow Jackets avenged the upset the previous year. Things went from bad to worse as the Jayhawks lost their final 10 games, giving up 40 or more points in eight games. Seeing no positive developments on the field, Zenger relieved Gill of his duties and set off to find the next coach.

Two years is not a long time to build a program, but with a 5-19 record, Gill did not have Zenger's confidence he could turn it around. From a personal standpoint, I felt bad for Turner. He was a good person and was good to deal with on and off the field. He had a wonderful family and they were great ambassadors for KU. I am happy for him that he found considerable success at Liberty after leaving Mt. Oread.

Many names were thrown out by the media in Zenger's one-man search party for the next coach. Southern Mississippi's Fedora, Air Force's Troy Calhoun and that of former Texas Tech coach Mike Leach added some intrigue. Leach would take himself out of the running when he took the Washington State job. Zenger surprised everyone when on December 8, 2011, he hired former Notre Dame head coach Charlie Weis, who was the offensive coordinator at Florida at the time. I'll admit it -- I did not see that one coming, and neither did anyone else.

The attention turned to basketball as the Jayhawks, smarting from the loss to VCU, were retooling just a bit for the 2011-12 campaign. The Morris twins declared for the NBA draft after their season, while dependable seniors Tyrel Reed and Brady Morningstar graduated. The leadership would fall on the shoulders of senior Tyshawn Taylor, while front line reserves Jeff Withey and Thomas Robinson would be called on to step up.

My feeling was the expectations for this team were probably the lowest for a Jayhawk basketball squad since the 2008-09 season when Self had to replace the entire starting five from the national champions. The Jayhawks were picked No. 13 in the preseason polls, and that was largely on reputation. Perhaps the turning point in the season came in early December, hosting No. 2 Ohio State in Allen Fieldhouse. Standing at 6-2 with losses to No. 2 Kentucky and No. 6 Duke, this was a game the Jayhawks needed for confidence and RPI bolstering. They caught a break when Buckeye big man Jerad Sullinger did not play due to a back injury. Kansas won

78-67, thanks to a 14-point performance by reserve forward Kevin Young on 6-of-8 shooting. A late transfer from Loyola Marymount, Young would be a key performer the rest of the season.

By now, the goal of an eighth straight Big 12 title was more of an expectation. Kansas would be pushed by outstanding teams from Baylor and Missouri. A February 25 matchup with the No. 3 Tigers in Lawrence would be pivotal. The Tigers had won 74-71 earlier in the season at Columbia, so a sweep would make things difficult to not only win the title, but secure a Midwest Regional berth in the NCAA Tournament. Self told me in taping his pregame interview that he felt more nervous about the game than any other regular season contest he had coached.

Missouri came out on fire in the first half and led by 12 heading into the intermission. The lead would swell to 19 before the Jayhawks rode the emotion of a home-court crowd to tie it at 75 as Robinson sent the game into overtime by blocking Phil Pressey's layup as time expired. Conner Teahan, who growing up in Kansas City had seen more than his share of KU-MU games, was 4-of-4 from three point range. And down the stretch, Robinson and Taylor made play after play. A chess game ensued in overtime and. It was clear the team and Self fed off a jacked up environment in Allen Fieldhouse that day for the win.

I look at the Kansas-Kansas State and the Kansas-Missouri rivalries a bit differently. The Jayhawks and Wildcats are both Kansans, kindred spirits you might say. I liked both growing up. Many families had members go to both schools. But going back to my days in college as a history major, you understood the philosophical differences between the Jayhawks and Tigers. Kansas was a free state and Missouri was a slave state. The Missourians invaded Kansas and were met by the fury of John Brown. Kansans **DO NOT LIKE** Missourians. As a family, you were one or the other. Of course, I did not necessarily take it to the extreme others did. I enjoyed broadcasting the Missouri games in 1983 and the people in the athletic department were good to me. But nothing spices up sports like a good rivalry.

Of course, the fervor for the game was turned up a notch as Missouri had earlier announced it was leaving to the SEC. The Big 12 had gone through some transition with Colorado and Nebraska heading to the Pac 12 and Big Ten, respectively the previous year. Texas A&M would join Missouri in leaving to the SEC, while the Big 12 added TCU and West Virginia. It's a shame Missouri and Nebraska are no longer in the same league as Kansas and Kansas State. But it was their choice. I'm not so sure the Tigers and the Huskers have benefitted from the moves.

I had noted that Bill Self's celebration following the win over Oklahoma State in 2005 was among the best, but the one following the Missouri victory has my vote for **THE** best. A fist pump, a twirl, a hug of staff, a big smile and a glance at the family told you all you needed to know about how much it meant to Self. Did the fact that he got passed over for the Missouri job in favor of Quin Snyder add to the emotion? Maybe, but it surely did not detract.

This team, which wasn't picked to do anything at the start of the year (2011-12), had moved from No.17 at the start of January to No. 3 heading into the Big 12 Tourney. A second round tourney loss to Baylor dropped the Jayhawks off the No. 1 seed line, but they did get sent to nearby Omaha. A win over Detroit and a 63-60 squeaker over Purdue meant a short trip to St. Louis. The Jayhawks ran over the state of North Carolina, beating the N.C. State Wolfpack, 60-57 and North Carolina, 80-67.

The win over North Carolina was special as the Jayhawks cut down the top seeded Tar Heels with a 12-0 run to end the game, thwarting them with a triangle and two defense. The Kansas starters accounted for all but four of the team's points.

So, it was an unexpected trip to New Orleans and the Final Four, and a rematch with Ohio State, this time with Sullinger in the lineup. The Jayhawks were on the verge of being blown out as the Buckeye lead grew to 13 with 1:32 left in the first half. Kansas would chip away and not take a lead until it was 56-55 when Travis Releford hit a free throw with 2:48 remaining. The lead would change hands until Taylor's free throws sealed the win.

The title game was a rematch of the Champions Classic game versus Kenucky in early November when the Wildcats took a 75-65 win in New York. Kentucky was dominant in the first half, jumping to a 41-27 lead. The Wildcats controlled the paint as the Jayhawks simply could not score. At one point, Wildcat center Anthony Davis blocked two shots in a row without leaving his feet. He was a man among boys around the bucket. He would finish with only six points, but collect 16 rebounds, record six blocks and alter about a dozen more. Chris and I could only look at each other in amazement.

Give credit to Self and his team for hanging in there. They came out in the second half and chopped the lead to 63-57 with 1:11 remaining. Elijah Johson then hit a three to cut it to three, but he was called for traveling and Kentucky iced the game at the line. Kansas would end the season at 32-7, No. 6 in the final *Associated Press* poll and win the hearts of fans for its never-say-die attitude.

Jayhawks football coach Charlie Weis spent his first fall at Kansas taking his lumps, finishing at 1-11, with the only win a season-opening 31-17 decision over South Dakota State. In fairness to him, the turnover of coaches in a short period only meant recruiting would be more difficult. Recruits build their relationships with assistant coaches over years and as the assistants come and go, so do the relationships. Still, he had coached at the highest levels and his paycheck was hefty. No one would feel sorry for him.

The 2012-13 Kansas hoops campaign opened with a few question marks. Could Elijah Johnson move over to the point and replace the graduated Tyshawn Taylor? Could Jeff Withey handle the load inside with Thomas Robinson departing early for the NBA? And, perhaps most importantly, could Greg Gurley follow in the footsteps of Max Falkenstien and Chris Piper as my broadcast partner? Piper, who is the owner of Grandstand Glassware in Lawrence, was becoming increasingly busy as his company grew, and he also had children involved in sports. It made sense for him to move over to television where he had fewer games. Greg, who had done Jayhawk Network Television for five years, was also working in the athletic department, so the switch made sense. My evaluation of the two is that Piper was a better defender, while Gurley was a better shooter.

Former Kansas guard Greg Gurley joined the radio network as the analyst in 2012-13.
Credit: Kansas Athletics

Kansas entered the season No. 7 in the *Associated Press* rankings and went 12-1 in non-league play, losing only to No. 21 Michigan State, but owning a win over No. 7 Ohio State on the road. Johnson, Withey, Releford and Young were four experienced seniors, while freshman Ben McLemore was a versatile athlete who could play all over the court. From a league race perspective, it was a bit of a bizarre series of events. Kansas and Kansas State would tie for the title at 14-4, and Oklahoma State a game back at 13-5. Kansas defeated Kansas State twice in the regular season and then again in the Big 12 tourney championship. For only the second time in the Bill Self era, his team lost three games in a row: to Marcus Smart and Oklahoma State, 85-80; at TCU, 62-55 and at Oklahoma, 72-66 The loss to the Horned Frogs had Self calling it the worst performance for a Kansas team "since Dr. Naismith lost to the Topeka YMCA." It was the first time in 264 games Kansas lost back-to-back-to-back games.

The Jayhawks righted the ship in tying for the title (ninth straight) and winning the conference tournament. Their reward was placement in Kansas City where they snuck past Western Kentucky, 64-57, and blitzed North Carolina 70-58. The Jayhawks trailed 30-21 at the half, but outscored the Tar Heels 49-28 in the second period to give them their third straight win over Williams and the Heels in NCAA play. It was on to Dallas for the Sweet 16 where the Jayhawks let one get away versus No. 10 Michigan. Leading most of the way, Kansas allowed the Wolverines back in thanks to some hot shooting by guard Trey Burke. In fact, a 30-footer by Burke sent the game into overtime and the Wolverines rode the momentum to an 87-85 overtime win. Still at 31-6 and No. 3 in the final poll, it was another outstanding season.

The season was witness to one of the better individual performances of the Bill Self tenure. In a 108-96 win at Iowa State, Elijah Johnson scored 39 points. That in itself is impressive. Johnson exploded for eight points in the final 29 seconds of regulation and 12 in overtime (20 points in 5:29) to lead the Jayhawks back from a five-point deficit with :44.5 left in regulation.

Passion and excitement are hallmarks of a Bob Davis broadcast. Credit: Kansas Athletics

The 2013 football season showed some improvement with a 3-9 finish, including a league win over West Virginia, 31-19. But the fans were restless. The program had gone from a No. 2 ranking in 2007 to near the bottom of the Power Five structure. Weis decided to take a gamble and amp up the junior college recruiting. There were some successes such as defensive backs Fish Smithson and Dexter McDonald, both who played in the NFL. But of the 26 juco signees in his first two classes, eight never played a down for the Jayhawks. Weis' 2014 class was much more high school focused, but with the juco departures of the previous two classes, the Jayhwawks were precariously low in numbers.

Bill Self said the 2013-14 season would be like starting over as he lost Withey, Releford and Johnson to graduation and McLemore to the NBA. There was excitement for the new recruits which included Andrew Wiggins, Joel Embiid, and Wayne Selden, plus Wichita Heights product Perry Ellis was back as a sophomore. It was similar to what Self faced following the 2008 national championship season.

I would venture to guess it was one of the more frustrating seasons as well. There were high points such as a 94-83 Champions Classic win over No. 4 Duke, a stretch of four straight wins over ranked teams, and a 10th consecutive Big 12 Conference title. But you could sense the team was running out of gas. Joel Embiid hurt his back and did not play in the Big 12 or NCAA tournaments. The team had to go to overtime to beat No. 9 seed Oklahoma State in the opener of the Big 12 Tourney, then lost to Iowa State in the semis. The opening round of the NCAA Tournament was a pedestrian 80-69 win over Eastern Kentucky, and the season ended at 26-10 with a 60-57 loss to Stanford. As Self would say, a good year, but not great. I know a lot of coaches who would have taken it.

Sheahon Zenger needed the football program to show some hope in 2014, but it did not come. In a somewhat surprising move, he fired Weis four games into the season. Kansas was 2-2, but was non-competitive in losses to Duke and Texas. Zenger said he was not seeing any progress on the field and turned to defensive coordinator Clint Bowen to finish the season. Bowen, a Lawrence native and long-time KU assistant, was a favorite son and it was difficult to see him be put in this position. It was nice to see the team respond for him in a 34-14 win over Iowa State, but the 3-9 finish for the second year in a row put the program behind the eight ball. I felt sorry for the coaches, players and fans as the season wound down. I also could not help but feel terrible for my broadcast partner David Lawrence. After the final game of the year, he looked like he had his heart ripped out.

Weis wasn't around that long, but he gave me one of my better compliments -- at least I took it that way. Given his gruff personality, my perception was he was not prone to tossing out bouquets. After a coach's show he remarked to me: "I hate to do these, but at least you make them tolerable."

Unlike the process Zenger used to hire Weis, he created a search committee to seek a successor. The committee focused on hiring someone with strong high school ties. The name that jumped to the top of the list was former Kansas and current Rice assistant David Beaty. Previously on Mark Mangino's staff, Beaty impressed the search committee with his ties to Texas high school football and understanding of the challenges he would face at KU. Energetic and personable, there was hope again for the football program, but also the realization it would take time.

Rarely do coaches have to re-tool in consecutive years, but in the era of the one-and-done, Bill Self found himself in that position for the 2014-15 season. Wiggins was, not surprisingly, a one and done and a lottery pick in the NBA Draft. Embiid's departure was not a shock either, at least after the halfway point of the season. He came to KU ranked outside the top 100 freshmen, but quickly developed into the No. 3 lottery pick. That left Self with a starting lineup of junior Perry Ellis, sophomore Frank Mason, sophomore Wayne Selden, freshmen Kelly Oubre and the last spot split between junior Jamari Traylor and sophomore Landen Lucas. Not the most experienced roster Self ever had, but pollsters still had Kansas No. 5. It was clearly evident in a 72-40 blowout loss to Kentucky in the Champions Classic that the young Hawks weren't quite ready for the big stage. The Jayhawks responded with a 61-56 win over No. 20 Michigan State in Orlando and a 63-60 win over No. 13 Utah in Kansas City.

The quest for an 11th straight league crown would be a challenge as a balanced league race was predicted by the media and coaches. In the end, there were five teams within two games of each other and each of those were in the final AP poll. The Jayhawks were solo champs at 13-5, while Iowa State and Oklahoma were 12-6 and West Virginia and Baylor were 11-7. The key was an undefeated league record in Allen Fieldhouse. Iowa State defeated Kansas in the Big 12 tourney title game, 70-66. The Jayhawks were the last of the No. 2 seeds for the NCAA Tournament and opened with a 75-56 win over New Mexico State. That set the stage for a matchup with a Wichita State team led by the fantastic junior backcourt of Ron Baker from Scott City and Fred Van Vleet. The Shockers limited KU to 35 percent shooting in a 78-65 win.

I began the 2015-16 school year knowing it would be my last one. I let those with the Jayhawk Network know, but there was no public announcement made at that point. I did not want a year-long going away celebration. I was not dying, I was still going to be around. But as a means to identify my successor, it was announced November 23 while Kansas was playing in the Maui Classic that this would be my last year.

The David Beaty era began with many challenges. He did not have a chance to recruit extensively upon his arrival and the player turnover under the previous staff was considerable. The fans knew the prospects were not that good, so while they were disappointed by an 0-12 season, I cannot say they were surprised. The defense struggled mightily, allowing 40 or more points in eight games. Undaunted, Beaty sent his staff to visit every single Kansas high school to build relations and meet coaches and players. Rome would not be built in a day.

Kansas opened the basketball season ranked No. 4 and followed a loss in the Champions Classic to No. 13 Michigan State with a Maui Classic title, defeating No. 19 Vanderbilt. There were 10 consecutive wins to follow, including the wildly exciting 108-106 triple overtime win over No. 2 Oklahoma in Allen Fieldhouse. I thought it said a great deal about the Kansas fans as after the game Sooner guard Buddy Hield came out of the lockerroom after scoring 46 points for an ESPN interview and was met with a standing ovation by the remaining fans. Wins over ranked opponents Baylor, Kentucky, Oklahoma (again), Texas and Iowa State built up the Jayhawks' RPI and secured their 12th consecutive Big 12 title.

The win over the Cyclones will always be special for me. That was my last game at Allen Fieldhouse as a broadcaster and the Jayhawk athletic department organized a nice celebration at halftime. Afterwards, Bill Self surprised me by recognizing me as the "fifth senior" participating in his last game. I was very much a senior. But seriously, it was extremely nice of Bill to recognize me and I am not surprised he did it. He is so good at expressing his appreciation for others. He always treated me as a member of the program. They say you should go out on top. I was 32-0 on senior nights.

The Kansas athletic department honored Bob Davis at the final game of the 2015-16 season.
Credit: Kansas Athletics

To show you how round the world is, my first game as the Kansas basketball play-by-play announcer was at the Great Alaska Shootout in 1984. There was a Manning (Danny) in the starting lineup and a Coach Manning on the bench (Ed). In my last home game, there was a Manning in the starting lineup (Evan) and a Coach Manning (Danny) in the crowd. Senior nights at Kansas are special. First of all, the Jayhawks haven't lost one since 1983. Second, there are 16,300 people who stay for the post-game, and lastly, the raw emotion of the seniors knowing they just played their last game in the fieldhouse is palpable.

A victory over Texas Tech on February 27 moved Kansas to a No. 1 ranking. Wins over Kansas State, Baylor and West Virginia in the league tournament secured a No. 1 seed at the Midwest Regional in Des Moines. The Jayhawks took down Austin Peay and Connecticut, then moved onto the Midwest Regional in Louisville. It was now setting in that my career would come to an end with a loss. In the Sweet 16 Kansas out-physicaled No. 18 Maryland, 79-63 coached by former Jayhawk Mark Turgeon.

Standing between Kansas and a second Final Four in four years was a talented Villanova team. The Wildcats seized control 10 minutes into the game and it wasn't until 13:24 left that the Jayhawks had retaken the lead. I'll never forget at halftime, CBS broadcaster Jim Nantz got up and came over, noting the 32-25 Villanova lead, and said to me: "we've got to get some more scoring to get you another game." With 8:42 Villanova took the lead for good, but it never got larger than five. The nail in the coffin came when Devonte Graham was called for a foul going for a loose ball with :34 left. The Wildcats hit 18 of 19 free throws, including all eight in the final 33 seconds. Kansas dug a hole by turning the ball over 16 times and were outscored from the line by 11 points.

The reality set in after I signed off that my broadcasting career was over.

Chapter 10 Sidebar: Within Earshot

There are times when something goes out over air as a result of someone -- not part of the broadcast team -- making a comment that got picked up by a mic. This is usually the result of crowd mics picking up this sound. It is truly one of the joys and perils of live radio.

With better equipment and delays, those instances are less frequent, but in my early days there were many voices on the broadcasts. In doing high school basketball at both Hays High and Thomas More Prep, my broadcast positions were literally among the fans. I not only had fan reaction go out, but people would come and say hello while I was on the air. I really did not mind either situation. When fans came by to say hello, they were just being their nice, friendly selves.

But I do recall a few instances where the "extra" voices got a reaction from the audience. I was doing an American Legion baseball game at Larks Park, a Works Project Administration baseball stadium built in 1940 in south Hays. It was constructed of native limestone, like the municipal pool, many buildings on campus and a few buildings in town. The public address announcer was Hank Speier, a great guy and big supporter of baseball in the community (the little league baseball complex on south Vine Street is named in his honor). I was doing the game and had recently purchased one of those wide-brim bucket hats. Well, the inning finished and Hank got up and took a stroll in the press box. I was actually still on air and Hank gave me a little pat on the back and said in a loud voice, "Bob's got a helluva hat there." For a few weeks, wherever I went, people were asking about my hat.

A few years later, I was in the press box at Lewis Field Stadium doing a Fort Hays State football game. John Smiley was the public address announcer at the time and his voice could be heard over the air, although it was somewhat muffled in the background. After one particularly ineffective play, John accidentally left his microphone on. He incredulously uttered, "why are you calling that play, coach?" The crowd and the audience heard it go out. It got quite a chuckle. And thanks to a good sense of humor on behalf of the coach, John kept his job.

When I moved onto KU, our basketball broadcast position for the first few years was next to the Kansas bench. Occasionally we'd get a look from the coaches asking if we agreed with an officials call. The position was good from the standpoint we could hear an occasional comment from a coach or player. It was bad from the standpoint that we were blocked from play from time to time.

One of the funniest player-coach interactions was between Iowa State guard Justus Thigpen and head coach Johnny Orr. The Jayhawks were on fire from the opening tip and were putting it on the Cyclones pretty good. It was in the first half and Thigpen was bringing the ball up the court and was being closely guarded. He was obviously frustrated and picked the ball up far from the basket, not too far from us. Suddenly he turns back to the bench and yells at Johnny Orr: "Coach!...Coach!... This shit ain't working!" Orr called timeout, gave Thigpen a tongue lashing and sat his star for the rest of the game. Kansas won 91-60.

We later learned that Orr and Thigpen had a heated conversation on the bus on the way to the Lawrence Airport, and then another talk the next day in Ames. With No. 2 Oklahoma State coming to Hilton Coliseum on Saturday and an NCAA bid slipping away, the prospects weren't looking too good for the Cyclones. The Cowboys of Byron Houston, Bryant Reeves, Darwyn Alexander and Corey Alexander were up by 18 at halftime. But all's well that ends well. Thigpen, who was held out of the starting lineup, hit all seven of his second-half field goals for an 84-83 overtime win. He would go on to be named Big Eight Player of the Week.

We were probably next to the bench on the road, more than at home. On the road, you're more likely to get into a conversation with the head coach because you are one of the few friendly faces in the arena. I remember we were playing on the West Coast and had Pac 10 officials working the game. Roy Williams was not particularly fond of a certain referee and after a call went against the Jayhawks, he whirled around walked up to us during action with fists clenched to his side and snarled: "Have we *ever* won a game with him?"

Another light-hearted moment came in Norman where the Jayhawks and Sooners were locked in a heated battle. The game was physical and a bit chippy. Just before the start of the second half, veteran official Rick Wulkow brought the two coaches together to tell them they were going to call it a bit tighter so the game wouldn't get away. Fans might remember Wulkow, who was a fine gentleman and executive director of the Iowa High School Activities Association, was missing most of his right index finger because of a farming accident. So, if he had a foul on number 11 or had to signal a one-and-one, he did it by showing his two pinky fingers. The conversation with Roy Williams and Billy Tubbs was just a few feet away from Max and me.

Rick is extremely serious in starting the conversation and so were both coaches as they listened -- until all of the sudden Billy Tubbs interrupts and says (forgive me for taking some literary license here): "Hey Rick. If they could sew that 'thing' back on John Bobbitt, why couldn't they do the same for your finger?" The three broke out in laughter and the game was played without further incident.

Sometimes, the interesting comments came from the broadcasters themselves. We've all been there.

Working with Max was interesting because Max was interesting. During a game he might point out some dignitary in the stands, the news of the day, or an oddity that might or might not have anything to do with the game. One such moment happened shortly after KU signed the new zillion dollar deal with Nike. There was so much hoopla about the new uniforms for the Jayhawk sports teams. The first home basketball game the team is playing in these beautiful new white uniforms. All of a sudden, in the middle of the game, Max says, "What's that little checkmark on their shirts?" I said, "Well, that's the Nike swoosh that they've spent about a billion dollars on."

As the football sideline reporter, you see things a bit differently than you do up in the booth. In a game versus Texas Tech in Lawrence, the Jayhawks were playing toe-to-toe with the heavily favored Red Raiders. At that time, Tech head coach Mike Leach had employed the use of the wide receiver screen with great frequency. It eventually became a part of almost everyone's playcalling, but at this point it was still unique. Kansas was doing a great job getting its hands up and deflecting these passes. After it happened for maybe the third or fourth time, David Lawrence became excited and blurted into his microphone interrupting Max and myself: "the reason the Raiders cannot move the ball is because the Jayhawk defenders are getting their hands on (quarterback) Sonny Cumbie's balls!"

There was a slight pause in the broadcast as I had one of those "did he just say what I think he said" moments. Next to me, Max was giggling like a little child. That was not unusual. Even at 70-plus, Max was a little kid. He was so tied in knots that I had to transition out of it, even though I too let out a chuckle. I simply said, "And *that*, ladies and gentlemen, is live radio. Live with it."

David showed he was a quick study as a sideline analyst. We were playing Missouri at Columbia and I noted the visiting team had moved from in front of the

Tigers' student section, to the other side of the stadium where the alumni sat. When patrolling the sidelines in front of the students, David was occasionally the target of empty liquor bottles. During the broadcast I noted that change and suggested David would not be in the line of fire anymore. To which he replied: "My guess is the bottles will still come. But I do expect they will represent a higher grade of whiskey."

Baseball lends itself to many interesting on air comments because the games tend to be longer, there is more time for conversation and there are so many games. This was long before my time, but many longtime Royals fans will remember Denny Matthews and his promotion of Guy's snack foods. He closed the promo by saying, "so the next time you are at the store, grab some Guy's nuts." That line gained a life of its own over the years.

I was working on television with Paul Splittorff and one of the objectives he had was to eventually be able to do play-by-play in addition to color analysis. So we worked him in, starting with what we call "drop-ins." Those are the short 15-to-30 second promotional messages you hear between batters or during a mound visit. They are written on index cards and the producer hands them to you and you fire away. You generally go over them before the game, but you don't have time to review them once the game starts.. So Paul gets the card and begins to read it. *"The First Five Thousand Fans Should Flock to Kauffman Stadium to get Your Free Flag Friday Night."*

You can imagine getting tongue tied reading that. Well, Paul was determined to get it right and kept getting in deeper and deeper as he repeated it. The 15-second read was well past 30 by now and I am frantically giving him the cut signal. Being the competitor he was, he crumpled up the card, took off his head set, and had some choice words for himself. All the while, the rest of us are busting a gut.

We were at old Tiger Stadium and Juan Encarnacion is coming up to bat for the Tigers. Well, the name doesn't look that hard to pronounce, but it does not roll off the tongue easily. It is almost as if your jaw locks up trying to get it out. Well, one time it took awhile for Splitt to get it right. He could not get past the "En-car-nnnnnnn" before he looked like he needed someone to do the Heimlich Maneuver on him. Of course, it doesn't help when the guys in the truck are laughing their butts off. No one is safe with those guys.

As I noted, every broadcaster or announcer has been there. And when you find out even the top dogs in the business do it, you realize your screw ups aren't so bad. The late Bob Sheppard was the longtime public address announcer for the New York Yankees. He had that deep voice that absolutely scared the hell out of you. I asked him if he ever had a "hot mic" moment where something went out erroneously. He told me about the time he was doing the Army-Navy football game and President Kennedy was in attendance. As is the practice, the President sits on one side for the first half, and at halftime moves to the other side for the second half. The day was bitterly cold, but Kennedy was only wearing a top coat and no hat or headgear. Thinking his microphone was off, Sheppard remarked to a full stadium: "can you believe the President is not wearing a hat!"

Chapter 10: Friends of Bob

Bill Self: Head Basketball Coach, Kansas, 2004 - Present. Bob is excellence. He's the best I have heard. But he is even a better person than he was a broadcaster. I enjoyed being around him and miss him now that he is not around us on a daily basis. I miss his dry humor as much as anything. He loved telling jokes and was so good at it. And, he was a great storyteller and the consummate pro. Bob called it like he saw it, and that was refreshing. If things were going well, there was definitely a little more "umph" in the broadcast. I know our fans loved that about him.

We got along so well because we both understood each other so well. Bob got me, and I got him. He knew when to interject, and when to chill and listen. I felt and acted the same way when I was around him. I knew when to step back and let him do his job. It was comfortable working with him.

I knew Bob when I was a graduate assistant in '85-86, but I really didn't "get" him until I came back as the head coach and understood the magnitude of his relationship with the people of the state of Kansas. I came to realize rather quickly the impact the broadcasters had on the people, especially in the rural areas where there might not be access to cable or they were far from Lawrence and could not get to games very often. Being the "Voice of the Jayhawks" had stature and of course he was so good and had such great respect. He and Max were together for 22 years and I doubt you'll ever see that again.

I loved the lunches I had with the media after our weekly press conferences during the season. I'd gather with our core media and we'd sit around the table and talk about anything and everything: politics, sports, you name it. And, of course solving the world's problems in the process. A lot of times we wouldn't even talk about college basketball. Bob always sat to my immediate right and was always a big part of the conversation.

I probably listened to him do Royals baseball more than his doing us. He was really good at baseball. He was fun to listen to. I would listen to clips of our games, but to me the biggest compliment of how good he was came from what people would tell me about his calls. My wife Cindy can be a tough critic, and she thought he was great.

There is one clip which will always stick with me and that was in the national champion game against Memphis. When our team ran out on the court Bob talked about the potential for this team to be mentioned alongside the '52 team and the '88 team. He lists the names of Lovellette and Hoglund and Lienhard and Kenney and Hoag; and then he transitions to Manning and Piper and Newton and Gueldner and Pritchard; and then our guys. For someone who got to know the guys on the '52 team, and then was involved in coaching or recruiting everyone on the '88 team, hearing that just reinforced the importance of the legacy of the program.

John Morris: Baylor Radio Network. I first knew of Bob and his work from the NCAA Women's Basketball Championships he would do for national radio. When Kansas and Baylor became charter members of the Big 12 Conference, I was really looking forward to meeting and getting to know Bob when the Jayhawks and Bears met. He is truly one of the guys that I admire the most in this profession. Each year at the Big 12 Basketball Tournament the "Big 12 Voices" get together for dinner the night before the tournament begins. It is one of the few times we are mostly all in the same city at the same time and it has become a highlight event on our yearly calendar. You can imagine with this group the stories that are being told around the table but a common theme every year is the tremendous respect all of us have for Bob Davis. Even in retirement, we make sure Bob joins us for dinner each year and he remains the best storyteller in the group. Retired or not, Bob will always be a valued member of our Big 12 broadcasters fraternity to which Bob would quip "Why would I want to be part of a fraternity that would have me as a member?"

John Morris: Baylor Radio Network. It was February 4, 2014, and the Kansas Jayhawks defeated the Baylor Bears in a Big 12 Conference game in the Ferrell Center in Waco, Texas. KU and BU are both schools whose multimedia rights were held at the time by IMG now Learfield – IMG College. Earlier that week, all the IMG announcers, both play by play and color, had received a strongly worded memo from Chris Ferris who was head of the radio division for IMG clearly stating in no uncertain terms that announcers should not drink before game broadcasts. Apparently that had been an issue at some IMG school or schools to the point that Chris felt the need to send out the memo.

Well Bob and Greg Gurley, and Pat Nunley and I had a good laugh about it before the game then we all went to work. Kansas won the game, but afterward there was bad weather in Lawrence or Topeka so the KU travelling party had to spend the night in Waco instead of returning immediately after the game on its charter. That prompted a late-night voicemail message from Bob asking if it was okay to have a drink that night since it was after the game or was it technically before the next game so they couldn't. I have kept the voicemail message on my phone to this day.

Chris Piper: Basketball, Kansas, 1984-88; Jayhawk Television Network, ESPN+, Jayhawk Radio Network, 2007-12. In my time being associated with KU, the three basketball coaches have been Larry Brown, Roy Williams and Bill Self. Great coaches. Yet, very different personalities. Completely different. But they had two things in common. First, they all adhered to that Kansas basketball philosophy of Phog Allen and Dean Smith of moving the ball from side to side. Ball movement and unselfish play is important. And second, they see everything and tolerate no slippage. Coaching is exhausting, especially when you are like those three where the attention to detail is so great. That is why they are winners.

Back to the Station

UNLIKE MY TIME in Hays, my role as play-by-play broadcaster for Kansas did not include a position at a radio station. That has been one of the biggest changes in the industry as colleges began creating their own networks that weren't tied to a particular radio station.

Unless you were well off financially, being a college play-by-play broadcaster was not a full-time job. Many of my peers were employees of athletic departments as directors of broadcasting. That is becoming more popular as digital audio and video production has ramped up. Some were in private business. And, others worked at radio stations in various capacities. Shortly after we moved to Lawrence, I took an advertising sales position with KLWN in Lawrence. The owners were the Booth family, among the many great broadcast pioneers in the state of Kansas.

One day I went to lunch with Shannon Zenger and Jack Layton, both who worked for an advertising agency in Kansas City. If those names sound familiar, they should. Shannon was the older sister of future Kansas Athletics Director Sheahon Zenger. Jack was the Royals public address announcer. They mentioned that KMBZ radio in Kansas City was going to hire for a sports director position. That was only about half a year after I began working at KLWN, but the Booths were understanding. I applied for the job, went to the station to read some copy and was offered the position shortly thereafter.

KMBZ was a well-respected operation with a long history in the Kansas City market. Ray Dunaway was a morning host and was such a talent. He would move to Hartford, Conn., and was replaced by Noel Heckerson. Noel is from Kansas City, but had spent time on both coasts and is a legend in the Kansas City radio scene. Like Dunaway, he was an outstanding talent. He had a great personality and sense of humor. Ellen Schenk was a co-host, too. She was a Missouri fan, but that was the only bad mark on her resume. She was really good. We also had who I consider to be one of the best "street" reporters I had ever heard, Dan Verbeck. He was dogged and determined. If anyone was going to get the story, he was.

Growing up in the golden age of radio and being a radio junkie, I loved being back in the studio. As you might imagine, the newsroom for a news talk station in a metropolitan area is a beehive of activity. There was always something going on in the city and reporters were coming and going.

The station was interested in ramping up its sports production as it had the broadcast rights for the Kansas City Royals and the Kansas Jayhawks. They already had a sports talk radio show. Don Burley actually started it in the 1970s, was followed by Kevin Wall and John Doolittle, then Don Fortune followed. I would be a guest on the talk show, and I hosted or co-hosted it a handful of times. But truthfully, I was not interested in being a talk show host. I did not have the time for it, nor did I have the personality. In my opinion, to be a good talk show host, you could not afford to be too tied down by other obligations. You had to be free to do research and to get to a variety of sporting events and activities. Then of course, there was the need to be a personality with appearances on onsite broadcasts. My work at KU precluded me from doing that.

My role was to do the morning sports report, aired two times each hour on the hour, between 5 and 8 a.m. I would also host a Sunday night radio show with Kansas City Royals Manager Dick Howser. That lasted a year because the logistics just did not work. Sunday was often a get-away day, so the team was involved in travel. Howser was an excellent manager and had a good personality, but the timing was tough for him as well. Of course, the positive that season was the Royals won the 1985 World Series.

I would later host pre- and post-game shows for Royals broadcasts with Paul Splittorff, although it was not part of the Royals Radio Network. I had actually met Paul in Hays when he was part of the Royals Caravan program in the offseason. The franchise would send players and staff to cities of network affiliates in the Midwest and visit with fans and take photos. It was essentially a goodwill tour, but important for ticket sales because the Royals attracted fans from all over the region. Paul was sent to Hays a few times and I got to meet him and develop a bit of a relationship.

Splitt, as he was known, was tremendous to work with. When the Royals were in town, we did the shows at the stadium. We'd hole up in a small booth and talk baseball and broadcasting. I learned so much about the game from him. And I tried to share as much as I could about broadcasting. Paul wanted to be known as a broadcaster. He did not want to be thought of as a former player just hanging around the ballpark. When the Royals were on the road, we worked out of the KMBZ studio. We'd take a few calls, but the focus was on the interviews and analysis.

Paul would actually further hone his skills by broadcasting Blue Springs High School athletics on local radio. He worked hard and became a good broadcaster. When WDAF won the rights to televise Royals games in 1988, he was added as an analyst. He would continue in that role until his passing in 2011. He also added to his schedule games as a basketball analyst for the Jayhawk Network and the Big 12 Conference Network.

By now, you are probably wondering about my schedule given I did KU games, worked at KMBZ and did Royals pre- and post-game shows. My first priority was to KU, so I did not miss any games on account of the Royals schedule when I started doing games in 1997. The only conflicts were with KU football games in August and September. The alarm came early at 3 a.m. and I would drive from Lawrence to Kansas City Monday through Friday to do my sportscasts. I would stay in Kansas City to do the pre- and post-game shows, then get back home by midnight. I was not really an early, early morning person, so it could wear on a person. I'm not too proud to admit it was a grind at times.

Of course, when I was on the road with the Jayhawks, my studio was my hotel room. To make sure Max got his sleep, my roomies were usually Richard Konzem, Doug Vance and Jeff Bollig of the athletic department. I tried to be as discreet as possible, but they often had to hear my reports in the wee hours of the morning. They were great about it. It was always a bonus to have a hotel room where the bathroom had a phone. It would become my studio.

It would not be unusual for me to grab a bit of sleep on a couch at KMBZ after getting home late from a Jayhawk or Royal road trip. I'd go straight into the station to do the reports. I worked at KMBZ for 20 years. I truly enjoyed my time there, working with some great people and making numerous friends in the Kansas City media market.

Chapter 11: Friends of Bob

Noel Heckerson: Kansas City radio personality, 1960-2005. Bob is an easy guy to get to know. After you've been with him for only a short period of time, it is as if you've been friends for years. There's no pretense -- with Bob, what you see is what you get. He is a fun kind of a person who makes any radio newsroom, any place really, a happy place to be. We worked together at KMBC on what they call the drive time shift -- those folks who are going to work in the morning. Bob not only has an easy going way about him, but his personality rubs off. If you were moving at half speed when you got there around four in the morning, Bob Davis and a few cups of coffee got you going.

Bob has an incredible storehouse of jokes piled away in his memory. I don't think he's forgotten any joke he's ever heard. The thing that is funny is he and I see each other for the first time in the morning and he had a certain smile. I said to myself, "hmmm" I betcha Bob has a new joke. We didn't take ourselves all that seriously, but at the same time thrived on being what they call, in our business anyway, consummate professionals. I enjoyed hosting parties at our house in Mission. They included snacks, drinks, music and plenty of stories. More than a few times I'd walk up to a lively group and there'd be a bunch of folks. And, there was Bob, right in the middle telling the assembled about his latest road trip and for sure he added a joke.

Whenever the topic turns to radio play-by-play announcers, so many people praise Bob's style, knowledge, personality and certainly his way with words. There are people who can recall what Bob said word for word during key moments in crucial games, basketball, football or baseball.

My two sons and I were recently in Lawrence and we decided to go by and visit Allen Fieldhouse. Even though it was off season, all the lights were on, but there was a quiet in the stands. Anyway, as we looked around and remembered all the great games. My son left me to myself for a while and I closed my eyes for a bit. And, you bet, I could hear that old familiar voice from the KU courtside -- Bob Davis.

Nate Bukaty: Football Sideline Reporter, Jayhawk Network, 2001-15. As a kid who grew up listening to Kansas football and basketball on the radio, it was an absolute thrill for me to get the opportunity to work with Bob for 15 years. I had set the goal of becoming a sports broadcaster when I was in fifth grade, and Bob was always one of the role models I admired. You have to remember that back in those days (late 80s, early 90s) not every game was on television. In fact, if my memory serves correctly, the majority of KU football games were not televised, so many of my memories of Kansas Football in those days were pictures painted by Bob, Max and David. I was a couple of years out of college when I began to get the opportunity to work with and around Bob, at News Radio 980 KMBZ.

At that time, Bob was announcing play-by-play for the Royals, Kansas football, and Kansas basketball, as well as anchoring the morning sports at KMBZ. It was an incredibly demanding work schedule, yet I never heard Bob complain about it. In fact, I remember, as a young aspiring broadcaster at that time, I asked Bob how he was able to juggle so many jobs, on such little sleep. "Oh, let's be honest," he laughed, "this work isn't that hard. There's no heavy lifting involved." So, the first lesson I really learned from Bob was work ethic. Maybe more importantly, he taught me perspective to remember: what we do for a living is a labor of love. It's not actually "work." If we ever find ourselves complaining about the hours, we should probably find something else to do. There are a lot of people who would love to get paid to talk sports for a living.

Always Royal

BASEBALL HAS ALWAYS been my first love -- when it comes to sports.

I loved everything about the game, the traditions, the strategy and the setting. When my dad was covering the Class D Independence Yankees for the *Independence Reporter*, I eagerly looked forward to going to the ballpark. Nothing like the green grass, the aroma of the popcorn, the crack of the bat and the pop of the mitt.

That passion was further fueled by my listening to major league games on the radio. The broadcasters were so good in describing the action. I felt like I was right there with them. It was something I decided I wanted to do, even at that young of age. As I grew older, I thought it was a heck of a deal to watch sports, talk about sports, and get paid doing it.

As professional and collegiate sports organizations sought to increase revenues, broadcast rights grew to be a prime source. No only as part of national packages, but through their own productions. Radio networks were well established, but television was beginning to expand beyond local packages to regional sports networks. Fox Sports created a group of regional networks and almost every game was on television.

I came to the realization many years ago that I would likely not be a broadcaster for a major league team. I just did not fit into the path of how people make it to the majors in the broadcast industry. And I was okay with that. My experiences in Hays and now with KU were wonderful and fulfilling.

However, one day the phone rings and Paul Splittorff is on the other line. He tells me that Steve Busby would not be returning as the Royals television play-by-play announcer. Was I interested? Does Carter have pills? I met with a variety of officials from the network and the Royals, and got the job beginning with the 1997 season. My dream became a reality. And to make it even better, Paul would be my partner. I would do television from 1997-2007. From 2008-12 I did radio with Denny Matthews. I enjoyed both experiences and my partners were obviously pros.

Make no mistake, the Royals were not a successful franchise in my time broadcasting them. The only season where the organization was in a position to make the playoffs was 2003 when we were 83-79. Overall, I think it was four, 100-loss seasons, a 19-game losing streak, one manager, (Tony Muser) who wanted more whiskey drinkers and fewer milk-and-cookie guys. We had Tony Pena, who leaped into the shower fully clothed to inspire the troops, and we had Buddy Bell, who said, "'Don't ever say it can't get any worse because it can."

And worse it did get, but not from a wins and losses perspective. Splitt began to fight a private battle with oral cancer and it made it hard for him to do the games. It became public in mid-May 2011, and on May 25, 2011 he passed away. It was a crushing loss for me personally. He was a great friend and a heckuva broadcaster. He had been a member of the Royals organization in some form or fashion since he was drafted in the 25th round in 1968.

Paul Splittorff and Bob Davis had outstanding chemistry in the booth and were best of friends. Credit: Kansas City Royals.

Because I had worked with Splitt doing the pre-and post-game shows on KMBZ, we had a good feel for each other and how to broadcast the games. He was meticulous, prepared, focused and wanted to be known as a broadcaster. He purposely did not interject his career or past performances into the broadcast. He would take copious notes and make it a point to know the last detail about a team and its players. He feigned displeasure if you uncovered something he did not know.

One time we were doing a game in Minnesota and I had mentioned on air a particular note about a player. Suddenly, Paul was busy scouring his notes and looked panicked that he could not find this particular piece of information. He looked at me incredulously like "where in the hell did you pull that out from?" I just smiled, and pointed at the scoreboard where the information was displayed. After that, whenever anyone worked with Paul, they'd mention something and then point to the score-board with the grin of a Cheshire Cat. Paul was so good at sticking the needle in you, it felt good to get him back.

The broadcasts allowed us to bring the legends of the game to the fans. I remem-ber on one television pregame show for the Royals-Cardinals series we had both George Brett and Stan Musial on, arguably the two biggest names in the history of both franchises. The way they dissected hitting was amazing. And to top it off, Musial played the harmonica on air for us.

Another time, Splitt and I had legendary announcers Red Barber and Ernie Harwell on to talk about their broadcasting careers, especially their time together with the Brooklyn Dodgers. They talked about doing the games at the Polo Grounds, where they were virtually right right on top of the action. They had great fun talking about there being no bathroom on the top level and problems that caused.

Speaking of being on top of the play, old Tiger Stadium in Detroit gave you that feel. Being in the press box makes it seem like you can reach out and touch the catcher. We were closer to the game than I was at some high school games. In the middle of one game, Royals catcher Mike MacFarlane turned to the press box and looked up at us and yelled, "hey, can you keep it down up there. I'm trying to work!"

Mac was one of the good guys I encountered over the years with the Royals. And there were a lot of them. He was a no-nonsense player and one of the veteran leaders by the time I joined the network. He was winding down his career, but was certainly a positive influence on the younger guys.

The road trips could get long and the travel would get to you, but the radio and television guys were great fun. Outside of baseball, there was eating, many jokes and a lot of needling each other. We had a great time.

Our meals were never designed for those who were on a diet. The greasier the better -- and of course it was our responsibility to make sure the buffets always turned out to be a bargain. When we got served or arrived back at our table and saw the amount of food on the plate, Paul would remark, "this is a no bullshit meal!" Splitt would also make sure we treated the help who had to put up with the group at the various eating establishments well. He'd encourage a big tip when our server was in ear shot by saying, "we don't want to lose this one, let's make sure she is back the next time we come here."

Obviously, economics played a role in the ability to sign and retain talent. And, the ownership uncertainty that existed before the Glass family purchased the team in 2000 did not help. The lack of an owner and being a small-market team worked against the Royals. But I did not let the losing get me down. The broadcast team,

Royals administration, coaches and players were great people with whom to work. As Splitt and I would say, "someone has to do the games, it might as well be us."

I joined the Royals (1997) during a challenging time for the franchise. It was owned by the Greater Kansas City Charitable Foundation as part of a transition in ownership after Ewing Kauffman passed away. David Glass would chair the board overseeing the franchise, and Herk Robinson was the general manager. The managerial situation was even more tenuous. Bob Boone lasted through the all-star break that year. From a purely historical perspective, he was fun to talk with because his dad Ray, and his sons Aaron and Bret also played professionally. Boonie, as he was known, was a Stanford guy so his explanations and theories always had a bit of technicality to them. I remember we got into a discussion about how hard it must be for a catcher to chew tobacco while playing. He gave us a detailed description of the process used to keep the mask and gear from becoming full of tobacco spit.

Tony Muser followed Boone and was my favorite Royals manager to work with. He was unbelievably funny and very self-deprecating in his humor. The guys liked him because he was a hard worker as a player and manager. From a broadcaster perspective, he always had time for you. Splitt and I would go down to his office before the game and one of us would peek our heads into his office and ask: "You open for bullshit?" He'd give us this wry smile and say, "get your ass in here." We'd have great conversations. He loved talking baseball. After the game, he would regularly stop by the production truck in the parking lot as would Paul and I. We'd rehash the game, mixing a few jokes and stories. With any bit of talent, he would have been successful.

It had been a while since I was on television on a regular basis, so I had to brush up on a few things in that first season. I was not concerned about the actual broadcast differences such as letting the pictures tell the story on television. My concerns were more about the on-air presence and to some degree the flow of the broadcast. I have to admit there were some nerves and butterflies leading up to that first game, but we had an excellent crew headed up by producer Kevin Shank. He made it so easy.

My first game would be opening day versus Baltimore at Oriole Park at Camden Yards. At our workout the day before I noticed there were law enforcement officials everywhere, including stationed on the roof of the stadium with rifles in hand. We came to find out that President Bill Clinton was coming to the game. So we got to the ballpark the next day: excited for opening day, excited to do my first game, and excited for the pomp and circumstance. The weather was great, but curiously started to hear rumblings that the game might be postponed. It was ultimately called, and later we found out for what I believe was a first -- it was called because of the potential for high winds.

We were all a little dubious of that reasoning. A game called for weather that **might** happen? More likely was the fact that the Orioles' Brady Anderson and Mike

Mussina were not quite ready to go. I was crushed. You get ready for a big game, and then find it's cancelled and you have to come back the next day and do it all over.

So the next day, April Fools no less, the Orioles take the first game of the season, winning 4-2. Anderson was 3-for-4 with a run scored and an RBI - he recovered quickly. Nevertheless, it was good to have game number one under my belt.

After the 1997 season, the Royals had the opportunity to move to the National League, but declined even though the Indians, White Sox and Twins all had good young talent and offered a tougher option than the National League. I was happy tradition won out. Kansas City has always had an American League affiliation with the Blues as the Yankees Triple A farm club, followed by the A's and then the Royals. There was a slight improvement on the field in 1998 as the team went from 67-94 to 72-89.

The 1999 season was a significant step back record-wise at 64-97, but young talent was beginning to step forward. Jeff King retired abruptly early in the season, making way for a young Mike Sweeney to play regularly at 1B/DH. You might remember he was the last player to make the opening day roster that year (as a third catcher) as he would have been exposed to waivers. He went on to hit .322 with 44 doubles, 22 homers and 102 RBI.

Sweeney was almost too good to be true as a person. If you hadn't seen him in a while you were going to get the biggest bear hug known to man. He was a heck of a hitter, and he was always so positive. If you were having a bad day, all you needed was a little Mike Sweeney. He was a deeply religious person and lived out his Catholic faith. When he retired, he bought over 300 bibles and had them individually engraved for everyone in the organization. He also signed them. It meant a great deal to me when he came to Allen Fieldhouse for my final home game as the Voice of the Jayhawks.

That year was also the season of "Dos Carlos" as rookies Beltran and Febles made the big league team. Beltran was the AL Rookie of the Year hitting .293 with 22 HR, 108 RBI and 27 steals. He was the first 20/20 Royal since Bo Jackson a decade earlier. Defensively, Beltran was part of an outstanding outfield flanked by Johnny Damon and Jermaine Dye. Coming over from Atlanta, Dye hit .294 with 44 doubles, 27 homes and 119 RBI.

When I joined the Royals, Fred White was paired with Denny Matthews as the long-standing radio team. But in 1999, the Royals replaced Fred with Ryan Lefebvre, a young 28-year old broadcaster who had been with the Minnesota Twins organization. Fred took a position with the Royals alumni association, but the move was difficult for all involved in the beginning. Fred and I were friends from years ago when he worked at WIBW and did Kansas State games. Ryan, who came with great credentials, incurred the wrath of fans who had been long-time followers of the Royals.

But all of the credit goes to Fred and Ryan, who became close friends, for making it work and diffusing a potential lingering negative situation. Fred would later work for Metro Sports in Kansas City and actually returned to the Royals television network on a part-time basis. It was great to have him on the road with us. For our part, Splitt and I felt the best way to make Ryan feel at home and accepted was to treat him like everyone else. He would get needled and be the object of good-natured ribbing as well. By the way he dished it back out, I could tell he appreciated our approach.

I actually didn't do much broadcasting with Ryan. I was totally on the television side from 1997 to 2007, then moved to radio from 2008 to 2012 to work with Denny Matthews. When Denny pulled back a bit from some of the road trips, Ryan would move over when the games were not being televised. He was quite good from the beginning and became outstanding in a short time. I thoroughly enjoyed doing the games with him. And as good as he is as an announcer, he is a better person.

The 2000 season was one of significant change. David Glass bought the team and he elevated assistant GM Allard Baird to the top spot in June. Whether it was coincidence or not, the team improved to 77-85. Still, the small market challenges remained. There are those who felt Glass was not spending enough to build a winner, but give him credit for building a World Series champion. David Glass kept a low profile and did not particularly enjoy interacting with the media. But when you talked with him you understood how his country smarts made him such a successful businessman with Walmart. My lasting memory of Baird was him working 24/7 and always having a phone pressed to his ear. It was an unbelievably tough situation for him to be in to bring in and keep talent.

Beltran spent significant time on the DL, but Sweeney, Joe Randa (second-year hitting .300+), Damon and Dye kept hitting, setting a franchise record for runs scored at 879. Sweeney had a franchise record 144 RBI and hit .333. I contend that he and Manny Ramirez were the best two right-handed hitters in the AL during a three-to four-year stretch. Dye hit .321 with 41 doubles, 33 homers and 118 RBI. He was voted the first Royal to start the All-Star Game since Bo Jackson in 1989, and was the first Royal to win a Gold Glove since Bret Saberhagen and Bob Boone in 1989.

The 2001 season revealed the challenges of small-market teams. Damon was nearing free agency and traded to Oakland in the offseason before the season began. The team was 15 games below .500 before the end of May and the fire sale began. Dye and shortstop Rey Sanchez were traded, although Dye had a year left before being a free agent. I think the fanbase lost some hope with the departures as the team fell to 65-97.

There was not much reason for optimism in 2002, but there was still reason to enjoy Sweeney, Beltran and the steady Raul Ibanez. On the mound, Paul Byrd gave the Cy Young award a run with 17 wins, including seven complete games. But the bottom line was the squad was not winning. Muser was fired at the end of April as the team began 8-16.Tony Pena replaced Muser and had instant credibility as an outstanding former player in his time. He was full of chatter and constantly looking to motivate the team, hence the shower with his uniform on.

Ibanez had the nickname of "Mayor" because he was such a good leader and had the respect of everyone in the clubhouse. He was such a classy person and had great character. My guess is he will be an excellent manager or general manager in the future. You might remember the Royals brought him back late in the 2014 season just to be a positive influence in the clubhouse. He was the one who called the famous team meeting in Chicago where he told his young teammates that they were indeed capable of winning the pennant. And furthermore, he told them no one wanted to play them. I am not sure the Royals would have won the pennant without his influence.

Pena began 2003 with the slogan Nosotros Creemons -- "We Believe."

And believe they did. The team started the season with a nine-game winning streak, including a home opening 11th inning walk-off win thanks to a Ken Harvey home run. The record would improve to 16-3 and the team jumped to a 7.5 game lead in May. It fell to second place in June, but rebounded with a 10-3 start in July to retake the 7.5 game advantage. They would hold onto the lead until that last game of August, finishing in three games back of the White Sox at 83-79.

Among the bright spots was shortstop Angel Berrora, who earned AL Rookie-of-the-Year honors, hitting .287 with 17 HR, 73 RBI and 21 SB. An unconventional 29 pitchers took the mound, including 15 different starters. We even had a little fun with Jose Lima "Time" -- signed out of the Independent Atlantic League. Pena earned AL Manager-of-the-Year recognition.

In the broadcast booth, the Royals formed an in-house television network (Royals Sports Television Network), one of few such arrangements in the majors. We would televise more games, especially from home. It was a difficult sell because cable companies were reluctant to incur the additional fee that would be passed along to a wary fanbase.

The 2004 campaign had great build-up and a 9-7 opening day win did nothing to dampen the spirits. The White Sox had a 7-3 lead in the bottom of the ninth, but a three-run Mendy Lopez game-tying homer followed by a two-run Beltran walk-off triggered delirium on the field and the stands. But the bottom fell out. Veteran sign-ees Benito Santiago and Juan Gonzalez did not pay off as they played only 49 and 33 games, respectively. The team started 8-20. Seeing free agency on the horizon, Beltran was traded in late July. The team finished 58-104.

Things did not get much better in 2005 after an 8-25 start, Pena was let go on May 10 and replaced by Buddy Bell. Like Boone, Buddy was a member of a three-generation family to play in the majors. I really liked Buddy. He was a nice man and cordial. He had an excellent sense of humor. He got worn down by the losing. But he never let it affect how he dealt with people. There was a franchise record 19-game losing streak from July 26 - August 19, and a second-straight 100-loss season ensued at 56-106. The bright spot might have been drafting Nebraska standout Alex Gordon with the second pick in the June draft.

Dayton Moore replaced Baird as the GM in 2006 and benefited from a better ownership situation that started to spend more money on attracting and keeping talent. I think Moore was more comfortable than Baird in the position. Some of that had to do with his being a disciple of former Royals GM John Schuerholtz, working with him in Atlanta. John is still revered in Kansas City and in the organization. The other thing Dayton had going for him is he knew the region. He was born in Wichita and moved away after kindergarten, but came back to Garden City Community College to play baseball and became a Royals fan. You might remember the story where he and his college roommate drove to watch game seven of the 1985 World Series. Tickets on the open market were too expensive, so they ended up watching from their car parked on the shoulder of I-70.

Moore is one heck of a gentleman. You could tell early on that he would be a good fit. He has a certain magnetism about him. People are attracted to him in a way that commands respect and attention. But he doesn't have an oversized ego, is easily approachable and relates well with people. He is also heavily involved in the Kansas City community. The combination of David Glass and Dayton Moore will be held in high regard forever for delivering the excitement of 2014 and 2015.

The team started 10-35 and for all intents and purposes, the season was over. The only record set was for most letters in the last name of the right side of the infield with Gold Glove winner Mark Grudzielanek at second and Doug Mientkiewicz at first. That's a combined 23 letters of last names. The Royals had the first draft pick and selected pitcher Luke Hochevar out of Tennessee.

For those of you keeping score at home, the Royals were 62-100, marking their third consecutive 100-loss season. During those years there were several unusual occurrences including a first baseman getting hit in the back by a throw from the outfield; an outfielder climbing the wall trying to prevent a home run, only to have the ball fall on the warning track; and two outfielders converging on a ball then looking at each other, and then jogging for the dugout while the ball landed behind them.

As difficult as it was for the owners, management, players and fans to go through the losing, I felt for the managers. They didn't go to battle with the talent or experience to compete. The season is long and it can be draining. And everyday, they had to face the media and keep a positive attitude.

The long climb out of the cellar began in 2007. Moore brought in veteran pitcher Gil Meche and signed him to a five-year $55 million salary, matching the franchise record of Sweeney. Gordon was inserted as the starting third baseman and Billy Butler's bat was added as designated hitter. The farm system was being rebuilt and with the No. 2 pick in the draft, the Royals tabbed third baseman Mike Moustakas. There was a seven-game improvement to 69-93.

In 2008, there were changes in the dugout as Trey Hillman replaced Bell as manager. He was somewhat of an unusual hire because he had no experience in the majors and was the first manager ever to be hired from the Japanese Baseball League. Hillman was a good athlete. There would be times when he went out to argue a call that he did not use the steps, he just hopped the railing and charged the umpires. He would also take a unicycle out to the warning track and ride it to keep in shape. Another change was in the press box as I moved over from the TV booth to radio. While I would miss working with Splitt, I was happy to work with someone as talented and respected as Denny Matthews.

Bob Davis and Denny Matthews worked together to broadcast Kansas City Royals games on radio from 2008-12. Credit: Bob Davis

The steady improvement continued - I believe because the powder blue jerseys returned -- and the club finished at 75-87 in Hillman's inaugural season. Talent continued to be added as first baseman Eric Hosmer was the No. 3 player taken in the draft.

The next season was one of investment. Facility-wise, there was a major renovation of Kauffman Stadium completed in time for Opening Day 2009. It was an impressive renovation and completely transformed the outfield look and experience.

The big move before the season was to sign pitcher Zack Greinke to a four-year extension. He had one of the best seasons for a Royals pitcher with a 38-inning scoreless streak (beginning in 2008) and led the league in ERA. He would go on to win the Cy Young Award and was one of the best young athletes to play for the Royals in my opinion. He could have been a position player, he was that good. I never got to know him well and was aware he did suffer from anxiety-related issues. You had the feeling he was never going to be a long-term Royal. I always had concern for his well-being. He was so young and it was obviously a tough situation for him.

The team started 18-11, but lost 20 of 25, and was out of the race early. The team took a step back to 65-97.

The 2010 season is when you can trace the championship drive of 2013-14-15. Moore reached back to his Atlanta roots to hire Ned Yost to replace Hillman in May. It was not a surprising hire as during the winter, he was signed by Moore to be a special assistant to the club. He would be entrusted with developing the young players drafted and signed in recent years. Yost was an old-school manager who ran a tight ship. He was liked by the players because he never publicly demeaned or criticized them. His job was to build them up.

Another area of improvement was the farm system where it was returning to the strength it had in the 1970s and 80s. It was regarded among the best, if not the best, in baseball. There was slight improvement as the team went 67-95.

Prior to the 2011 season, at his request, Greinke was traded to Milwaukee -- which brought four players including Alcides Escobar and Lorenzo Cain. Both cracked the starting lineup. That added to the influx of young talent that included Alex Gordon, Billy Butler, Eric Hosmer, Salvador Perez and Mike Moustakas.

Interestingly, our son Steven, who broadcast games in the Royals minor league system, actually got to see the potential of Gordon, Moustakas, Perez and Hosmer before I did. He had Moustakas and Hosmer at Idaho Falls (Rookie League) and Northwest Arkansas (Double A), while Gordon and Salvy also played at Northwest Arkansas. That led Hosmer to keep the Davises straight by calling the young kid Steven and referring to me, the old man, as Mr. Davis.

Gordon, who moved to left field in 2010, proved to be a quick study. He won his first Gold Glove, recording an impressive 20 assists. The team took its lumps, but you knew the young players were going to be good. They were competitive on the field and getting better. I thought their 71-91 record did not reflect the improvement from the previous year.

My last season in the booth was 2012. I was looking forward to an enjoyable year but did not have expectations of significant improvement in terms of wins and losses. I probably mirrored the fans in that we were content to see development as a group that would lead to future success. Perhaps the biggest downer was the poor start with a 12-game losing streak in April. The team did have a winning record in May, June and August - but the final record was only 72-90.

The season was also an opportunity to show off the shiny new renovations to Kauffman Stadium with the Major League Baseball All-Star Game. The weekend got off to a great start with the first time the MLB Futures Game was sold out. Three Royals farmhands participated and George Brett managed the U.S. Team. Billy Butler was selected as the Royal representative to the game but was not chosen by captain Robinson Cano to participate in the Home Run Derby, despite Cano saying he would likely select someone from the hometown team. As result, Cano was roundly booed by the fans every time he was introduced at events. He had a sub-par derby and game.

That event was the highlight of my final season. You could see Yost and the youngsters were headed in the right direction. He would lead the team to an 86-76 record in 2013, the Royals' first winning season since 2003. With 16 years in the books for the Royals, it was time to pull back. I had left KMBZ in 2006 and the timing was right for me to step down broadcasting the Royals. I was 68 years old and had put on a lot of miles with the Jayhawks and Royals in over years. It was a great run and obviously a dream come true to do Major League Baseball. I'll always be Royal.

Chapter 12 Friends of Bob

Lynn Splittorff: Wife of the late Paul Splittorff, Kansas City Royals, 1971-85; Royals Broadcaster, 1988-2011. They (Davis and Splittorff) were great friends long before working together announcing the Royals. They met in the early 70s during a Royals Caravan in Hays and became friends when Paul started doing Big Eight and then Big 12 basketball games. Paul thought the world of 'Bobby D' as he called him. He would always remark about Bob's wonderful sense of humor and being so quick-witted. I thought they played off each other remarkably well, both on and off the screen. They were truly special friends.

But they also liked to have fun at each other's expense. Paul and Bob were on a trip to our property in northern Minnesota. They drove up on an off day playing the Twins. Bob was impressed with the lake property and asked if there were bears there. Here is how that conversation went:

Bob: Are there any Bears on the property?

Paul: Yes

Bob: Are they fast?

Paul: Yes

Bob: What happens if one comes after us?

Paul: We run

Bob: You think we can outrun a bear?

Paul: I don't need to run fast, I just have to run faster than you!

Denny Matthews: Kansas City Royals Radio Broadcaster, 1969 - Present. When Bob came over from television in 2008 it was about as smooth a transition as there could be for the both of us. Obviously, we both knew each other and how each other broadcast games. There was no stepping on each other. Bob knows baseball so well. When it's 2-1 in the bottom of the eighth, your focus is on every pitch. If it's 10-1, then you're doing everything to keep the listener engaged. That is when it's time to tell the story. Bob knew exactly what to say and when to say it. I thought we played well off each other. Bob is quick and has a great sense of humor. There was good chemistry. Interestingly, we both share the influence of Buddy Blattner. Of course, I started with the Royals in 1969 with Buddy. And Bob spent his youth, teens and then into his early professional years listening to Buddy. There weren't many as good as Buddy. Bob and I came up when radio was the only means to get live baseball short of being there in the stadium, so we have a deep appreciation of making sure the listener feels like they are there.

Stuart Shea: Author, *Calling the Game: Broadcasting Baseball From 1920 to Present.* (Bob) Davis and (Denny) Matthews, working together, presented baseball the way it was heard 30-40 years ago, with excitement and geniality, but without the unneeded flash or silly catchphrases.

Ryan Lefebvre, Kansas City Royals Broadcaster, 1999 - Present. The first thing that stands out about Bob is the voice. It's so powerful and classic. He reminds me of those legendary people I listened to on radio and TV growing up. When he spoke, you could feel your ribs vibrate. That is how powerful it was. He made all of us feel like we had the voice of a castrated goat. But there was nothing fake about it. He did not go into "anchorman voice" to call the games. Second, he was just so quick and witty. He'd come up with the perfect response right away. He left us saying, "why didn't we think of that?" I think that is the one thing a lot of people do not realize. He is extremely funny, but he respected the game and the listeners so much that he did not want to make it about himself or degrade it into a comedy. Sure, he had fun, but he did not go overboard. And lastly, he loved his teams. He knew he was broadcasting for a fan base who wanted to enjoy their teams. And that is okay. When you broadcast for a team, you want to be passionate about them, and Bob was.

All of this is supported by an extremely impressive work ethic. When he worked at KMBZ, he did two sports reports each hour at 5, 6, 7 and 8 a.m. This was while he was doing KU and much of it while he was doing the Royals. So think about this. He's done a night game at Kauffman, then gets on a bus and rides to the airport to catch a charter. We might get to the hotel anywhere from 1 - 2 or even later in the morning. While the rest of us are sleeping in, he's up and doing these reports for KMBZ. Plus, he had to lug this extra equipment around. Yet, not once did you hear him complain. He was just so dedicated to his work.

Ryan Lefebrve, Kansas City Royals Broadcaster, 1999 - Present. A highlight of the road trips were the meals. Bob and I had our favorite breakfast places to go around the league. In fact, I'll get a text from him today when we are on the road and he'll ask me how the food is right now at such-and-such a place because he knows I'll be there. We'd often go out as a group of the radio and television personnel and it was a constant string of jokes and needling each other. One day we are in Cincinnati and of course you have to go to Skyline Chili when you go there. In fact, it was right across from the hotel.

But Bob wanted to go to Montgomery Barbecue. Here are a bunch of guys from Kansas City who can get barbecue on any street corner anytime we want. However, we relented and ended up walking what seemed like a mile in the sweltering sun to get there. We arrive, all sweaty and tired. We've really been giving it to Bob by now, especially Splitt. So we go in and it is a nice place. We go around the table and everyone orders ribs or burnt ends or brisket. But not Bob. He says, "I think I'll have the BLT." I thought Splitt was going to come unglued. "What!" he said in an exasperated tone. "We walked all this way in the hot sun to a barbecue joint and you order a BLT?" Bob never lived that one down.

Tony Muser: Manager, Kansas City Royals, 1997 - 2002. I love Bob Davis. He is one of the best people I have worked with in my life. We did not have great success in Kansas City, but I loved the people there, and of course he was at the top of the list, along with Splitt (Paul Splittorff). When we first met, I could tell he was a person of high character. I grew up listening to Vin Scully and he had a voice that connected with the fans. Bob was the same way. He had that deep, calm and soothing voice. The kind you could listen to all day.

I gained a greater appreciation for what he and Paul did -- and really the whole television team -- when I was suspended for eight games after we got in a brawl with the Angels. I could be there for batting practice and pregame, but had to leave once the game started. (Television producers) Kevin Shank and Big John (John Dennison) said I could watch the game in the TV production truck, so that is where I kept up with the team. My God! You think it was wild in the dugout! There was so much yelling in that truck. It was more entertaining watching them than the games, sometimes. But it gave me a chance to watch Bob in action and I really saw just how good he was.

Kevin Kietzman: Kansas City Radio and Television Personality. I think the one thing that Bob Davis does better than anyone else is he lets you know how the game is going, not by telling you the score over and over again, but by his emotion and tone. It is not forced or canned. From a fan perspective, that is what you want. You want the story of what is happening and you don't want it bogged down by a lot of stats or jargon. Everyone one knows the famous expression Bob uses for KU basketball -- "*SWIIIISSSSSHHHH!*" But he does not use it every time a basket is made. He uses it when the situation dictates: a key shot, a long scoring run or even when the opponent makes a big play.

I think sometimes we get bogged down by what the consultants tell us. I remember listening to him do a Royals game and thinking he just did the best inning of baseball I have ever heard. I actually played it back on the air. Baseball is a slow sport. You need someone who can keep the listener engaged and interested. Bob did that so well. Sports broadcasting needs all the Bob Davis's it can get.

Kevin Shank: Producer, Royals Television, 1994-2011. I met Bob Davis when I started working Big Eight Conference basketball games in the mid-1980s then worked with him as producer for the Royals on television. He is one of the funniest persons I have ever met. But you never got all of that from him because he respected the game too much to make it a comedy show. He did not want to be silly. Actually, I think people would have absolutely loved it, but I understood and respected his perspective.

He had so much passion that he could tell the story of an ant crossing a table and make it exciting. He had this true gift to be so descriptive of the action. We used to laugh at him when we were on the road with the Royals and we'd be walking down the street in Chicago or San Francisco and he'd see something odd or unusual and would break out into play-by-play. *"There's a silver Honda and it swerves quickly to avoid the red light. He misses the lady in the crosswalk and everyone is okay."* We'd be laughing so hard, people would look at us like we were crazy.

But that was Bob's gift. He was not contrived. He was not full of cliches. A lot of guys would write out what they were going to say or have several catch phrases written down. That was not Bob. He could walk in, sit down and do a game. And one reason was because he was so prepared and did his homework. But he was also so quick and could process what was happening and be so smooth in getting it out.

On a personal note, my mother loved Bob's voice. I used to think she watched the games because she knew I was the producer. But she would always talk about Bob and his voice. But she was not the only one. He was popular with the fans - because of his demeanor and his voice. I admired his work ethic. When we went from

100 to 150 games on television, that meant Bob had no downtime between KU and the Royals. Plus he was doing the morning sports on KMBZ starting at 5 a.m. every morning. He was incredible from that standpoint. You have to remember there were some 100-loss teams and he made them fun to listen to. That wasn't easy.

Max Utsler, Associate Professor of Communications Emeritus, Kansas. When I first heard Bob Davis was hired by KU to be the new radio voice of Jayhawk football and basketball, I thought, "What a great hire." When I first heard Bob Davis was hired by the Royals to be their new TV broadcaster, I thought, "Huh?"

Sure, Bob had done baseball before. But it was always high school, NBC or low-level minor league, and it was always *for radio*. As a long-time broadcast professor (and admittedly an under-performing play-by-play guy myself), I understood the great difference between broadcasting a game on radio and doing a game on TV. I also knew the path most other Major League Baseball announcers had taken to get to "The Show." John Rooney had left Mizzou football and basketball to toil in Triple-A baseball in Oklahoma City and Louisville. Ryan Lefebvre had grown up in Major League ballparks and started his broadcasting career as a student at the University of Minnesota. Ex-players such as Mark Gubicza, Jeff Brantley, Bob Brenly, Buck Martinez, Ron Darling and Tim McCarver had their faces on a baseball card before they got their faces on TV.

So yes, Bob was an unusual hire. And, it's a credit for him to make it as he did. It didn't take long to see he knew his way around the diamond just as well as he knew his way around the court and field. And the return to the television booth? It's like he never left.

Mike Sweeney, Kansas City Royals, 1995-2007. I love Bob Davis. Being around Bob was a blessing because he was such a good person and so positive. He had an awesome personality and sense of humor. You just liked being around him. I feel like we were part of each other's families. I got to know Linda and Steven and enjoyed them very much. And because I had family all over the United States, they would watch or listen to Bob over the internet doing Royals games. He was a part of their lives. I would make it a point to listen to him doing KU games when I could because I just loved his voice. It was smooth and powerful.

One of the really wonderful moments for me came when I had the chance to go to KU for the senior night basketball game. That is such an emotional night, but this one was even more so because after the players talked, Coach Self introduced Bob after his final game. The crowd was so loud in cheering for Bob. That told me how much an impact he has had on people and how much they loved him. Emotion came over me and I had tears running down my cheeks. I remember giving him a hug that night and congratulating him, but really thanking him for being such a great friend. You look back at all the games he's done over the years and how many people he's touched. When you have that kind of impact, you are special.

Don Free: Kansas City Royals Radio Network Engineer, 1986-2017. I first met Bob when he came to KU and I was working in television production. I would help with the Big Eight Game of the Week. We hit it off then, and have been friends ever since. You won't find a nicer, more fun-loving guy than Bob. I was happy for him when he got the Royals job because he loved baseball. Even though he did television for the first 10 years or so, we always went to lunch as a group. You had better own a good sense of humor to be a part of that group. There was a lot of good-natured ribbing going on. Bob had an amazing sense of humor. Whenever he had a new joke, he'd get this big grin on his face like he was going to tell us a big secret. As he told the jokes, he'd have us in stitches.

As a broadcaster he was so good at telling the story. He did not get caught up in all of the stats. There's a saying, "I saw it on the radio." That is what I feel when I hear Bob. The picture he paints is so vivid. He was a true professional on the air, but I did get a kick out of the times he would get mad at a play that went wrong. He'd take the pencil he'd be scoring with and toss it. Sometimes up, sometimes down -- occasionally you had to take cover.

Another thing I appreciated was the great relationship Bob and Splitt (Paul Splittorff) had. They were inseparable. Both had a great sense of humor and they played off each other so well. They carried that over to doing the games. It was fun for the viewer I'm sure.

Mike Scott: Baseball 1970-72, Hays High School; Assistant Sports Information Director Baylor; Assistant Service Bureau Director Big Eight Conference. I was working for AT&T in Lawrence when I was transferred to Seattle, so I made it a point to connect with Bob when the Royals were in town. He invited me to sit in the booth with him and Paul Splittorff at Safeco Field as they called the game. What a great night that was hearing their stories and seeing them play off each other. It was there where I learned their rule about eating at buffets while on the road. They said, "it's up to us to make sure this buffet is a bargain!" What a rule to live by.

Mike Swanson: Vice President of Communications, Kansas City Royals. From a professional background, I don't think there's anybody who brought more excitement to the booth than Bob Davis. In the active sports, like basketball and football that he calls for Kansas, the excitement is already there on the field. In baseball, it takes a while to get excited. It's not every play that has that. But Bob could make the routine sound exciting.

My Partners

ONE OF THE best pieces of advice I received came early in my career from an industry veteran who told me that for the broadcast to be a success, you have to want your broadcast partner to look and sound good. There are plenty of stories where the two (or more) people broadcasting the game could not stand each other and it showed up in the broadcast.

In addition, there are so many people who are crucial to the success of the broadcast. Whether you work for a radio station or a network, there are the support people such as administrative personnel, the sales staff, off site and on site engineers and many others. The voice(s) are just one part of the puzzle.

For the first 16 years of my career in Hays, I really did not have a consistent analyst or partner. The station did not have the staffing and for someone in the community to do it, you had to not only have time to do the games, but put in some time to prepare. There were occasional contributors, however. When I moved to Lawrence, the crew got a bit bigger. I no longer had to do my own engineering on site. Plus there would be a color analyst and in football a sideline analyst. With the Royals, there was your primary partner, but there were a host of guests from time to time, plus a few who would move between radio and television as fill-ins.

But suffice it to say, I have been blessed to have worked with some great individuals over the years and they have all played a key role in any success I had. Here's a look at some of them:

Gene Jacobs, Fort Hays State Sports Information Director. While I did not have an "official" broadcast partner, Gene was as close as I came to having one in Hays. He was the Fort Hays State sports Information director -- or SID -- as they call them. Gene is perhaps the funniest person I know and a source of many of my jokes. He'd sit in with me on some Tiger broadcasts and some of those for the two local high schools. He was the first SID I worked with and so helpful to me in getting started in my career that I called him "Uncle Jake."

Speaking of SIDs, I would be remiss if I did not mention how valuable these individuals were for me and the other media members. SIDs are the professionals who provide the services to the media to help cover games in addition to their efforts to publicize the school's athletics departments. I worked with so many talented and dedicated professionals at Fort Hays State and Kansas. I am deeply indebted to them.

It is just not the SIDs for the teams you are covering. Those from other schools were extremely helpful. For them, it wasn't about competition, it was about service. SID titles have changed over the years, but not their value. Their counterparts on the professional level were equally helpful. There is so much that goes on behind the scenes and without these people, broadcasters could not do their jobs.

Max Falkenstien, University of Kansas broadcaster. Max was around so long and had so many experiences that he had *two* books written about him. He is so well-known among the Kansas fan base that I doubt there is anything I could add would be considered breaking new ground. But even as well-known as he was as an announcer, not as many listeners knew Max the person. First, he was astute financially. He would travel with a yellow legal pad where he tracked his commodity purchases and was quite good in trading - which was difficult to do. We would rib him about his yellow notepad, but it worked for him.

Second, he was not an athlete, but he was competitive as hell. That earned him the nickname "Game Little Fighter" often shortened to "Fighter." He stayed active riding a bike into his 80s - although Jayhawk hoops standout and classmate Jerry Waugh said, "you had to drive a stake in the ground to discern any movement." He loved a good golf match and had regular games at Topeka Country Club where a few dollars exchanged hands. He would regularly take coaches with him to play as a way to get to know them better and to let the coaches meet longtime Jayhawk fans. Max also had his handball group, which as the years passed, was composed of members younger than him. I believe his habits played a big role in extending his life to the age of 95. On the morning of game day on the road, Max and Roy Williams would often go on long walks.

Animals tugged at Max's heartstrings. When on the road, if our hotel had the Animal Channel, he would have to tune in on the happenings. When the Topeka Zoo acquired a baby gorilla, Max was on the plane to go get it. The gorilla would later be named in his honor. After Max retired I would text him photos of animals. It was my way of checking in with him.

Max was a man interested in current events and enjoyed discussing the issues of the day. He wasn't necessarily a debater and I would not say he was absorbed by politics. But he was learned and truly interested in what others thought. Accordingly, he liked to meet people and get to know them -- whether they were public figures or your average man on the street. He struck up friendships with officials, coaches (both sides), athletes, and media. But he'd do the same with cab drivers, servers at restaurants, security guards, cashiers, etc. He was a people person.

Lastly, Max liked being around young people. I know they kept him young at heart. He would strike up conversations with the athletes and always want to know where they were from and what they were studying. He was quick to give them common-sense financial advice to help them get off on the right foot. If wealth were measured by the breadth and depth of friendships he had, then Max might just have been the richest man to walk the earth.

Bob Newton, Engineer, Jayhawk Television Network. Forget Max and me, Bob Newton was the most important person on our broadcast. He was the technical guru who made everything work and kept it working. I thought it was ironic that Bob was not really a sports fan. He appreciated the effort required, but he was not a religious follower. It certainly did not affect the quality of his work. I appreciated that he was a professional and committed to our broadcasts sounding that way.

He joined the network when I did and retired after 34 years of outstanding work. I do know that it is not always easy taking care of the announcers and that you have to go with the flow due to changes in schedules and sometimes finicky coaches. I never saw Bob get overly upset or flustered. He was also well-known for having every tool or cord packed away in the event someone with a different network needed it. He helped many a broadcast crew by doing something that got them on air.

Bob was also heavily involved in the emergency preparedness system for Douglas County and the Lawrence Community Theater. He had immense pride in the community and was a true volunteer. If anyone asked Bob for help, he was ready and willing to give it.

Bob Davis was inducted into the Kansas Sports Hall of Fame in 2016.
Credit: Kansas Sports Hall of Fame (KSHOF)

David Lawrence, Jayhawk Network, 1994 to Present. When you look in the dictionary at the definition of "good guy" David is high on that list. An All-Big Eight Conference pick at offensive guard, David was a member of the 1981 Jayhawk Hall of Fame Bowl squad. A native of Parsons, he had spent some time doing color analysis for Sunflower Cablevision in Lawrence, which aired games on a delayed basis. He joined the Jayhawk Radio Network for football as a sideline reporter in 1994 and then became my partner in the press box when Max retired (for 2006 season). He also contributed to Kansas men's and women's basketball radio broadcasts.

I used to think no one was more passionate about Kansas football than the late Don Fambrough, but David gives him a run for his money. No one cares more than he does. Those years where the Jayhawks struggled were tough on him. I appreciate David's analysis. His knowledge and insight adds so much to the broadcast. He really knows what he is talking about. Of course, there are some times where he might get a little too excited, but I love his energy. And while he loves KU, he does not pull punches. He is honest in his critiques. David fit right in when he joined the team. He enjoyed a good joke, our needling each other and of course, any greasy spoon. He is also a hard worker when it comes to preparation. He is not a broadcaster by training, but he puts in the hours getting ready for broadcasts.

Nate Bukaty, Jayhawk Network Football Sideline Reporter. If you think it is easy being a sideline reporter, try spending about six hours in the elements loaded down with various electronics and trying to take notes on a notepad. At the start of the year, it is scorching and by the end of the season you're freezing your butt off. But Nate was a real trooper. There is also the hazard of interviewing the losing coach -- at halftime and then in the postgame setting (now carried on live radio). He had the glory years under Mark Mangino, but there were some lean years as well. Nate was always well prepared and worked hard in roaming the sideline to get the best perspective. He's obviously developed into a fine broadcaster and displays his breadth and by hosting a talk show, having traveled with the Royals, and serving as the voice of Sporting Kansas City.

Josh Klinger, Jayhawk Network Football Sideline Reporter. When Nate Bukaty's soccer duties began to conflict, Josh Klinger stepped in to do the sideline reporting for my final season. Like Nate, he has had a tremendous amount of experience as what I call "a young gun." He is the co-host of an early morning radio show (I have a special place in my heart for the early-morning guys), but also does play-by-play for KU women's basketball, baseball and soccer. He also contributes to the basketball broadcasts (including pre- and post-game shows) on occasion. He recently added a plum assignment as the sideline reporter for the Kansas City Chiefs Radio Network. His great sense of humor should continue to serve him well.

Chris Piper, Jayhawk Basketball Network (Radio and Television). Those in

Lawrence are probably aware that Chris Piper is an extremely successful business owner. His company Grandstand produces printed products on just about any surface you want: glass, plastic, cloth, stainless steel, aluminum - you name it. But he has long been a successful basketball analyst as well. He started out on the Jayhawk Television Network and then moved over to radio when Max retired. While on the television side, he was an analyst on the Big Eight Conference Basketball Studio Show and did some Big Eight and Missouri Valley Conference games. Of course, most people remember Chris as a captain on the 1988 Jayhawk NCAA championship team. That gave him instant credibility as an analyst.

People don't realize just how good of a player Chris made of himself. It's not that he was highly recruited - he was offered scholarships only by Washburn and Hutchinson Community College. Kay Johnson, the wife of former Kansas athletic director Monte Johnson, was showing Larry Brown homes to buy and told him about Chris. The Johnson's son, Jeff, played with Chris at Lawrence High and they won the Class 6A title in the Spring of 1983 when Brown was hired. They gave Brown a tape of the title game and that led to a meeting with Piper and eventually a scholarship offer. Quite a testimony to his work ethic, talents and mental make up.

With his business and family commitments, Chris chose not to pursue a television career that would have him on the road a great deal of time. But I can say with great confidence, if he had, he would have been a first-tier analyst for any of the cable or regional sports networks. Chris knows the game and his ability to recognize how small items can lead to big results was amazing. He was extremely cerebral as a player and that came across in his analysis. He was a natural in his position. He knew when to jump in and when to hold back. He could be critical when necessary, and complimentary as well. He never got too up or too down. In many ways, he was like my baseball partner Paul Splittorff. He was a former player himself, but he did not make the game about him, his career or how he played. He was great to work with and did it professionally.

Greg Gurley, Jayhawk Basketball Network (Radio and Television). When Chris Piper's family commitments grew with a daughter and son heavily involved in youth sports, it made sense for him to move back to television where his schedule was not as heavy. Greg Gurley, who had been doing Jayhawk television analysis, moved to radio beginning with the 2012-13 season. He has had a long association with KU athletics, starting as a basketball player under Roy Williams from 1992-95, then working as a television analyst for Sunflower Cablevision and Metro Sports. He joined the athletic department in 2011 as a fundraiser.

Greg, like Chris, had a great feel for the game and the transition from my perspective was quite smooth. He had solid relationships with coaches in the Big 12 and had national connections which allowed him to give perspective. His late father, Jim, was also a coach on the high school and youth levels in Kansas City, so he also had good area connections. I do not think it is a must to have someone with Jayhawk bloodlines on the broadcast, but it helps to have the historical perspective. Both Chris and Greg provided that. It was more than a job for them. They were emotionally invested.

Greg and I got along well because we both enjoyed a good joke. And they could come at any time - away from the game, at a commercial break, during the game - whenever the feeling hit us. Greg would humor me by scribbling a punch line to a joke one of us had just told and hand it to me during the game or a break. It broke the tension. One thing you learn quickly that when you are on air, people critique you. Some can be biting and some do it in jest. Bill Self does the latter. And with Greg doing postgame, he gets his share of grief and good natured ribbing from the head coach. I think it is his ability to laugh at himself that has allowed him to improve over the years and be confident in his delivery.

Paul Splittorff: Kansas City Royals Television Network. When you get to work with one of your best friends, it really doesn't seem like work. Paul Splittorff was my partner from 1997-2007 as we called Royals baseball on television, but our relationship started in the late 1980s when we hosted KMBZ radio's pre and post game show. Sadly, Paul passed away at the age of 64 on May 25, 2011. His passing left a huge void in my life and I still miss him so much today.

We hit it off right away, in large part because we loved baseball, a good joke, didn't mind needling each other, and devoured barbecue. What impressed me about Paul from the beginning is he worked extremely hard to become a good broadcaster, not only as an analyst, but also as a play-by-play announcer. Before we began doing games together, I remember Paul and I would sit alone in a booth and talk baseball and broadcasting all night. I learned so much from him about the game. Obviously, he made himself into a good broadcaster. You might also remember he did basketball games for the Big 12 Conference. He loved basketball, and just like he did in baseball, he became a solid good broadcaster for hoops. He played the sport in high school and while in Omaha with the Royals farm club, he would officiate scrimmages for Eddie Sutton's Creighton teams.

We both felt the games should be fun and we did not take ourselves too seriously -- and even less seriously away from them. You might have noticed that one aspect of our telecasts, and it came at Paul's insistence, was we did not talk much about his career or his stats. He wanted the game to be about the players on the field and their accomplishments. It wasn't about him.

When Kansas would play football games versus Missouri, Splitt would meet us on our way home at Zarda's in Blue Springs. Whenever a game would be done, he'd like nothing more than to rehash it with a beer. Splitt could drink some beer. We'd sit down and he'd order one, finish it quickly and then the waiter would return. Splitt would say, "Now I'll have my first beer, that was my emergency beer."

Paul was a friend to all. There wasn't a person who had anything bad to say about him. He was a true blue Royal, drafted by the franchise in 1968 and making his big-league debut late in 1970. When he retired in June 1984, he was and remains the team's all-time winningest pitcher at 166-143.

Fred White: Kansas City Royals Radio Network. I had known Fred for a long time as we met when he was at WIBW radio in Topeka and did Kansas State sports. He was a great friend and is sorely missed. You might remember Fred was Denny Matthews' partner from 1974-98, then went into alumni and radio affiliate relations for the Royals. But Denny cut back his schedule later on and Fred came back to fill in on radio and television, so we worked together a few times. You won't find a person to say anything bad about Fred White. He was just a good guy and was helpful to me when I joined the Royals. I felt Fred was comfortable to listen to and came across in his broadcast as your good friend. I really enjoyed our meals together on the road. He had a great sense of humor

Ryan Lefebvre: Kansas City Royals Television Network. I actually did a few games with Ryan, usually teaming up with him when Denny Matthews did not travel and there was not a televised game. However, we spent so much time together on the road that I felt we were on the same crew. Ryan grew up around the game as his dad, Jim, played for and managed the Dodgers. You might remember him from a highlight of one of the more impressive plays in Royals history. In 1989 in Seattle, Bo Jackson threw out Mariner second baseman Harold Reynolds trying to score from first on a hit that Jackson fielded in the left field corner. It was so unlikely that Jackson would make the play that former Royal broadcaster Denny Trease called Reynolds safe before the throw even made it to catcher Bob Boone. Lefebvre sprang out of the dugout to argue the call, chasing umpire Ken Kaiser around the field. I'm not sure he was arguing the call or claiming Jackson's play was not humanly impossible.

Ryan, who played collegiately at Minnesota, is such a talent with a great under-standing of the game and a wonderful sense of humor. I truly enjoyed being in his company. I don't think people realize how difficult it was to replace Fred White. Both handled it so well and it is a testament to them that they became great friends. He makes the game fun to watch. My hope for him -- and selfishly for the fans of Kansas City -- is that he spends the rest of his career with the Royals. He is a treasure.

Denny Matthews: Kansas City Royals Radio Network. Denny's been there from the beginning -- meaning 2020 was his 52nd year. That's amazing. And of course, he has been honored with the Ford C. Fricke award by the Baseball Hall of Fame for major contributions to the game.

All of those games and all of those road trips can take its toll, but he has had remarkable stamina. He was helpful to me when I joined the Royals and even more so when I moved over to radio for those five years. He was a great collegiate athlete at Illinois Wesleyan, playing both baseball and football. I think that makes him a bit unique in that he is equally good as a play-by-play person describing the action as he is as an analyst in explaining why things were happening. He's precise in his calls.

We actually have a connection to Buddy Blattner, the original lead play-by-play voice of the Royals. Obviously, Denny worked with him, but when I was growing up, I was listening to him do national radio games before he joined the Royals. Buddy was one of the big influences in my career. I think one reason Denny and I really meshed on air is we both grew up and fell in love with the game when radio was virtually the only source of baseball. You had to paint the picture for the listeners. I'm not saying we had the same style, but we had the same influence on our calls.

Chapter 13 Sidebar 1: And Thanks to Our Spotter, Linda Davis

My run at single life ended a few years into my career. I was introduced to Linda Michaelis of Russell by two women who worked at Hadley Hospital in Hays, Jane Roberts and Rene Kritz (who was a friend of the Michaelis family).

Linda was working at Camp PECUSA in Stockton in the summer of 1970, and I called her up and asked if I could see her. So I drove up there and treated her to a Coca Cola at the Dairy Queen. You could say it was our first date. We got married June 12, 1971, at the Methodist Church in Russell. She liked sports, so we were compatible, at least in my eyes.

It wasn't love at first sight because Linda was fond of telling everyone that she really missed Keith Cummings as the play-by-guy. She said it was really a case of "love at first ticket" because she got into the games free by dating me.

While at KAYS, I was a solo announcer for the most part, which meant keeping stats and engineering the games myself. In 1973, I asked Linda if she wanted to be my "spotter," which started out as identifying the tackler for football, but expanded to statistician shortly thereafter. She continued that until the 1979 season. In 1981, Steven was born and that ended her career in the press box.

Linda made it on the air only once -- after I broke the first rule of broadcasting if you were flying solo. The first thing you did upon arriving in the press box was to find the restroom and get a seat to it as close as possible. Well, at Emporia I was further away than usual and Linda was forced into action reading the halftime stats.

For her work, she got to eat at numerous fast food joints and pregame press box meals on our road trips. Part of my sign off was always to recognize her in the closing credits: "And thanks to our spotter, Linda Davis."

We had great fun traveling the backroads of Kansas. And I could always count on her to keep me grounded. When I would get home and walk in the door, a frequent refrain was, "Davis, you didn't say the score enough."

Chapter 13 Sidebar 2: Max and Me

People frequently ask me what it was like to broadcast with Max Falkenstien. And everytime, my answer is: "It was great."

I could talk all day about our time together. It is somewhat remarkable that we never had one argument or major disagreement in our 22 years. I don't think you could find a married couple who accomplished that. You would be surprised, but oftentimes the play-by-play guy and the analyst do not get along.

Max pumped a lot of life out of that little body in 95 years. He was active and had a sharp mind, up until his passing. He was young at heart and enjoyed being around the young athletes. He related to them remarkably well and was a mentor to them in many ways. You might remember the Late Night with Bill Self video where he played the old man character (Blue) in the movie Old School. He just loved doing it and loved the reaction from people.

Max knew everyone, and everyone knew Max. That was helpful for me as I met so many people through him. You have to remember he was born in Lawrence and graduated from KU. He was a Beta, with his fellow fraternity members including Jayhawk basketball standout Jerry Waugh, future KU track coach Bob Timmons and future Kansas governor Robert Docking.

Max actually began broadcasting at WREN while in high school. He enrolled at KU in 1942 and left for the Army after one semester. He came back in March 1946 and went to work again at WREN. His first sports broadcast was in an NCAA District game in 1946 between KU and Oklahoma A&M (State) in Kansas City's Municipal Auditorium when he was only 21. He graduated from KU in 1948 with a math degree. Among his duties were to broadcast both KU and K-State games. During that time Big Eight Conference Commissioner Wayne Duke asked him to become the first television play-by-play announcer for league basketball games. Max later moved to WIBW and in 1971 began a banking career at Douglas County Bank. It was owned by Ross Beach, the same individual who was co-owner of KAYS radio in Hays (where I first worked).

People might be surprised that prior to working with me, Max never worked for the Jayhawk Network. He was in a sense " a competitor." In fact, prior to my time at KU, Max's broadcast would often feature the KU athletic director Bob Marcum as his analyst during basketball season. Even he was drawn in by Max. The network became the exclusive rights holder in our first year together.

Max had a wonderful sense of humor and loved to hear and tell a good joke. We had so much fun on our broadcasts that he often got worried he might get caught laughing on the air. There were times before I could get out the punchline that he would chuckle and say, "now don't make me laugh!"

We often created our own humor by playing off each other during the broadcast. In the 1992 Aloha Bowl at Honolulu, BYU scored almost immediately after we returned from a break for the opening kickoff. I did my best to give a Hawaiian welcome and wish everyone a Merry Christmas, so I said: "There's the kickoff, Mele Kalikimaka and Hema Heimuli goes up the sideline for a touchdown." We go to a commercial after the extra point, and Max takes off his headset and asks, "who scored that touchdown." I said it was Hema Heimuli. He said, "oh hell, I thought you were wishing us a Merry Christmas and a Happy New Year." It was tough to keep a straight face the rest of the game.

A lover of nature, when we were on the road Max would often seek out the Animal Channel and become enamored by the documentaries. He would be on the edge of his bed watching the cheetah's stalk and chase down the antelopes. And when the pace would quicken and the capture was seconds away, Max would turn the channel. "Oh hell, I can't watch this. That poor antelope is in trouble" he would say.

Another story involving animals resulted in Max getting head basketball coach Roy Williams in hot water. We were in Florida and the team took a side trip to SeaWorld. At the end of the dolphin show, we went up to the edge of the water to get a closer vantage point. Roy wondered out loud if dolphins liked popcorn. Max said, "sure, I don't see why not." So Roy tosses a few kernels in the water and the dolphins devour them. A few seconds later, a guard comes streaking toward the group, loudly chastising them for feeding the dolphins. Roy was the target of the guard as Max had eased himself far from the scene of the crime.

Max was so trusting of people, including strangers. We were in New York walking down the street looking for Beefsteak Charlie's. Suddenly we couldn't find Max. He had stopped a stranger in a station wagon about 100 yards behind us to ask for directions. Max yells at us, "hey, come back, this nice man is going to give us a ride. It's too far to walk!" So the four of us pile in and away we go. I mutter under my breath that I hope he's not going to dump us in the East River.

Sometimes you make friends who turn out to be someone you did not expect. We had one of those Saturday-Sunday doubleheaders in 1985 where the Hawks won at Colorado when Calvin Thompson hit a last-second shot to beat the Buffaloes, 70-68. The team was going to fly on a little charter to Ann Arbor, Mich., for a nationally televised game the next day against the Wolverines. There wasn't room for our two-man radio crew, so Max and I had to drive back to snowy Denver to catch a commercial flight to equally snowy Detroit, late Saturday night.

About midnight, we were trudging out in the snow in Detroit to rent a car to drive to Ann Arbor. Dead tired after this long day, Max and I were the only two guys on the rental-car bus headed over to where they parked the cars. The bus driver had this long, beautiful, wavy blonde hair. Max, who's always friendly with people and doesn't really know a stranger, says from the back of the bus, "Honey, how far is it up to Ann Arbor?" The bus driver turned around — showing a great big, blonde mustache — and said in a deep voice, "About 30 minutes." Max and I had many great laughs over the years, but I got to enjoy that one all by myself.

If Max made friends out of strangers, he even made acquaintances better friends. His routine at basketball games included greeting everyone in the media room, saying hello to the opposing coach during pregame shootaround, conversing with the visiting radio crew, then offering a word of welcome to the game officials. It was something to watch. It was like Max was royalty and the honored guests were in awe. It wasn't unusual for the officials to have a running dialogue with him as they ran up and down the court.

There are certain people who light up the room when they enter, and that was true of Max. His bright smile was as welcoming as one could have. He was approachable and went out of his way to make you feel welcome and important. He was as comfortable shaking hands with the governor as he was with the guy who swept the Allen Fieldhouse floor. And he treated both equally well. This played out in public spaces as well. We had somewhat of a regular lunch group in Lawrence featuring some media, KU athletics staff, current and retired coaches and businessmen. We would circulate among salad bars at Dillons and Hy-Vee, Wendy's, Backyard Burgers, Sub 'N Stuff, Goodcents, any one of the many barbecue joints, Morningstar's Pizza and Runza. When Max walked in, heads turned. It might take 30 minutes for him to order after working the room and saying hello to others.

Speaking of food, Max had a remarkable ability to put it away despite his small frame. My guess is he was all of 5-8 at best. But even the all-you-can-eat buffet at Border Bandito was no match for him. And not only was his capacity underrated, so too was his ability to handle even the most challenging foods. The greasier the better. Among his road favorites were Hickory Park in Ames, where he could order a Green River; Bob's Sirloin Room in Seneca, Kan.; Biffles BBQ in Concordia, Mo. (not wanting to spend any money in Columbia), Zarda BBQ in Blue Springs; Guy and Mae's in Williamsburg, Kan.; and the Pizza Hut in Wamego, Kan. If it looked like a place our wives wouldn't enter, we were eating there.

Most people don't know that Max didn't drink alcohol -- no beer, wine or mixed drinks. In fact, Max's favorite drink was caffeine free, Diet Mountain Dew. So I asked Max, "What's the point of drinking Mountain Dew if it's both caffeine free and diet -- why don't you just pour it in the toilet and eliminate the middleman?"

I was not aware that Mountain Dew came in a diet or caffeine free form until we were in Ames for a basketball game. Ames was one of the test markets for the drink. Max was excited to see this new soda (it was my opinion it removed the guilt of the pregame meal of barbecue and halftime ice cream cone) and as we sat down to eat proclaimed: "I know this looks like horse piss, but to me it is nectar of the gods!"

Max was an honest person, and even brutally more so off the air or with close friends. His evaluations were vivid, and sometimes a bit off color. Bob Valesente was the football coach who replaced Mike Gottfried for the 1986 and 1987 seasons. Val, as we knew him, was a wonderful person. Kind and caring. Although he did not find much success on the collegiate level, he had a long career in the NFL. Everyone cared for Val and worried about him as the losses mounted. After one drubbing by Nebraska, I asked Max how Val looked in the postgame interview session. Max got quiet, then said: "he looked like he had just been pulled through his asshole."

Max had been around sports all of his life, so he had a great perspective on winning and losing. The games were played to be won, but to him it was also about the relationships and honorable competition. He had friends at every Big Eight stop and was treated somewhat like royalty. He did Kansas State broadcasts for several years, along with the KU games. He had many friends at Kansas State, and always made it a point to seek them out. It was telling to see former Kansas State head football coach Bill Snyder at Max's memorial service in the summer of 2019. He even had many friends at arch-rival Missouri, although he would joke "they still have a lot of sonsabitches."

His even-keel perspective spawned one of the great and enduring lines among our radio crew. Typically, we all travelled together, either with the team or driving in a van. The trips with the teams afforded Max the opportunity to get to know the student-athletes and coaches better. No one worked an airport gate area better than Max. His inquisitive nature was certain to uncover many interesting nuggets of information. When we traveled by van, we'd regale each other with jokes and stories, many re-used from the previous year with a touch more embellishment. We'd stop at the greasy spoons and favorites to chow down. We weren't a rock band by any stretch of the imagination, but we did feel Max had a bit of star quality about him.

So, while the road trips were long and packed with many activities in a 36-48 hour period, they were still fun. During one football season that was not going particularly well, the sting of losing started to take its toll. After a drubbing at Nebraska, our van pulled up to the Falkenstien house just after midnight. Our first stop was always at Max's. Being in the business 60 years earns you that. On this particular trip, Max slowly departed the van, grabbed his luggage without saying a word, and shuffled to his front door. After a few steps, he turned around and flashed that Kirk Douglas look alike smile and said, "boys, this would've been a great trip if we didn't have to do the damn game!" He chuckled, turned and slowly walked to his front door.

They say that behind every successful man, there is an equally successful woman. Isobel Falkenstein was that woman for Max. She would dutifully pack Max's luggage for every road trip. Everything was accounted for, including his sleepwear. No T-shirt and shorts for Max. He would have the best silk or flannel pajamas you could find. He was styling staying at a Super 8.

Max's pajamas were a secret among a tight circle in the travel party, but they became the subject of discussion in a full airport waiting area while the basketball team was getting ready to board the plane. It began when Richard Konzem and I were awakened in the middle of the night by a sound in our bathroom. I looked at Konzem's bed and he was still there. Who in the hell was in our bathroom at 3 in the morning? The door swung open and it was Max. He just smiled and waved as he sauntered back through the unlocked door that led to the adjoining room. We later found out that his roommate, basketball sports information director Dean Buchan, was using their restroom. Then next evening at the airport, we were telling this story and suddenly the team, the coaches and the travelling party were huddling around. Head coach Roy Williams became incredulous. Not so much because Max snuck in our room, but because he wore silk pajamas. "You wear silk pajamas?" Roy said in his Carolina drawl. Max came back with the quick retort, "What do you wear?" Roy, paused, then said, "gym shorts." Max, with a look of disapproval, said, "don't you get cold. Not even a T-shirt in the winter?" And the boarding began.

One of Max's many qualities was the ability to diffuse a situation when that meant letting people down. But he did so gently. On one road trip to Honolulu, Max was walking down the street with KU assistant athletic directors Richard Konzem and Doug Vance. An extremely attractive and much younger woman came up to Max and asked him if he wanted to enjoy the evening with her. Without missing a beat, Max said, "I'm sorry honey, but I'm with these guys, maybe some other time." He turned around and gave us a wink. He was so suave.

There will never be another Max.

Chapter 13 Friends of Bob

David Lawrence: Kansas Football Letterman, 1978-81; Graduate Assistant, 1982; Jayhawk Radio Network, 1994 - Present. I was asked to be the football sideline reporter for the 1994 season. I was not a newbie, but certainly not a seasoned veteran. As a football graduate assistant in 1982, I joined Tom Hedrick on the broadcasts. I left Lawrence to coach high school football and later returned to teach junior high and coach football. I also did analysis for the local Sunflower Cablevision.

Just before the 1994 season began, I got together with Bob and Max and they could tell I was a bit nervous. So, in the perfect Bob Davis manner, he broke the tension. He said, "David, this is easy. There are only three rules you need to remember. No. 1, get in and out of breaks quickly. No. 2, get in all of your commercials; and No. 3, don't say EXPLETIVE on the air!" There was a pregnant pause by us all, then Bob burst out laughing. I felt at ease.

So, fast forward to the 1995 season. We are playing at Cowboys Stadium in Irving, Texas against a solid North Texas team. We won the game 27-10 and I assumed my position for the post game interview of head coach Glen Mason. We had just gone to a commercial break when Mason came out and said "Let's go." I explained we were in a break and it would be about a minute. Win or lose, coaches are generally impatient people. While we are waiting, Bob is feeding me stats on the game. Quarterback Mark Williams had a solid game, so I was hearing Williams this and Williams that. So, they throw it to me, and I say: Coach Williams, what did you think of the game in general?" There was a long pause and Mason's face went beet red in color. Eventually he answered. In my ear, I hear the deep voice of Bob Davis slowly say: "REMEMBER RULE NO.3." I chuckled to myself and finished the interview.

A few weeks later, Bob told me that he amended what he had told me and said there was a fourth rule: Always call the head football coach by his last name, and not that of the basketball coach.

Greg Gurley: Kansas basketball letterman, 1992-95; Jayhawk Television Network 2011-12; Jayhawk Radio Network, 2013 - Present. Growing up in Kansas City and being around KU, I knew Bob Davis was a good broadcaster. But once I started working with him and seeing how he did his job, I was in awe. The thing that stood out to me was his passion for his job and KU. He connects with the fans because of that. He was very helpful to me. I was nervous moving over to radio from television to work with him. I remember our first game was against a smaller school and it had the potential to be a blowout. Bob told me to treat it like a Final Four game - focused and analyze the play. And of course, he is so funny. A road trip with Bob Davis is a treat.

From my position as a fundraiser for the athletic department, Bob was an excellent ambassador at our events. He has such a presence. When he gets up to speak, that voice, passion and humor creates a positive environment. Our fans loved Bob and they considered him their close friend.

Chris Piper: Basketball, Kansas, 1984-88; Jayhawk Television Network, ESPN+, Jayhawk Radio Network, 2007-12. Bob is so good. I knew that by listening to him, but once I started doing radio it really became apparent just how good he was. My transition from television was easy because of Bob. He sets you up so well and makes his partner sound like a pro. I could have come in off the street and done the games with no prep because of the way he went about his work. He has such a good feel for the game and how the broadcast should go. I think the combination of his voice, his passion and ability to tell the story is amazing.

Another thing people may not realize about Bob is how competitive he is when it comes to his work. He has that humorous, folksy delivery. But he is a perfectionist. He would toss his pencil down and I asked him what was wrong and he would say, 'he only has two fouls, not three.' The pencil toss is when you realized he was upset. But that is what made him so good. He was prepared and focused. And none of his work is scripted. Some guys write out their whole introduction and have various phrases written down to use in advance. That wasn't Bob.

Bob also liked to talk with his hands. Almost like he's conducting an orchestra. We are on the road at Oklahoma State and Bob is getting demonstrative with his hands flailing away. I don't think it helped that we thought the officials missed a few calls. So at halftime, Sean Lester (associate athletics director), comes out and tells us the officials want the radio crew to calm down a bit or they might eject them. That was the passion of Bob coming out.

Kevin Shank: Producer, Royals Television, 1994-2011. Bob joined the Royals at a tough time. The community foundation owned the club and the team was not good. So, I knew it would be difficult for anyone to make Royals baseball exciting, but Bob did it. Bob was just a joy to be around because of his personality, but also because he worked so hard. I think a lot of that had to do with his not wanting to let anyone down, especially Paul Splittorff. Paul was a big booster of Bob's to get the job. Bob had not done television for a while, so I would say he was a bit nervous at first. But he's so coachable and easy to work with that the transition was a quick study.

I remember his first game like it was yesterday. It was actually postponed the day before so my guess is he did not sleep at all the night before. We started the game and you could just tell how much fun it was going to be to have Bob working with Paul. The guys in the truck were just giddy because here is a guy who could bring passion and excitement to every pitch -- but not go overboard.

Paul's and Bob's relationship was beyond special. One reason was because they both felt they were taking care of each other. Here was Bob, new to Major League Baseball and Paul felt he needed to take care of him because, let's face it, there are some jerks out there. It's not like high school or college. Bob felt he needed to take care of Splitt to help him in his broadcasting and set him up so that he would be able to interject at the best moment. They really cared about each other.

Nate Bukaty: Football Sideline Reporter, Jayhawk Network, 2001-15. The first KU broadcast I was ever lucky enough to do with Bob and Max was the Sunflower Showdown in 2001. The game was televised on pay-per-view, and David Lawrence, who had been the sideline reporter for KU football on the radio at the time, moved over to do the color analysis on the TV broadcast for that game. So, they asked me to fill in for David on the sidelines for the Jayhawk Radio Network. I still remember meeting Bob, Max and Richard Konzem at the parking lot of McDonald's in

Lawrence, so that I could ride with them to Manhattan for the game. I was a young nobody as a broadcaster, just 24 years old, and I would be working my first ever Jayhawk Radio Network broadcast with two of my childhood role models, Bob and Max.

That was my first glimpse into the terrific sense of humor that Bob has. Anyone who knows Bob well will tell you that he is genuinely one of the funniest people you'll ever meet. I honestly had no idea about this sense of humor before this time, because Bob never really revealed this on the air. For the next couple of hours, Bob and Max had me in stitches as they exchanged witty quips on the drive to Manhattan. It was a great tension reliever for me, and helped relax me for such a big moment in my career. I will always appreciate the way they welcomed me in, and put me at ease.

The first word that comes to mind about Bob for me is "passion." I always admired Bob's knack for having his voice match the moment. The bigger the moment, the better his call was. And it wasn't because he overcomplicated his call. Many times it was as simple as a "SWIIIIIISH!" or "TOUCHDOOOOOWWWN!" or "THE DREAM IS REAL!" The calls were to the point, but the tone of Bob's voice always reflected a passion for the moment, and it was absolutely contagious as a listener. I believe that the great broadcasters have a way of conveying significance in moments that mean so much to so many people. Those moments deserve a passionate call, but some announcers have difficulty managing their voices in these moments, and they become abrasive or difficult to understand. Bob was as good at that as any broadcaster I've ever listened to in these moments. And there was never a doubt that his passion was genuine. There was nothing contrived or forced about it whatsoever.

John Rooney: Play-by-Play Broadcaster, St. Louis Cardinals. I first met Bob Davis in 1977 when I was broadcasting Pittsburg State and he was doing Fort Hays State. He was the dean of broadcasters in the league and everyone looked up to him. The best thing about Bob is he was approachable and always willing to help young guys advance in the business. As a broadcaster, Bob excelled because he was extremely prepared and he loved what he was doing. If you cannot have fun broadcasting a game, the audience is not going to have fun listening. He made it fun.

He's had such an outstanding career. I always thought it was great how much he meant to the people of Hays. You could tell they knew they had something special. I think that relationship is what kept him there for so long. He appreciated them and they appreciated him. Certainly getting to do KU and work for the Jayhawks was a major accomplishment. And then he got to do Major League Baseball with the Royals. He's always had a passion for baseball and to get that opportunity I know meant a lot to him. He's a dear friend and just a good person.

Jim Nantz: CBS Sports Broadcaster. Bob Davis was a broadcasting icon for nearly a half century. Everytime I called a KU basketball game for CBS I knew there was a legend sitting on press row just a few seats away who was giving his adoring audience a call that was better than mine. I heard enough clips through the years to appreciate the timbre in his voice, the excitement in his every call, the dramatic flare he brought to every game. What honor he brought to our profession. And to the state. And to the school. And how cool it is to be recognized for being as vital a part of the Jayhawk Nation as any athlete who ever graced the uniform. I'm lost in admiration.

Holly Rowe: Reporter, ESPN. I got to know Bob Davis covering Kansas basketball games for ESPN as part of the Big 12 Big Monday crew. It wasn't long before he introduced himself and we started chatting before every game. We have become great friends. Even after he retired, Bob keeps in touch with me. After big games in any sport I am working, I can count on having a text from Bob. When I would be getting ready for my cancer treatments, he would always text me and wish me luck. He is forever encouraging me, supporting me and telling me I did a good job. His voice gives me chills and his storytelling is intoxicating. I love that he has been such a huge piece of Kansas history. He is so classy and caring. I feel so lucky to be his friend and colleague. He is the best.

Al Wallace: Kansas City Sports TV Personality, WDAF-TV, 1985-2018. It's important that a play-by-play announcer, be it television or radio, know exactly what makes the team he is following, unique and important. It's not necessarily about the wins and losses. It's about their significance, their history, their fabric, and the way those who follow that particular team or franchise, feel about that team or franchise. It's that overall understanding that helps connect that announcer to the team he is covering. Bob Davis made his audience feel like they were connected to the team like family.

I believe, when it came to covering Kansas basketball and football, Bob Davis fit that definition to a tee. In my opinion, Bob Davis did it with the precision of a surgeon, and that's why for years, I called him "Dr. Bob." especially in reference to the way he called Kansas basketball games.

Andy Landers: Retired Georgia Women's Basketball Coach; ESPN Women's Basketball Analyst. I was just a coach with zero experience in broadcasting so I should have been petrified at the idea of doing color for an NCAA championship -- but I wasn't. I was petrified at the idea of working alongside the legendary Bob Davis! But, like all who are considered the best at what they do, Mr. Davis made it *SO* easy and comfortable for me. To this day, I have no idea how I did, but I do know this: Bob Davis was terrific!

CHAPTER 14

Believe in Yourself

WHEN YOU ARE in a profession where you rely on the public trust, you certainly never want to overstay your welcome. It is a discussion broadcasters have all the time as none of us wants to cheat the listeners. It is not my position to judge any of my peers as to when they should hang it up. We walk in our own shoes and know the best path for ourselves.

Still, my philosophy is it is better to leave a year too early than to hang around a year too long. My decision to leave broadcasting involved the input of a small circle - my family. From a personal standpoint, I have accomplished all that I dreamed of -- and more. I was comfortable in what I had done. Could I have continued and still upheld the standards I had set for myself in my previous 48 years? Yes, I could have continued.

But I was ready to step aside and spend more time with my family. Steven and his wife Katie, have four wonderful children. I thoroughly enjoy being a grandfather. In addition, many of you are aware my wife Linda has Parkinson's Disease. If there is a champion in our family, it is Linda Davis. Without her support over the years, I would not be where I am today. While physically Linda has been impacted, she remains as sharp as a tack and is a wonderful wife, parent and grandmother.

By pulling back, it also afforded me the opportunity to enjoy Steven's work as a broadcaster. The apple didn't fall far from the tree in that regard. I am biased, but he has a great feel for broadcasting and is better than I was at his age. His main job has been as a minor league broadcaster in Arkansas, and he has combined that with some small-college and high school football, and Missouri-Kansas City basketball. He has a great future.

Linda and I are both extremely proud of Steven - and blessed that he is our son. We had lost our first pregnancy and there is always the concern you might not be able to have children. When we later found out Linda was pregnant with Steven, we were both overjoyed and scared. He was born a healthy baby on a Wednesday and that Saturday Fort Hays State had a home football game. I went down to the field for my pregame meeting with Tiger head coach Jim Gilstrap, who was your typical, hard-nosed football coach. I sheepishly offered him a cigar and he grabbed my shoulder and whispered in my ear: "that baby is a gift from God." That is when I realized just how great fatherhood was going to be.

Bob Davis joined by wife Linda and son Steven for his induction into the Kansas Association of Broadcasters Hall of Fame in 2006. Source: KAB

I still have a love for sports and broadcasting. I still follow the Jayhawks and Royals religiously, and have so many friends with Hays connections that I keep up on the place that gave me a chance in 1968. But first and foremost, the aspect I miss the most are the relationships with my broadcasting peers, coaches, athletes, other members of the media and the countless others I have met along the way. That is truly the best part of the job -- meeting so many people and developing lasting relationships.

As a broadcaster, you don't get judged by whether your team wins or loses. But you do get evaluated by the fans after every game. I tried to never let the criticism get me down or the adulation go to my head. However, there was one moment in time where I let myself bask in the glow of approval. My father was driven and wanted me to be successful. At a young age when I was engrossed with *The Sporting News*, he encouraged me to read "non-sports" publications. When I went to college, he was dead set on me going to law school. He let me know he was disappointed when I decided to go into broadcasting.

But early in my career, I took my dad to a football game I broadcast and he got to sit in the press box and watch me call the game. Afterwards, as we walked out of the press box and down the stadium steps he said to me: "hey, you're pretty good!" A big smile came over my face and worked its way to warm my heart.

I guess that is the singular message of this book. If you have a dream, chase it. Work hard, develop relationships and take chances. But most of all, believe in yourself. Your dream can be real.

Chapters 14: Friends of Bob

Steven Davis: Broadcaster, University of Missouri-Kansas City, Arkansas Travelers

When you live with someone it's hard to see them as the world sees them. To many, Bob Davis was famous, but to me he was just my dad. He was the guy I wanted to run errands with as a kid even though I'd get stuck listening to old time country music while he sang along. Whatever his job may have been, that was my normal.

Now because of his job, I did get to experience numerous cool events throughout my childhood such as Final Fours, trips to fun places (always associated with a game except for one) and of course Saturdays at Memorial Stadium and going to every home game in sold out Allen Fieldhouse were expectations. The only trip that didn't involve a game was for my parents' 25th anniversary when they took 14 year old me along with them to Niagara Falls, the Baseball Hall of Fame and the Basketball Hall of Fame. Not the most romantic trip I'm sure, but it worked for our family.

Sports were always the focal point for us but other than high school football and basketball games when I was young it was a rare occasion for me to sit with my dad as a fan. But without a doubt, my love of sports was created and still thrives because of his lifestyle along with the support of my mom. We listened to every second of every game. I am quite sure that I've heard my dad call more games than any other announcer.

Even as a father and son who hung on anything and everything to do with their teams and games, I feel my dad and I became more close when he was working for the Royals. One of my first jobs was working in the TV production truck at Royals games while I was in college. Our time together increased dramatically driving back and forth (oftentimes I drove if he needed to catch a nap) and hanging out at the stadium before games. Crashing a few road trips and sharing a hotel room also helped our relationship grow. Being around him extensively, in his environment, also made me appreciate how others, especially his colleagues viewed him. As I was informed once on a Royals trip, "Your dad is a lot cooler when you're not around."

Yet, even having grown up with a walking, talking, grammar correcting broadcast text book for a dad and having pretended to announce any game I might be playing around the house, becoming a broadcaster was the last thing I expected to pursue.

Working in sports was the only place I could see myself but simply not in broadcasting. A revelation hit me one day about a year before graduation from college; I'd always told my dad that what he did was easy, so I should give it a try!

Turns out what he did wasn't easy - he just made it look easy!

My appreciation and respect for Pop grew greatly as I went through my own trials and tribulations in the sports broadcast industry. Working in the same profession and being able to share experiences -- rather than just hearing what he said as stories -- made for a tight relationship even though the physical distance between us was greater than ever.

He also went to great lengths to show his support for me. My dad (with an assist from Father Mike Scully) drove from Denver to Casper, Wyo., on a Royals off day in 2005 to be there for my first solo broadcast. The next few years, he and my mom spent the Major League All-Star Break trekking to wherever I was broadcasting. Looking back, it fit who they were, but it really meant a lot that his 'vacation' time each summer was to come support me and my career. Then and now, any chance Pop has to tune into a game I'm broadcasting, I know he'll be listening.

I think it is safe to say that Bob Davis is not only my dad, but also my friend and most importantly my No. 1 fan. And for that I can't thank him enough.

Afterword

By Wyatt Thompson, Kansas State Play-by-Play Announcer

FAR BE IT for me to compare any success I have had in my career to that of Kansas State head football Coach Chris Kleiman or Kansas head basketball coach Bill Self. But I do have a deep appreciation for what they were able to accomplish in replacing their successful and popular predecessors. Kleiman, of course, followed a legend in Bill Snyder and has done quite well in his own right. And Self, a hall-of-famer himself, succeeded one of the all-time winning coaches in college basketball in Roy Williams.

In the summer of 1984, I accepted the sports director position at KAYS radio in Hays, Kan., following in the footsteps of Bob Davis. I'm not so sure my challenge wasn't greater than Kleiman's or Self's.

Not only was Bob an outstanding broadcaster. But he was then, and is today, even a better person. Though some 36 years removed from being a Hays resident, Bob could return there today and be elected mayor. I am not sure there was a more popular person in Hays when I arrived than Bob Davis. I was already acquainted with Bob through my work broadcasting high school sports in the state at Goodland, Abilene and Great Bend.

By the time I entered the broadcast business, he was -- especially in the western part of Kansas -- considered an established star. For me to say I wasn't nervous would be disingenuous. But my transition could not have gone better. One reason was the wonderful people at KAYS specifically, and in Hays in general. And second, it was because Bob Davis was there to provide any assistance, answer any questions and speak on my behalf. He had no ego and only wanted the best for me and the sports fans of Hays.

*Wyatt Thompson, Voice of the Kansas State Wildcats, and Bob Davis
share a laugh and a long-time friendship.*

Since those early days, our friendship and my admiration for Bob has only grown. I look forward to the Kansas State - Kansas matchups because I know I will learn at least one new joke from Bob Davis. I'm usually laughing seconds after our handshake. Our conversations are wonderful and enjoyable. The only challenge is there is almost a constant flow of interruptions as it seems **EVERYONE** knows Bob Davis. Patient, approachable and genuine, Bob never turns down a handshake or chance to say hello. One thing about broadcasters is they are never too experienced to learn from others. I think I learned something from Bob every year until he retired. And that was not only based on observation, but also because he is so giving of his time. The stories of him reviewing tapes and offering immediate feedback are voluminous. He truly loves the profession and people.

Like so many others have said, Bob stands out with the booming voice, vivid descriptions and passion in his call of the game. But what I believe distinguished him the most from was his outstanding -- and no doubt natural -- voice inflection. He was mesmerizing in his broadcasts. When you listened to Bob, it was from the edge of your seat.

I am truly happy for all of Bob's success. Every accolade, honor and award has been well-deserved. I am also full of gratitude for the trail he blazed for people such as myself and others who got their start doing small-town radio with the goal of advancing their careers. He, as Tom Hedrick said, was a "major leaguer in a small market." He gave everything he had to KAYS and the people of Hays, and when the opportunity to advance presented itself, they were genuinely happy for him. That tells you all you need to know about Bob Davis. They were so thankful for what he gave them, that they only wanted the best for him. That is how we all fell about Bob Davis. We are thankful for all he gave to us.

Yes, his dream was real. And it was a heck of a ride.